JERRY ROBINSON

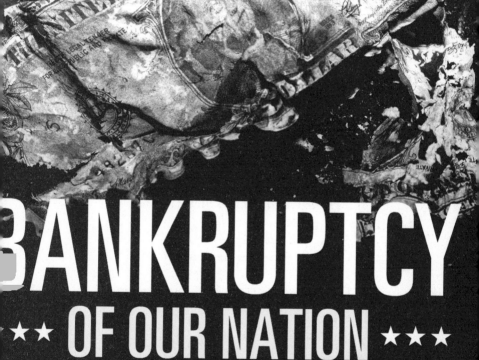

BANKRUPTCY
★★ OF OUR NATION ★★★

12 KEY STRATEGIES
FOR PROTECTING YOUR FINANCES
IN THESE UNCERTAIN TIMES

First printing: March 2009

New Leaf Press, P.O. Box 726, Green Forest, AR 72638.

ISBN-13: 978-0-89221-693-2
ISBN-10: 0-89221-693-X
Library of Congress Catalog Number: 2009923747

All Scripture quotations in this book, unless otherwise noted, are taken from the New King James Version of the Bible.

Printed in the United States of America

Please visit our website for other great titles:
www.newleafpress.net

For information regarding author interviews,
please contact the publicity department at (870) 438-5288.

New Leaf Press
A Division of New Leaf Publishing Group
www.newleafpress.net

*To my two precious daughters
whom I treasure and adore:
Genesis Makayla and Isabella Rose.*

Acknowledgments

Writing a book is a daring feat. And because it takes a team, there are many people to thank.

My wife, Kristy, for her loving patience and her wise counsel.

Rick and Cris Lenard for their encouragement, prayers, feedback, and massive amounts of proofreading of the early drafts of this book. I am grateful to you. Thank you.

My literary agent, Jeff Dunn, for his belief in me and in the message of this book.

To all those at New Leaf Publishing, especially Tim, Laura, Judy, and Stacey for their hard work to make this book a reality.

And finally, a warm thanks to all those who have supported our ministry — and our message — for the last several years. Thank you for your continued support.

Contents

Introduction

America is in deep, deep trouble.

As a nation, we are surrounded by a whole host of political and social problems:

- Internal terror threats
- Loose immigration and border control problems
- The institution of the family and of marriage is under vicious attack
- There are great issues in the area of bioethics, such as a blatant disregard for the sanctity of human life
- And of course, the U.S. economy seems to be teetering on the edge of disaster

Without a doubt, America has become a house-flipping, day-trading, non-saving, debt-exporting, Chinese-importing, oil-sucking, money-printing, credit-loving, entitlement-demanding, foreign-financed nation.

And because America has enjoyed such immense economic prosperity, many Americans have been lulled into a sense of economic complacency. But the recent tremblings in the global economy have demonstrated that the United States may not be as strong as was once thought.

When I first started writing and speaking about the economic ills of America, it was not well received. Some even considered me to be unpatriotic to expose the deficiencies of my own homeland. And while those early days brought little interest in our message, now that the economy is tanking, I find that I am busier than ever. Though you would think that this newfound awareness of America's economic vulnerability would make my message easier, it has actually made it more difficult. The reason for this lies in the simple fact that humans have a tendency to cast blame when things go wrong. This "blame game" mentality started in the Garden of Eden when Adam blamed his sin on his wife, Eve. Eve then proceeded to blame the serpent who had so craftily deceived her. But in the end, humanity's sin was to blame.

The blame game continues today within the realm of our financial crisis. Democrats blame Republicans, Republicans blame Democrats, others blame corporations, while still others blame government and its institutions. Those who fall for this blame game are thoroughly deceived. In this book, I will demonstrate many of the problems that are facing America. Problems will be found in nearly every area of our society. But this book is different in that in my final analysis, there will be one overarching theme. That theme is man's inability to effectively rule himself. And the reason that man cannot rule himself effectively is very simple: he was never created or designed to rule himself. Man was created to be ruled by his Creator God. Man's rebellion against God's rulership in the Garden of Eden has led to nearly 6,000 years of failed human government. The chaos, disorder, and confusion in America's economic and political arenas are ultimately due to one single factor: man cannot rule man. In fact, the problems confronting our nation and the world at large serve to prove God's point that we need Him more than ever. As a follower of Christ, I believe that Christ is going to return, judge the nations of this world, and set up His own Kingdom here on the earth. My faith is in that Kingdom. All other kingdoms are rooted in false hopes. They are cheap imitations. And they all end in disaster.

The kingdom of America is no different. The American economic empire is facing an impending collapse. I believe that the coming crisis in the U.S. economy can become one of the American Church's finest hours for evangelism. However, it can only be an opportunity *if the Church recognizes it.*

But for the Church to recognize the opportunity, it must be watching. Unfortunately, much of the American Church today is *asleep.*

And not only are many of the churches in America asleep, they are also caught up in the same delusion as the world is. Many of today's churches are chasing after the same elusive and temporal things that the world is chasing after, so much so that it has become hard to tell the two apart at times.

This spiritual lethargy has allowed massive amounts of deceptive teachings to seep into America's churches regarding money and

Christian living. Of course, these false teachings then directly affect the theology of the Church, which leads to an even greater deception.

In 2 Timothy 3:1–5, the Apostle Paul describes what the very last days prior to Christ's return would look like. He said that men would be:

- lovers of themselves,
- lovers of money,
- without self-control,
- conceited,
- lovers of pleasures rather than lovers of God.

Do any of these things sound familiar today? America is ripe with this type of behavior. And while this type of behavior exists in the world, it has even become acceptable in many of America's churches. As this book unfolds, I will demonstrate why I believe that many in the American Church have been sucked into a great end-time money delusion in that they believe in this illusion of prosperity that surrounds them. Throughout this book, I will show why I believe that America is moving quickly toward a *hyperinflationary depression* in the coming years. As mentioned previously, I believe that this time of economic hardship will be one of the Church's greatest opportunities to witness and show the value of Christ to a deceived and broken nation that has placed its trust in man's ability to rule and govern himself.

But for the Church to take advantage of this opportunity, it must not be sucked into the illusion of prosperity that has so greatly affected this nation.

The American illusion of prosperity has been built upon several premises that are faulty. This book will identify five economic trends that point to this faulty foundation.

- This book will explain why the purchasing power of your U.S. dollar is declining and why the dollar is doomed.

- It will detail how America became the greatest debtor nation in world history, built upon foreign-financed entitlement spending, and why this will lead to massive inflation in the future.

- It will point to America's dependence upon foreign nations for its energy supplies and how this could lead to massive disruptions in both the American economy and our entire way of life.

- It will expose the fraudulent debt-based monetary system employed by America's central bank, the Federal Reserve, and how it has turned America into a "bailout nation."

- Finally, this book will seek to shatter the myths of the American mindset regarding the American nation, and its trappings of over-consumption and lack of sacrifice.

After a complete discussion on these five topics, which will include a few forecasts, I will conclude with 12 key strategies that any American can use to protect his or her finances in these days of economic uncertainty. These strategies have already been used by many who have heard me speak and teach on this topic. I believe that they will help you, too, as you seek to protect yourself and your family from whatever financial turmoil may lie ahead.

A Final Word on Awareness

During my studies in college, the two topics that I naturally gravitated toward were economics and theology. I remember a few of my academic counselors were slightly confused by the two seeming incompatible disciplines. However, as long as I can remember, I have always seen a direct link between economics and the study of theology and the Bible. This is perhaps because I do not view economics as the study of money. Instead, I view economics as the study of choices and decisions. In this world, we all have to make decisions. In fact, our lives consist of the choices and decisions that we make on a daily basis. We can choose the good. Or we can choose the bad. We can choose responsibility. Or we can choose recklessness. Our daily decisions do not only affect our lives, but they affect those around us as well. Each decision we make contains within it the opportunity to make this life, and the next, more sweet, or more bitter. We have been blessed and endowed by our Creator with the blessing of being able to choose. Of course, this freedom of making choices is a double-edged sword. History is proof positive of this.

The information concerning mankind's history, and our present day, that is presented in this book will be both exciting and weighty. In one sense, this information is exciting because it will shed much light on the confusion that exists in our nation and our world. In the midst of so much confusion, it is highly exhilarating to gain clarity. However, the information is also extremely weighty in that "to whom much is given, much is required." The truths that you will learn in this book will forever change how you view the world around you. It will lead you to greater awareness — which is ultimately the first step in any direction.

Awareness is important for another important reason, as well, for those who view the world through biblical lenses. Most sincere followers of Christ believe that these are the last days and that Christ could return at any moment. If that is true, then it must also be true that these are the most deceptive days the earth has ever experienced. This is because the Bible indicates that great deception would be a sign of His return. And if these are truly the final days before Christ's return, which I believe they are, then we are living amid more deception than we could ever begin to realize. Awareness regarding the lateness of the prophetic hour urges us to be ever vigilant and watchful. *Anything is possible in these days of deception.*

The reason for this deception is simple: Satan is operating with very little time, and he desires to lead the whole world into deception. His very first recorded act in the Garden of Eden was rooted in deception. In Revelation 12:9, the Bible calls Satan the devil, "the deceiver of the whole world."

But Satan's dominion over this earth will come to an end. And that time is coming soon. All of creation will rejoice and be glad in that hour.

In the meantime, however, God has not left the Church powerless against the deceptive wiles of Satan. In fact, we possess the strongest weapon imaginable to counter Satan's efforts to deceive. That weapon is the Word of God.

As children of the Most High God, we are commanded not to be ignorant of Satan's devices. Instead, we are expected to exercise the light of truth from God's Word to expose and confound the dark deceptions of wickedness. While Satan's power is found in his lies, our strength is found in the truth.

In this book, I will expose the deceptive lies about money that have infected the American culture, and the American Church. The only way to arrive at a place of truth regarding these matters will be to recognize these deceptions about money for what they are, and then to confront them with the truth.

This is my prayer for you, for the Church, and for the nation.

Chapter 1

Welcome to the End of an Empire

"History is a vast early warning system."[1]
— Norman Cousins

In an era full of doomsayers and gloomsters, it was my sincere hope that my first major book release would be on, let's say, a milder topic. Maybe even something light-hearted, such as a book on how to leash train a Rottweiler, or a beginner's guide to French wines. Or even better yet, a pictorial tourist guide for Southern Europe.

But instead I have written this tome on the decline of the American experiment and how mankind is about to enter the greatest financial crisis in world history. Depressing, huh? Well, yes. But to those who are familiar with economic history, it is simply the natural ebb and flow of competing interests. According to the laws of physics, an apple thrown upward into the air will be pulled downward by the invisible force of gravity. And while history does not necessarily subscribe to a set of laws, it does teach us great lessons. These lessons can even be forceful at times. *It is often said that while history may never truly repeat, it does at least rhyme.* And unfortunately, in the case of the inevitable American economic decline, we have a wide array of historical precedents, which we will examine in later chapters.

But even more than the lessons of economic history (which we will examine more closely in chapter 3), we have even greater evidence that the global influence exerted by America, both economically and politically, will decline considerably in the not-too-distant future. Our source: the Holy Bible. Despite what the Western-centric thinker may suggest, the ancient writings of the Christian Bible are clear. They confirm that the biblical prophecies concerning the "last days" are Israel-centric and Middle East-centric. *They are anything but America-centric.* God's Word clearly states that the global stage will be firmly transferred to this volatile region just prior to the return of Christ.

As a believer and follower of Christ, it is my earnest belief that hope is never completely lost, because God's sovereign plan of the ages will forever prevail — no matter how desperate things may appear. But as a believer, I have also learned that only a fool places his trust in man's ability to rule man. If history is a guide to anything, it is a guide to the consistent knucklehead acts of mankind throughout the ages. Mankind's predicament stems from the fact that man was not designed, nor was he ever meant, to rule himself. According to an orthodox view of the Christian faith, mankind has rejected the omnipotent rule of his Creator. Instead, man has opted for self-rule. This ancient act of rebellion explains the last 6,000 years of pain and suffering and more recently, why the 20th century was the bloodiest century on record. (Ironically, the 20th century has also been labeled the "American Century.")

America represents the culmination of all that man has ever aspired to: wealth, fame, self-love, self-importance, and freedom to do whatever the heck he wants (otherwise known as independence). But as men have engaged themselves in this "American experiment," the inward corruption of mankind has bubbled to the surface. Unable to rid himself of his true sin nature, man attempts in vain to cloak his deficiencies. Unfortunately, America is following the same path as every economic empire before it. And lest we confuse ourselves, Western Christians must quickly grasp this point: America is not the light of the world. The sun shone before America was here, and it will continue to shine long after our self-inflicted demise. So let us not proceed in shock or surprise at the complex webs that America has weaved for itself. Its fall is historically identifiable, though unfortunate. And it is all but certain.

The Excesses of Empire

Over the last few decades, certain economic trends have pointed toward an eventual day of reckoning for the U.S. economy. For example, over the last several years the United States has outsourced the majority of its domestic manufacturing to foreign countries, opting instead to specialize in consumption. This specialization in consumption has meant that for the first time in the nation's history, the personal savings rate of Americans has dipped below 0 percent. Today, the U.S. credit industry has trumped the manufacturing industry in total revenues. This as the consumer-crazed nation purchases everything in sight through the use of high-interest credit in an effort to feed the hungry credit beast that they have created. And this "buy now and pay later" mantra is not contained to, nor did it originate within, the consumer credit market. Evidence of it is found in government as politicians promise the unborn grandchildren's money to pay for the luxuries of the grandparents.

It is demonstrated in the poor monetary policy decisions that have systematically devalued the empire's choice of currency, the U.S. dollar. Today, thanks to our nation's fiat currency system, it takes one dollar to purchase what five cents could purchase in 1945.

Evidence of this "buy now, pay later" attitude that threatens America is demonstrated in American foreign policy as modern wars are fought without an appeal to national sacrifice. Instead, foreigners fund America's wars through massive capital inflows that serve to prop up U.S. consumption and conquest.

America has reaped what it has sown by creating an *entitlement generation* that expects perpetually low tax rates and interest rates. It also expects unrealistically high government entitlement spending and investment returns. This new entitlement generation considers the concepts of sacrifice and saving as unnecessary relics worthy of the dustbin of history as modern Americans refuse to deny themselves any delight or delicacy. The American economy represents nothing less than a feeble house of cards completely vulnerable to the inevitable external forces that await every declining empire.

Many authors and commentators have highlighted the striking similarities between modern America and former empires such as Rome and Great Britain. Those who are not familiar with such comparisons would greatly benefit from researching this material, as it will provide a much-needed historical context to the impending American economic crisis. Therefore, I will avoid belaboring the historical and cultural comparisons here. I do not believe, however, that one must understand the historical cycles to appreciate the fact that America is facing great economic jeopardy.

The painful truth expressed in this book is that the end of the American experiment will, more than likely, come sooner rather than later. The reason behind this looming decline is due to the fact that the United States of America is standing on the precipice of a self-imposed economic calamity. America's ascendance into the heady realms of economic empire began in the post-World War II Bretton Woods era when it was the world's greatest creditor nation. Today, just over 60 years later, America now stands as the *greatest debtor nation in world history*. Decades of financial excess, coupled with an entitlement mentality, has left America as financially bankrupt as it has become morally. America clearly represents a reluctant economic empire in decline. And like all empires that have gone before it, its days are numbered. The death of an empire can be quick and painless; however, that is rarely the case. Instead, empires tend to die slow, painful, and humiliating deaths, and their demise is usually accompanied by at least two things: an overextension of the empire's military and extreme economic overindulgence and depravity. America exhibits excesses in both of these categories.

U.S. Military Overextension

To confirm America's overextended global military presence, one must look no further than the more than 700 U.S. military bases located in over 120 nations. That means that America's military is located in over half of the world's nations. The American obsession with maintaining global hegemonic power through military force is justified in the name of protecting the important causes of freedom, democracy, and justice worldwide. Or as former President William McKinley put it, "The American flag has not been planted in foreign soil to acquire more territory but for humanity's sake."[2] However, acting as the ever-vigilant and ever-present global policeman requires an annual budget over $600 billion.[3]

- That is 10 times larger than China's $65 billion annual military budget.
- 12 times larger than Russia's $50 billion.

- 120 times larger than North Korea's $5 billion.
- 140 times larger than Iran's $4.3 billion.
- And that's around 5,000 times more than Afghanistan's $122 million.

In fact, funding the American military machine costs more than all of the rest of the world's militaries' expenses — *combined*. And while these exorbitant costs spent to maintain militaristic dominance is typical of an empire, it also is clearly unsustainable.

U.S. Consumption Levels Require Foreign Creditors

The American empire's economy has become grossly indebted to foreign creditors through a shameful lack of sound fiscal stewardship. The empire's total current national debt stands at a colossal $9 trillion and is growing by the billions every single day. Foreign countries own more pieces of America than ever before. Not only do foreigners own a large amount of America's real wealth (real estate, corporations, etc.), they also hold vast amounts of our government bonds. The repercussions of this large foreign ownership of American interests will be discussed at length in upcoming chapters.

As this book will seek to demonstrate:

- American prosperity is denominated in a debt-based and debt-backed currency, the U.S. dollar. But this illusion of prosperity in America is hardly recognized or highlighted by the financial elite or the nation's media.

- U.S. over-consumption, coupled with American military adventurism since the Vietnam era, has been financed by foreign creditors. With huge trade deficits and a growing national debt, indebtedness to foreign creditors leaves the United States in a highly vulnerable position.

- U.S. and global demand for energy resources are increasing at a rapid rate. Unfortunately, global energy production is not going to be able to keep pace with global demand. A growing depletion of cheap energy resources, coupled with a threatened petrodollar system, will more than likely force America into becoming militarily aggressive in future resource wars with other growing nations (i.e., China, India, etc.).

- American consumer debt has reached all-time highs. This year, more Americans will declare bankruptcy than will divorce, graduate from college, or get cancer; 43 percent of American households spend more every month than they earn. Clearly, this lack of fiscal discipline must eventually end. Behind all of this lies a monetary system that is based upon debt. This book will explain in stark details how the monetary system of the United States of America is a debt-based system. In fact, money *is* debt. To understand this concept, we will examine the Federal Reserve system and the mind-blowing money creation process that they employ.

An Illusion of Prosperity

Despite these facts, the majority of America's government's institutions, along with their sidekick, the American media, exploit the lack of economic understanding of the masses. In the face of a weakening U.S. economy, those with the loudest voices and largest platforms within the empire have rushed to the nearest microphone urging Americans to continue their overconsumption. They gently assure Americans that the economy is "resilient" and "strong" enough to weather any storm. As the *Titanic* coasted through the Atlantic that fateful night, no one believed that the mammoth ship would ever meet its demise on such a routine voyage. Nevertheless, as the *Titanic* began to sink, the majority of its passengers remained in disbelief. The horror of that fateful evening unfolded against the backdrop of big band music, dancing, and free-flowing cocktails. The music played until the very end. Likewise, everything is perpetually peachy on the inside of a declining empire. But to believe that the current excesses of the American economic empire are eternally sustainable is about as wise as taking time to rearrange the furniture on the sinking *Titanic*.

It is understandable why some Americans would still feel optimistic about the nation's economic future when one simply looks at the recent performance of the U.S. stock market. Over the last several years, the nominal returns on many domestic stocks have been extremely healthy. Since 2000, for example, the Dow Jones Industrial Average has provided the average investor a return on investment of around 36 percent. However, *all of the returns reported to American investors are calculated based upon the empire's currency, the U.S. dollar.*

What the typical American investor does not realize is that the gains that he has made in his U.S. stock portfolio have actually been losses due to the declining purchasing power of the U.S. dollar. So in the past, when the average American examined their 401(k) plan statements, they may have seen a positive return on investment, but in all reality, their investments have lost value, internationally speaking, due to the declining dollar.

We can see more clearly how much the U.S. dollar has been devalued through a series of bad monetary policies by simply considering an example using the aforementioned Dow Jones Industrial Average. The Dow Jones, of course, is denominated in U.S. dollars and has increased 36 percent over the last seven years. But if we compare the Dow Jones to other prices besides the dollar for the last seven years, here is what we find:

- If the Dow Jones had been priced in euros rather than dollars for the last seven years, the Dow would have been a losing investment. In fact, it would have lost 40 percent. Therefore, Europeans who have invested in the Dow Jones for the last seven years have not gained 36 percent but, rather, have lost 40 percent.

- If denominated in milk prices, the Dow Jones now buys 35 percent less milk than it did just seven short years ago.

- If denominated in wheat or corn, the Dow now buys 40 percent less wheat and corn than it did seven years ago.

- If denominated in gold, the Dow now buys 50 percent less gold than it did seven years ago.

- If denominated in silver, the Dow now buys 55 percent less silver than it did seven years ago.

- If denominated in oil, the Dow now buys 70 percent less oil than it did seven years ago.

- If denominated in copper, the Dow now buys 80 percent less copper than it did seven years ago.

- If denominated in uranium, the Dow now buys 90 percent less uranium than it did seven years ago.

A sign that you are living at the end of an empire is that you think you are making money while instead you are losing money. The illusion created by the American economic empire has become extremely deceptive to millions of hard-working Americans. It is a lot like driving a beautiful luxury car with a broken fuel gauge. When the gas tank nears the empty mark and you are running on fumes, you will receive little warning, but you sure do look great. *Today, many Americans look rich on paper, but the purchasing power of their dollars is rapidly decreasing.* A simple jaunt to any American grocery store will confirm this bit of data. Grocery prices, gas prices, oil prices, and commodity prices are all increasing at remarkable rates and testify to the economic uncertainty fueled by a declining dollar. The inflationary pressures hitting the U.S. consumer have been anything but subtle.

For example, in 2000:

- Gold was $273 per ounce.
- Oil was $22 per barrel.
- National gasoline prices averaged at $1.46.
- The euro was worth $0.87 per dollar.
- The Canadian dollar was worth $0.68 per dollar.

In 2008, just a few years later:

- Gold soared to well over $900 per ounce.
- Oil broke through $140 per barrel.
- National gasoline prices averaged nearly $4.00 per gallon.
- The euro reached $1.46 per dollar.
- The Canadian dollar reached parity with the U.S. dollar.

Of course, in the face of such obvious inflation, the U.S. federal government has assured U.S. consumers that consumer prices are under control and are being "tightly monitored." In fact, according to the feds, the U.S. economy is strong and inflation is low. But the price of gold, oil, and gasoline do not lie. The purchasing power of the dollar is declining, and it has been for years. In the last five years alone, the U.S. dollar has lost 35 percent of its value against the euro. Open any newspaper and you will find that your hard-earned U.S. dollars are hitting all-time lows against other global currencies nearly every week.

Of course, average everyday consumers pay little attention to gyrations in the global currency markets. But they do understand that when the price of milk or bread goes up, they are able to buy less of it. So the price of gold is hitting all-time highs. Oil is hitting all-time highs, causing gasoline prices to rise. Food prices are rising. It appears that the price of everything is going up. However, the point is that prices are not rising as much as the purchasing power of the dollar is declining. Thus, the illusion of the dollar is simply that: a glorious illusion.

A "Global" War on Terror

In addition to economic illusions of prosperity, declining empires also tend to become rather ambitious in their military aims. The 21st century began with the largest terrorist attack on U.S. soil when occupied airplanes were used as missiles against the World Trade Centers and the Pentagon. In response, the Bush administration launched a global war on terror. Admittedly, hunting down those responsible for these egregious attacks upon thousands of Americans should be a priority of the U.S. government. But upon closer examination, an even larger problem exists: war is expensive. And initiating and conducting a worldwide war on terrorism is terribly expensive, even for the richest nation in world history. This is why every previous war in this nation's history has required some economic sacrifice on the part of its citizens. For example, in the wake of the Japanese attack on Pearl Harbor, President Roosevelt ended production of new automobiles, new homes, and new appliances in an effort to free up American manufacturing and labor resources for military trucks and tanks needed for the war. Food and gasoline supplies were rationed as the country mobilized for an expensive war that nearly all agreed was necessary for the future peace of the nation. Additionally, the federal government promoted and sold war bonds to the general public to obtain the funding necessary to pay for the ongoing costs associated with war. Understanding that wars cost money, U.S. citizens from that "great generation" *sacrificed* many of life's conveniences in order to prevent America from going into massive debt. Even in Vietnam, which was an American financial nightmare, a military draft ensured that sacrifice was exacted from American families.

In contrast, after the 9/11 attacks, President George W. Bush encouraged Americans to go shopping and to take vacations. In our modern era, little economic sacrifice has been requested from American citizens. So while the bombs drop and the rockets fly, most Americans yawn and turn off the television. The nightly news brings reports of war and chaos that might as well be happening on a different planet. Ask yourself: Where is the economic sacrifice in this new massive worldwide war on terrorism? Which of our nation's leaders are asking you to curb your consumption in an effort to fund our current global war? Oddly enough, in the midst of a costly global war, the nation's taxes have been lowered while government spending has increased. The sheer absurdity of this should be obvious. But apparently it is not, as clearly witnessed by American citizens who have apparently bought the government's line that "Americans can have their cake and eat it too." To tell the American voter anything to the contrary is too politically risky.

Since Americans are not being asked to fund the extravagant expenses of a global war with no end in sight, who then is footing the bill for America's war on terrorism? The answer: foreign countries, namely China and Japan. How are they funding the war, you might ask? Through their purchases of U.S. government debt, such as U.S. Treasury bonds. Since 2000, China and Japan have been rapidly increasing their holdings in U.S. debt instruments, to the tune of hundreds of billions of dollars. *In other words, China and Japan are financing America's war on terrorism.*

Emerging Nations as the New Global Consumers

Americans are "expert" consumers, and American consumption — until February 2005 — had been the highest in the world in nearly all categories. On February 16, 2005, a report was released by the Earth Policy Institute that confirmed what most of the world already knew: China is rapidly replacing the U.S. as the world's largest consumer. The report stated that "among the five basic food, energy, and industrial commodities — grain and meat, oil and coal, and steel — consumption in China has already eclipsed that of the United States in all but oil." China's insatiable appetite for commodities is both obvious and frightening. The enormous nation has 1.3 billion people who all desperately desire the same luxuries that Americans now enjoy, and they are willing to work hard to obtain them. Of course, one of the luxuries of a modern wealthy nation is automobiles. And automobile sales are increasing rapidly in China as the nation continues its industrial revolution — 21st-century style. Therefore, the price of oil is intricately linked to China's emergence from an agrarian society to a highly developed nation. And while China trails the United States as the world's second largest oil consumer, it is now the world's fastest net importer of oil. China's demand for oil is growing each year, and government estimates have stated that by 2030, China's demand for oil will eclipse U.S. demand for oil. In addition, China now boasts five of the world's ten largest companies, including oil production giant PetroChina. In November 2007 it was announced that PetroChina had become the first company in history to be valued at over $1 trillion, thus making PetroChina twice as valuable as the world's previously largest company, American oil giant ExxonMobil. China today is viewed by many as simply an economic bully. This may be true. But Americans do good to ask themselves: *How long before China's economic power turns into political power?* In fact, what else is a superpower if not an economic powerhouse with tremendous political prowess. As the Earth Policy Institute report concludes: "China is no longer just a developing country. It is an emerging economic superpower, one that is writing economic history. If the last century was the American century, this one looks to be the Chinese century." It is amazing when you think about it. America's population of just over 300 million has consumed more than China's 1.3 billion citizens for decades. This statistic alone displays America's staggering wealth and our consumption-driven economy. And China is not an isolated case. India, and its 1.1 billion citizens, is experiencing its own economic revolution as many of its impoverished citizens successfully embrace the tenets of capitalism in an effort to increase their standard of living. Add to this other countries such as Brazil, Russia, and a host of other nations that are all emerging as major global economic players onto the world's stage. They all come ready to compete for their share of the world's limited resources. Clearly, insisting that American hegemony is sustainable is not only unreasonable, but it is also highly irresponsible.

The Life Cycle of Democracies

Consider how the Scottish historian Alexander Tyler documented the typical life cycle of a democracy:

> A democracy cannot exist as a permanent form of government. It can only exist until the voters discover that they can vote themselves money from the public treasure. From

that moment on the majority always votes for the candidates promising the most money from the public treasury, with the result that a democracy always collapses over loose fiscal policy followed by a dictatorship.

Tyler continues with this amazing statement:

> The average age of the world's great civilizations has been two hundred years. These nations have progressed through the following sequence: from bondage to spiritual faith, from spiritual faith to great courage, from courage to liberty, from liberty to abundance, from abundance to selfishness, from selfishness to complacency, from complacency to apathy, from apathy to dependency, from dependency back to bondage.[4]

Does this sequence sound familiar? Where does this dependence upon others to pay the bills place the fragile American experiment on this life cycle?

So let us summarize our conclusions thus far:

- The purchasing power of our U.S. dollar is declining in value.
- The U.S. government continues to print more money.
- We are engaged in an expensive and endless global war on terror.
- We are obsessed with cutting taxes.
- We are raising government spending to all-time highs.
- We have requested little, if any, economic "sacrifice" on the part of our citizenry.
- Our trade deficit and budgetary deficits are at all-time highs.
- Our national debt is at an all-time high and growing exponentially.
- We are completely dependent upon foreign nations to fund our over-consumption through the sale of our debts.

As long as foreign countries purchase our massive debts, perhaps we can extend this madness. But what happens if foreign countries begin to decrease their funding of our debts? And what if America's foreign creditors decide to diversify their currency holdings into other currencies? The truth is, the American public is living in massive monetary deception. The direction that the American economy is heading is extremely difficult to swallow. However, if our aim is truth, then we will willingly embrace the facts and take the necessary steps needed to shelter ourselves and our families. Undoubtedly, the only real way out of the mess that has been created will also be the hardest. A glimmer of hope remains that the difficult steps that need to be taken will be embraced, especially by Christians. But regardless of whether this happens or not, there is still hope for the informed citizen. The message of this book is one of great hope. But it is not a hope that the global economy will never awaken to the harsh realities awaiting it. God's Word has clearly stated that man cannot rule man. Our failed attempts in this area continue to prove his point. Our hope is in knowing which direction the trends are taking us. It is in this knowledge that you will be able to protect and shelter whatever wealth you have already accumulated, and in addition profit from the greatest financial crisis that the world has ever witnessed. As you read the following chapters of this book, be of good cheer. Despite man's best efforts, God is still in control. And with God, the end is only the beginning.

Endnotes

1. *Saturday Review* editorial, April 15, 1978.
2. From a 1900 campaign poster for the Republican party, July 12, 1900.
3. http://www.globalsecurity.org/military/world/spending.htm.
4. David L. Wood, *Why Worry About the Gradual Loss of Our Liberties?* (Oakland, OR: Elderberry Press, 2003), p. 36.

Part I
The Demise of the Dollar

Chapter 2
What Is Money ... Really?

"Permit me to issue and control the money of a nation, and I care not who makes its laws."[1]

— Mayer Anselm Rothschild of the Rothschild banking family

"All the perplexities, confusion, and distress in America arise, not from defects in their Constitution or Confederation, not from want of honor or virtue, so much as from the downright ignorance of the nature of coin, credit, and circulation."[2]

— John Adams

OVERVIEW: Money has taken many different forms throughout history: shells, feathers, salt, gold, silver, and paper currency. This chapter lays the groundwork for understanding the current dollar crisis by examining the underlying concepts of money. What exactly is money? How is it measured? What gives it value? This chapter also explains three types of money that have been used throughout history: commodity money, receipt money, and fiat money.

There is an old joke about money that says that while money may not buy happiness, it sure does buy everything else. Benjamin Franklin referred to man's obsession with money this way: *"He that is of the opinion money will do everything may well be suspected of doing everything for money.*"[3] While each of us have varying views on the topic of money, one thing is for sure: *Money is a necessity for life in this world.*

I believe that a person's view of money is formed and fashioned by three prevailing factors.

The first, and most dominant, factor affecting a person's view on money is found in the foundations of the economic system into which a person is born. For example, a person born and raised in the United States of America is introduced to a capitalistic economic system from birth. The virtues espoused under a capitalistic system include the right to private property, the division of labor, and individual rights.

In contrast, those who are born in China view money through the lens of a predominantly communistic economic system. Under communism, individuals have fewer rights and the government plays a much greater role in every aspect of life. (More in-depth explanations of the various types of political and economic systems can be found outside of this book. My purpose here is simply to point out that a person's view on money is often directly tied to how his government teaches him to view money.)

The second factor that determines how a person will ultimately view money is found in his own family's financial philosophies. Parents are always teaching their children by their words, and more importantly by their actions! (Whether they realize it or not.) Parents who value consumption (that is, who love to buy lots of stuff) and who do not save are teaching their children the virtues of consumption and to not save money. Those who exemplify a strong work ethic for their children are teaching their children that money is best earned through lots of hard work. Other parents may be business owners and therefore teach their children that by employing the efforts of others, money can be accumulated.

> **Think About It:**
>
> *How have your own family's financial philosophies affected you?*

The third factor that determines a person's view on money is found in their religious and moral understanding of life itself. For example, those who have had a strict religious upbringing may view money as inherently evil. For example, I once knew a Christian woman whom I will call Margaret. Margaret is one of many Christians who view money as being inherently evil. When I asked her why she viewed money as being evil, she looked appalled and then said, "You are a minister! Don't you read your Bible? The Bible clearly states that money is the root of all evil." (I'll admit that I am bit Socratic in my discussions on Christianity. By Socratic, I mean that when someone asks me a question, I will often reply with a question of my own. This is a method that Jesus used quite extensively. And if it was good enough for Him, it is good enough for me.)

Margaret was a feisty thing. I responded to this dear lady by saying, "Well, I feel rather embarrassed. I was not aware that the Bible said such a thing. Here's a Bible. Would you please show me where it says this so I can help others understand this, too?"

"I do not know. But *it is* in there," she replied.

Knowing exactly the verse that she was taking out of context, I quickly turned my Bible to 1 Timothy 6:10 and read it aloud: *"For the love of money is a root of all kinds of evil, for which some have strayed from the faith in their greediness, and pierced themselves through with many sorrows."*

She quickly chimed in, "That's it. That's the verse that I was talking about. Haven't you ever read that before?"

My Socratic nature would not let me give her a straight answer yet. She had to see the folly of her logic. I responded, "Margaret, if this is true, do you realize how this changes everything I have ever known and taught about money? In fact, I am thinking of another verse right now that I feel we should read, too. Can I read it to you?"

With a smug assurance, Margaret nodded.

"Well, if money is evil then we better pay extremely close attention to this next verse. It is found in 1 Thessalonians 5:22. It says, 'Abstain from every form of evil.' Margaret, if this is true, and if money really *is* evil, then this means that you and I need to get rid of all of our money as quickly as possible!" I stated with a smile.

Margaret laughed nervously and asked what I meant.

With a more compassionate tone, I re-read 1 Timothy 6:10 to her and told her, "Margaret, the Bible never says that money is evil. What this verse is saying is that it is *the love of money* that is the root of all evil. If it were evil, then simply having any of it would violate God's Word. Do you understand why this is an important difference?"

> **Think About It:**
>
> *The morality of money is found in the intents of the user, not in money itself.*

Margaret took the Bible and read the verse again as if for the first time. "My father always told me that money was evil and those who had money were not godly. But this verse does not say that, does it?" she asked as her tone became accepting and friendly.

"That's right, Margaret. The Bible is balanced in its view on money. It never says money is good or evil. It is just an object. It is we humans who take money and perform good or evil works with it," I said with even more compassion.

Margaret's dogmatic approach to her view of money had meant that she had spent her entire life avoiding money out of fear that it was displeasing to God. While this may seem like a minor point, it is actually a huge distinction. It is important that we understand that *the Bible views money as being amoral.* In and of itself, money is not capable of being moral or immoral. It is merely an object. However, because humans have inherited a sin nature from the Garden of Eden, they often create idols out of things that they enjoy. Money is no exception. In fact, money has been the idol of choice for millions. But just because money is an idol to millions of people does not mean that it is inherently evil. Money can be used for very good purposes or very bad purposes.

Each one of us has had our views of money formed and fashioned by a combination of the three factors stated above. Understanding how our views of money have influenced our life's decisions can be very shocking, as in the case of Margaret. But in addition to examining our views of money, there are some important questions about money that we should ask. All people ask questions about money. Two of the most common questions people have are:

- How much money do I have?
- How can I get more money?

While these are the general questions that most people ask, there are other questions about money that most people never stop to think about. But if we want to understand the system that we depend on for our well-being, we should ask some foundational questions, such as:

- What is money?
- How is money measured?
- What gives money its value?
- And finally, if money can be printed, why not just print more?

You may be thinking, *I am not an economist, so why should I bother with understanding the answers to questions like these?* While these questions may seem irrelevant to you right now, it is my hope to demonstrate the importance of these questions. In this chapter, I will attempt to answer these questions and hopefully help you gain a basic understanding of the current monetary and banking systems, without boring you with all of the little details. Believe it or not, a large part of being able to protect yourself and your family is tied to your ability to understand and answer these questions. Now that I have your attention, let us proceed.

So What Is Money?

That is a great question — what exactly is money? How would you define it? If you answered that it is the paycheck that you receive at the end of every week from your employer, you would be only partially right. Economists have grappled with this question and have produced three basic answers to that one question. The three definitions of money are as follows:

- Money is . . . a medium of exchange.
- Money is . . . a store of value.
- Money is . . . a unit of account.

Medium of Exchange

Money is defined as something that is universally accepted as a payment for goods and services and repayment of debts. For example, in the United States a U.S. dollar is recognizable and is accepted as payment for any goods and service within the nation's borders. U.S. merchants who sell a good or a service do not accept U.S. dollars because they like the way they look or the way they smell. That would be ridiculous! The only reason that a U.S. merchant will accept payment from you in U.S. dollars is because they know that U.S. dollars are an acceptable means of payment for their needs. So they will accept your dollars as payment because they know they can immediately turn around and use those same dollars to purchase something for themselves. However, if you walked into a store and attempted to pay with a handful of bananas instead of dollars, then you would be out of luck. But this is only because bananas are not currently a recognizable and universal means of payment for goods and services. So money must serve as a medium of exchange for it to be effective.

A Store of Value

Economists also define money as a store of value. By this they mean that it can be stored away and used later. If money was perishable, then it could not serve as a very good store of value. This obviously can be applied to our earlier example of bananas. Within a week, bananas can rot. Money should be something that does not perish with time but can hold its value for future needs and wants.

A Unit of Account

Finally, economists consider money to be a unit of account. The prices of goods and services would be very difficult to determine without a universally accepted form of money. For example, without a single universally accepted form of money, how could storeowners price their items? What if you wanted to pay with your bananas and another customer wanted to pay with pineapples? How could the store owner possibly know how to price his goods under such a complex system?

Today's economic environment has become far too complex and people have become too interdependent to rely upon an antiquated bartering system. Today, people no longer have to produce everything they consume. They can trade money for the things that they do not, or cannot, produce.

The economy that mankind has engineered today certainly requires a cohesive and universal monetary system that can serve as a medium of exchange. In times past, people were not nearly as dependent upon each other as we are today. Today, economies and societies are highly interdependent. The roots of this dependency are found by examining a brief evolution of the concept of money.

The Brief Evolution of Money

The history and evolution of money is a story that spans thousands of years. And while money and trade have become more sophisticated over time, we have evidence that some early civilizations had some forms of advanced monetary systems. One of the first civilizations to develop a system of trade with a form of money was ancient Sumer. The Sumerians were highly advanced in many areas, including their system of economy and trade.

From the days of ancient Sumer to our present day, money and trade have taken many different forms. The most primitive type, and earliest form, of money is known as *commodity money*. Commodity money is a form of money that has an intrinsic value in and of itself. Early civilizations, for example, used common items as commodity money. These included items such as spearheads, shells, feathers, and salt. Commodity money is a unique form of money in that it serves a dual purpose. It can be used for trade or it can be consumed by the owner. In ancient times, for example, salt could be used for trading purposes. But the owner always had the option of consuming the salt for his own purposes. Salt could also be used for antiseptic purposes and for preserving food, among other uses. This is unlike our current paper money system, which serves only one purpose, that is, trade. Paper money has no other use if it is not backed by a commodity.

Over time, the portability and durability of money became all but necessary to merchants and traders as societies became more interconnected. And as the old saying goes, "Necessity is the mother of invention." This need for a more versatile form of money led to the rise of gold and silver as money. In addition to being easier to transport and more durable than most other forms of money, gold and silver were scarce and had the unique capability of being divided. Soon, gold and silver were being reduced into the form of coins with values stamped on them. This simple, but revolutionary, act made transactions more convenient and represented man's first real attempts at coined currency.

However, it did not take long for dishonest people to exploit the gold and silver system. Those who wanted to cheat the system did so by placing gold or silver plating over cheaper metal discs to fake the appearance of solid gold and silver coins. Governments often stepped into the "money-making business" to prevent such counterfeiting efforts. Despite these efforts, counterfeiting remained a constant challenge to most forms of money. This is true even to this day.

The superior aspects of gold and silver meant that they soon became the commodity money of choice for many people. However, as time went on, and as people began to accumulate large sums of gold or silver money, another concern arose: how to keep the gold and silver safe. Keeping large sums of gold and silver in one's house could be unwise and impractical. This need for safety led to the creation of goldsmith banking, which would eventually give rise to our modern banking system.

Under the system of *goldsmith banking,* which became popular in 17th century England, an individual simply deposited his gold with his local goldsmith. In exchange for keeping the gold in a safe place, the town's goldsmith would charge a small monthly maintenance fee. When a person made a deposit of gold with a local goldsmith, he would receive a paper receipt that stated the amount of gold on deposit with the goldsmith. To redeem one's gold, the individual simply had to return his receipt to the goldsmith. As trade grew, these paper receipts began to be accepted as payment for transactions because they were viewed as "good as gold." This is because the paper receipts were backed by the gold held in the goldsmith's vaults.

It was only a matter of time before traders and merchants who needed money began seeking out goldsmiths for capital in the form of loans. Most goldsmiths were willing lenders. To lend money, they would simply create a paper receipt for the borrower that made it appear that the individual had gold in the goldsmith's vaults. In reality, no gold was backing these loaned paper receipts, but no one could possibly know that except for the goldsmith himself. And because very few people ever had a need to liquidate their gold holdings, the goldsmith had relatively few problems, with little default risk, using this newfound lending system.

(This idea of lending money not currently on deposit became a highly profitable venture for bankers. It is known as fractional-reserve banking and is discussed at length in chapter 12, "Modern Money Mechanics: What the Banking Industry Does Not Want You to Know.")

As countries began to industrialize, small regional banks began competing with goldsmiths for the business of loans to merchants and traders. These small banks each issued their own bank notes, similar to the paper receipts issued by goldsmiths. But as a nation grew, too many forms of currency could overwhelm and stifle the flow of commerce. Often, the attempt would be made to initiate a unified paper currency system. These new paper currency systems were often backed by some form of commodity, usually gold or silver. As you can imagine, to implement, maintain, and then regulate a national paper currency required lots of vigilant oversight. Governments, especially in the Western world, typically responded by allowing the creation of a national central bank. Central banks were responsible for ensuring accessibility and an overall smooth functioning of the nation's currency system of choice, almost exclusively paper money.

But even under the central banking system, maintaining a commodity backing for every piece of paper money in circulation soon became a very laborious process and served to constrain the economy. If a nation's money supply was constricted to only the amount of a particular commodity, it would inhibit the growth of the economy during large boom cycles. In response, many governments would opt to remove a commodity backing from its national currency. When a nation allows its paper currency system to be removed from any and all commodity backing, it is then considered by economists to be a fiat currency. *When a currency is fiat, it is only backed by government guarantees, not a commodity.* Today, nearly *every* national currency in the world is fiat. And nearly all modern banking is built upon a fractional reserve system, which means that money can be created out of nothing! In our next chapter, we will examine a brief history of fiat currencies. You will discover why fiat currencies like the U.S. dollar have led nations to the brink of economic disaster every time they have been used by governments.

How Is Money Measured?

Regardless of the type of money a nation uses, one of the most important qualities that it should possess is that it should be measurable. This is especially true in the case of a fiat currency. When a currency is fiat, it means that the government is responsible for maintaining a public perception that it will keep the currency in a limited supply. This is to ensure that it does not lose its purchasing power through reckless overproduction of the currency. In response to our current fiat dollar system, U.S. economists have devised three categories to measure the nation's money supply. These three measurements are known simply as M1, M2, and M3.

M1: This measurement includes all coin and paper currency in circulation, demand deposits (checking accounts and NOW accounts), and traveler's checks. This is the narrowest measure of the U.S. money supply and only measures the amount of liquid money in the hands of the public.

M2: This category includes all of M1, but also includes all time deposits ($100,000 or less), saving deposits, and non-institutional money market funds.

M3: As the broadest measure of the U.S. money supply, this category combines all of M2 (which includes M1) plus all large time deposits ($100,000 or more), institutional money market funds, short-term repurchase agreements, and eurodollars (U.S. dollars held in banks outside the United States).

The M3 money supply is considered the broadest measure of the nation's money supply currently available. In chapter 4 I will discuss more about the M3 money supply and explain how it relates to our nation's economic crisis.

What Gives Money Its Value?

Another question that many have never stopped to think about is: what gives money its value? Since our discussion is regarding the modern economy, and the U.S. economy in particular, let's ask a more direct question: *what gives the U.S. dollar its value?*

If you have a U.S. dollar bill around you, pick it up. Examine it closely. Notice its many symbols and its colors. What is it about this dollar that makes people want it? Why do so many people work long hours for small pieces of green paper that have no other use than spending? As we have already discovered, fiat paper currency has no other real purpose, unlike other types of money from the past. As stated previously, many things have been used as money throughout history, and many of these different types of money had intrinsic value. When I say intrinsic, I mean that the "money" was valuable in and of itself. Therefore, it had more than one purpose. Take silver for example, which has been used for centuries as a form of money. Silver has many uses, including those in the fields of photography, dentistry, jewelry, mirrors and optics, and medicine, among others. With so many uses, it is no wonder that silver was so widely adopted as money throughout history. Silver and other similar types of commodity money have intrinsic value. Their value is tied to their usefulness. Compare that to the dollar in your hand. How many uses does a dollar have? I guess you could make a case that paper money could be used as firewood in enough quantities. (It was during the final hyperinflationary days of the Weimar Republic! See chapter 3.) Paper money is different from commodity money in that it has no intrinsic value. So back to our original question. If fiat currencies like the U.S. dollar have no intrinsic value, why do people agree to take them in exchange for goods produced and services rendered?

The answer is rooted in the public's trust in their government to keep the currency in scarce supply. The reason that the American public, or any society for that matter, is willing to accept a fiat currency in exchange for goods produced and services rendered is because they believe that the government will maintain the value of the currency by keeping it in limited supply.

This concept will become even more important as we proceed through the next couple of chapters. Recently, while watching C-Span (yes, I watch C-Span), a gentleman called in to a call-in show and asked this question: "Why doesn't the U.S. government just print a bunch of dollars and give them to the poor? Wouldn't this help the poverty levels of America?" You may be asking, however, why must governments keep their fiat money in limited supply? Why not print lots of the stuff? That leads us to our final question about money: If fiat money (like the U.S. dollar) can be printed, why not just print more?

In our next chapter I will answer that question with a look back at history. What happens when a government decides to print lots of a fiat currency? Does everyone get rich with all of the newly printed money? Does printing money solve problems or just create more problems?

Endnotes

1. Dallas D. Johnson, *Consume! The Monetary Radical's Defense of Capitalism* (New York: Dynamic American Press, 1940), p. 89.
2. Charles Francis Adams, *The Works of John Adams, Second President of the United States* (New York: Little, Brown & Co., 1853), p. 447.
3. Nathan G. Goodman, editor, *A Benjamin Franklin Reader* (New York: Thomas Y. Crowell Co., 1945), p. 288.

Chapter 3
A Short History of Fiat Currencies

"There is no subtler, no surer means of overturning the existing basis of society than to debauch the currency. The process engages all the hidden forces of economic law on the side of destruction, and does it in a manner which not one man in a million is able to diagnose."[1]

— Sir John Maynard Keynes

"With the exception only of the period of the gold standard, practically all governments of history have used their exclusive power to issue money to defraud and plunder the people."[2]

— Friedrich A. Hayek, Nobel prizewinner, economist

OVERVIEW: A fiat currency, like the dollar, is a currency that is not backed by any type of commodity. Since an underlying commodity does not give value to the fiat currency, only one thing can determine its value: scarcity. The government institutions, however, have a terrible track record of keeping fiat currencies in scarce supply. No fiat currency has ever succeeded. Ever. This chapter analyzes some of history's fiat currencies. Will America follow the same historical pattern?

"O Ye of Little Fiat . . ."

Fiat currencies are faith-based currencies. And people who live, work, and transact in a fiat currency system are a people of great faith. *Faith, you say?* What does faith have to do with a fiat currency system? Well, faith has *everything* to do with a fiat currency. As we have already learned, a fiat currency is not backed by any type of commodity. This means that your fiat dollars do not derive their value from anything tangible and they are not convertible into any other commodity on a fixed basis. The only real value of a fiat currency is its *scarcity*. This scarcity-dependent system means that those who choose to use and transact in a fiat currency system are expressing great faith in their government to keep the fiat currency in scarce supply. Fiat currency systems place an immense amount of responsibility upon the shoulders of the government to maintain the value of the nation's currency. To maintain the value of a fiat currency, it must be held in a limited and strictly measured supply. If the government chose to ignore this responsibility by producing massive amounts of the fiat currency, each fiat dollar would become worth less, if not worthless! Under such an irresponsible system, the citizenry would not want to hold the fiat currency. They would lose faith in both the sustainability of the fiat currency, and in the government that had chosen to overproduce it.

So I repeat, fiat currencies are faith-based currencies. The faith is in the government that issues the fiat currency to maintain its value.

Question: Is the U.S. dollar the first faith-based (fiat) currency in existence? And if it is not, what kind of historical track record do faith-based currencies have? Are fiat currencies more likely to succeed or to fail?

Answer: The history of fiat currencies has been one marked by consistent failure. Ever since the dawn of fiat creation, governments who have used fiat currencies have overproduced them until the currencies became worthless. This overproduction occurs when the government becomes seduced by the seeming ability to solve their economic misfortunes through the overly simple process of "creating money." But creating money "out of thin air," as the fiat currency system so easily allows, always comes at an enormous cost. History is clear. Every fiat currency ever devised throughout history has faced the same embarrassing and miserable death: *utter collapse by overproduction.*

Interestingly, an in-depth review of fiat currency history also reveals something else: a widespread prosperity just prior to the fiat currency's collapse. Of course, the prosperity that is experienced just prior to the collapse of a fiat currency is an illusion. As more of the fiat currency is pumped into the economy, a temporary rise in the average standard of living creates an illusion of increasing wealth in the nation. As real as the illusion may seem, this prosperity is an illusion manufactured and fueled by the government's overproduction of the currency. After the illusion of prosperity comes the death of the currency. The irony is cruel.

There Is Nothing New Under the Sun

According to the Bible, King Solomon was the wisest man who ever lived. As one of the greatest kings of ancient Israel, Solomon lived comfortably in the most upper echelons of his society. History tells us that his riches were immense. He was denied no request. His popularity and fame as a successful king were spread throughout the entire region. And at a first glance at his writings in the Bible, one can quickly gather that the man was full of great amounts of God-given knowledge, common sense, and wisdom.

However, when you take a deeper look at Solomon's writings, something else emerges from the pages: *a profound sense of despair.* Despite having everything that his heart could desire, Solomon soon learned that a life lived apart from God was futile and that humanity's quest for meaning strictly within the realm of this life would always be fruitless. To put it in his words: "All is vanity." Solomon's realizations helps one gain a greater appreciation for the phrase "Ignorance is bliss."

Another one of Solomon's famous quotes is found in the Book of Ecclesiastes: *"Generations come and generations go, but the earth never changes. The sun rises and the sun sets, then hurries around to rise again. The wind blows south, and then turns north. Around and around it goes, blowing in circles. Rivers run into the sea, but the sea is never full. Then the water returns again to the rivers and flows out again to the sea. Everything is wearisome beyond description. No matter how much we see, we are never satisfied. No matter how much we hear, we are not content. History merely repeats itself. It has all been done before. Nothing under the sun is truly new. Sometimes people say, 'Here is something new!' But actually it is old; nothing is ever truly new. We don't remember what happened in the past, and in future generations, no one will remember what we are doing now"* (Eccles. 1:4–11; NLT).

Norman Cousins would later paraphrase King Solomon in his famous quip: "History is a vast early warning system."[3] George Santayana said it this way: "Those who do not know history are doomed to repeat it."[4] This is not to say that history always represents destiny. However, we must admit that while history may not always repeat, it certainly rhymes. And the rhyming of history is what this chapter is about. While each historical case of fiat currency collapse is unique, it is all rooted in the same basic problem: human greed.

The Money Supply and Prices Are Directly Related

Before we take our brief excursion through history's pages concerning fiat currencies, let us illustrate an important concept about the overproduction of money. Imagine for a moment that two brothers — we will call them Bill and Bob — have become stranded on a deserted island. After a couple of desperate attempts to get off the island, Bill and Bob realize that the island may be their new home for some time. Bill soon discovers a fruit tree and lays claim to it. Under normal circumstances, Bob could pay money for one of Bill's fruits. However, Bob has no money, only a pocketful of eight golf balls. Bob and Bill soon decide that they will use the golf balls as the island's new official currency. Under their new "currency" system, each man gets four golf balls with which to trade for things that the other man may find.

Bob then offers Bill one of his own golf balls for a piece of fruit from Bill's tree. Just as the two men begin to negotiate, a very loud noise, like something striking the ground, is heard just a few hundred feet away. Bob and Bill run to investigate the noise and discover a very large wooden crate lying on the ground attached to a parachute. To their surprise, the outside of the box reads: "Golf Balls — 100,000 count." What effect does this new development have on the price of Bill's fruit? The answer is that the price for Bill's fruit goes way up instantly. With so many new golf balls now available, why would Bill want just one golf ball for his fruit? Why not ten? Twenty? Or even one hundred? When the golf balls change from having a scarce supply to an abundant supply, the prices of everything on the island rise. The money inside a modern economy operates much in the same way as our golf ball illustration. The more scarce the money supply, the lower the price of the goods and services denominated in that currency. And the opposite is also true. The higher the money supply, the higher the prices will be for the same goods and services.

This is because the amount of money within any economy is directly related to, and directly affects, the prices within that system.

So if the prices of everything seem to be going up within a particular economy, ask this question: *Is the government increasing the supply of money within the system?* Is milk more expensive? If so, either the business of milking cows just got more costly, or more money has been pushed into the system by the government.

Has bread become more expensive than it used to be? Either the costs of making bread have gone up, or the government is pumping more currency into the economy.

It may be difficult to determine which one is happening in some cases. However, determining whether an increase of currency is occurring within the system becomes very obvious when the prices of *everything* are all going up at the same time. When this happens it is called *inflation*. Inflation is basically a hidden tax on consumers and will be discussed in further detail in our next chapter. When inflation becomes uncontrollable, it is called *hyperinflation*. Obviously, hyperinflation is one of the most dangerous economic problems that a nation can face because prices rise dramatically and all in a very short time period. *Unfortunately, hyperinflation has been the doom of nearly every fiat currency–based system that has ever existed.*

A Brief History of Fiat Currencies

Let us now examine several fiat currencies that have been used throughout history. Each of them, of course, is now dead and gone. But let them serve as a testimony to man's tendency toward greed coupled with his consistent inability to rule himself.

Ancient Rome

The five centuries of the Roman Empire's dominance of the known world provides rich insights to those who enjoy researching history. And while the empire's rise was due to a variety of interesting factors, the reasons for its fall are rather predictable: government overspending and greed coupled with military overextension.

Obviously, the costs of financing the empire's perpetual wars and its numerous public works projects were immense. To fund the empire required ever-increasing taxes upon the Roman citizenry. But as time went on, many citizens could not bear the increasing taxes and sought relief through tax evasion. As many citizens opted to evade their taxes, the empire's tax revenues fell short. Instead of cutting its spending in response to the lower tax revenue, the empire moved to create a stealth tax that no one could hide from: inflation. Roman emperors began ordering the pure gold and silver coinage to be debased. To accomplish this, the silver content in the empire's coins was melted down and replaced partially with iron, and the gold was replaced with copper. Since it was done in limited amounts, few citizens noticed the new hybrid coins. By debasing the empire's currency, the government was able to raise large amounts of new money for the empire. However, the temptation to debase the currency became so much of an obsession that near the end of the Roman Empire, a Roman denarius coin was approximately 5 percent silver and 95 percent iron.

As the empire's financial needs grew, cheaper metals like copper and tin began to replace the gold and silver coins that had once been the empire's currency. These cheaper metals meant that more currency could be produced. This increased supply of currency naturally led to the higher prices of goods. In A.D. 301, Emperor Diocletian sought to end the increasing prices through price controls. By issuing the Edict of Prices, Diocletian threatened any and all merchants with the death penalty if their prices went above the empire's acceptable range. These policies eventually led to massive hyperinflation and the fall of the Roman Empire.[5]

China

China has had many experiences with hyperinflation due to its periodic attempts at creating a paper currency. One example occurred in A.D. 910, when China experimented with paper money. However, after a few centuries of currency overproduction and inflation, China decided to abandon the paper money system.

France

In 1720 a bankrupt France got a taste of paper money gone awry, thanks in part to John Law and his Mississippi Bubble scheme. Law convinced King Louis XV to adopt a paper currency and enforce its usage through making it the only acceptable form of payment for taxes. As the paper money became popular with the French people,

France began overprinting the currency and thereby further destroyed the economy.

During the French Revolution a generation later in 1791, France made another attempt at a paper currency. Four short years later, in 1795, inflation was growing at 13,000 percent. Napoleon Bonaparte ended the French Revolution and replaced France's paper money system with a gold-backed money system. This led to an era of prosperity.

But later, in 1936, France nationalized the Bank of France and removed the gold backing from the French currency. The new fiat paper currency became completely worthless just over a decade later.

Weimar Republic (Pre-Hitler Germany)

Hyperinflation struck the Weimar Republic of Germany in the post-World War I era of the 1920s. At the Treaty of Versailles, Germany accepted its defeat and was forced to pay war reparations to France. War-torn and humiliated, Germany had little money with which to pay its enormous war debts. By 1923 an impatient France became frustrated at Germany's inconsistent payments on its debt. In an effort to get their money, the French invaded Germany by marching into a German industrial area, known as the Ruhr, where Germany held much of its wealth. France occupied the area, threatening to bring Germany to its knees. Germany quickly responded by printing more money. As the German government began printing millions of marks to keep itself solvent, German citizens began to see an increase in their wages due to all of the excess money within the system. There are pictures from Germany showing workers being paid with wheelbarrows full of money. The problem, however, was that the prices of goods and services was growing at a faster rate than wages. For example, in 1922 a loaf of bread cost 160 marks. By the fall of 1923, the same loaf of bread cost 1,500,000 marks! To counter this, the German government made the situation even worse by printing more money. This, of course, had disastrous results. The overproduction of the German mark not only wiped out the life savings of much of the population, but it also made it so many people could not afford to simply eat due to rising prices. Mass hunger in the nation led to starvation in the poorest communities. Poverty was soon widespread as the prices of goods and services skyrocketed with no end in sight. As the marks became completely worthless, many families burned the marks, as it was cheaper to burn the money than it was to purchase firewood. Others used the marks as wallpaper. By 1924, Germany had replaced the failed mark with the new and improved currency "rentenmark." Additionally, France became more reasonable on a debt repayment schedule, providing some needed relief to the German government and its people. Later, in 1929 as the U.S. economy collapsed, Germany followed by falling into a deep economic depression. This economic meltdown led to social chaos, which provided the perfect breeding ground for the rise of Adolf Hitler.

Recent Fiat Failures

In the last century, the world has witnessed a number of fiat currency problems, and even collapses.

In 1922 Austria suffered from large amounts of inflation as high as 134 percent.

In 1932 Argentina's fiat currency system began a long and painful collapse. In the period just before the collapse, they were ranked as the eighth largest economy in the world.

DID YOU KNOW? On April 2, 1792, the United States Congress passed the Coinage Act. This act established the United States Mint and regulated coinage of the United States. President George Washington and the Congress strongly detested paper currencies and therefore made special provisions within the act to ensure that anyone who attempted to debase the currency would be put to death. Ironically, today George Washington's face is plastered on the front of the fiat U.S. one dollar bill — the same kind of currency that would have brought the death penalty just two short centuries ago.

In 1944 Greece suffered its worst inflation ever. The inflation reached 8.5 billion percent per month! During this period of inflation, prices doubled every 28 hours.

In 1946 Hungary's fiat currency suffered from 4.19 quintillion (4.19×10^{18}) percent inflation. (Prices doubled every 15 hours.) Each morning, millions of Hungarians listened to a radio broadcast just to keep up with how much their money was worth that day. This is one of the worst cases of hyperinflation in history.

In 1984, after battling inflation for a decade, Israel suffered an inflation rate of 445 percent, which was later tamed by price controls.

In 1990 Peru faced a monthly inflation rate of 397 percent, due to its poor monetary policies.

In 1992 Norway, Italy, and Finland experienced major currency problems with their fiat currencies.

From 1993 to 1994, Yugoslavia experienced one of the worst bouts of hyperinflation in history. Mathematical equations are required to measure the height of inflation that struck Yugoslavia during this time. The inflation rate during this period: 5×10^{15} percent!

From 1993 to 1995, the country of Ukraine suffered from hyperinflationary pressures. At one point, their inflation rate reached 1,400 percent per month!

In 1994 the Mexican peso collapsed in what was known as "the Tequila Hangover."

In 1997 the Asian Currency Crisis began as Thailand's fiat currency, the baht, collapsed. The effects of the collapse spread to other Far East nations.

In 1998 the Russian ruble collapsed. Like Germany's Weimar Republic, Russian workers were paid in wheelbarrows full of rubles. While the situation was far from comical, some in the working class joked about the worthless currency: "We pretend to work and they pretend to pay us."

Beginning in 2001, Turkey experienced major bouts with hyperinflation as its currency, the lira, became increasingly worthless. Currency reform came in 2005, when Turkey issued a new Turkish lira (1 was exchanged for 1,000,000 old lira).

In 2007, after several years of increasing inflation rates, the African nation of Zimbabwe was gripped by massive hyperinflation. By the summer of 2007, the inflation rate was 11,000 percent. One year later, the official monthly inflation figures were over 11,250,000 percent!

At this rate of inflation, Zimbabwe residents must spend their paychecks as soon as they receive them to keep the money from losing its worth as prices continue to outpace incomes. And if some estimates are correct, the worst is not over as Zimbabwe may be heading for one billion percent inflation in the near future!

The Failures of Fiat Money Ignored

In former times, many people were intimately aware of the grave dangers caused by fiat currencies. The French philosopher Voltaire once quipped: "Paper money eventually returns to its intrinsic value — zero."[6] All of earth's recorded history can quickly respond with a loud *"Amen"* to Voltaire's astute observation. While the landscape of world history is littered with failed fiat currencies, history is also replete with vigilant warnings from our ancestors regarding the inherent dangers of fiat currencies. Here I have compiled a list of warnings issued by some of the brightest men in world history regarding the failures of fiat-based money. You will notice their reference to gold and silver as a wise backing to a nation's currency. I will explain those references momentarily.

> *You have to choose [as a voter] between trusting to the natural stability of gold and the natural stability of the honesty and intelligence of the members of the Government. And, with due respect for these gentlemen, I advise you, as long as the Capitalist system lasts, to vote for gold.*[7] — George Bernard Shaw

> *Sound money still means today what it meant in the nineteenth century: the gold standard.*[8] — Ludwig von Mises

> *Paper money is like dram-drinking, it relieves for a moment by deceitful sensation, but gradually diminishes the natural heat, and leaves the body worse than it found it. Were not this the case, and could money be made of paper at pleasure, every sovereign in Europe would be as rich as he pleased. But the truth is, that it is a bubble and the attempt vanity. Nature has provided the proper materials for money: gold and silver, and any attempt of ours to rival her is ridiculous.*[9] — Thomas Paine

If you increase the quantity of money, you bring about the lowering of the purchasing power of the monetary unit.[10] — Ludwig von Mises

We are in danger of being overwhelmed with irredeemable paper, mere paper, representing not gold nor silver; no sir, representing nothing but broken promises, bad faith, bankrupt corporations, cheated creditors, and a ruined people.[11] — Daniel Webster

The governments alone are responsible for the spread of the superstitious awe with which the common man looks upon every bit of paper upon which the treasury or agencies which it controls have printed the magical words legal tender.[12] — Ludwig von Mises

Of all the contrivances for cheating the laboring classes of mankind, none has been more effective than that which deludes them with paper money.[13] — Daniel Webster

Based upon the preceding quotes and all that is known from recorded history, it is hardly conceivable as to why our modern society would dare to build and hold the majority of its wealth in a fiat paper money system. Yet today, every economy in the world uses a fiat currency! Why would the nations of this world place their wealth near the precarious slopes of fiat currency systems? Insanity has been defined as doing the same thing over and over again but expecting a different result. As we examine the consistent failures of fiat currency systems throughout history, you may find yourself asking why someone has not come up with a better system by now. If fiat currencies have a 100 percent chance of failure, then why are they ever considered by modern governments? The answer is not easy to find, but it can be found. Answers do not come simply because the question exists. Answers come only when enough people ask the question and demand an answer.

One obvious answer is human greed. Fiat currencies allow governments, businesses, and consumers to spend more than they actually have. This is because modern fiat money is debt-based money. Today's monetary systems are based and rooted in debt. *Today, money itself is simply debt.* While many financial commentators are quick to point out that you should "get out of debt," this book is going to explain that the money you hold in your pocket is debt itself. The current system is entirely flawed. How all of this is possible is completely exposed in chapter 12 (What the Banking Industry Does Not Want You to Know). In that chapter, I will unveil another possible reason why the nations of this world have opted for fiat currencies over more sound and honest money. What we will discover in that chapter will be shocking, to say the least.

God's View of Fiat Currencies

One of the tragedies of our modern day is found in the passivity of the population regarding its government's monetary policy. For the most part, economic literacy levels are at all-time lows around the world. Part of this is due to the increasing complexity of the global financial systems. But it is also due to a growing apathy among the citizenry of various nations. This apathy has allowed government to grow, both in size and in strength, virtually unchecked. The larger the government, the more severe the problems eventually become.

For those who belong to the Kingdom of God, the answer is not found in political or economic activism, but rather in simple awareness. This awareness of the monetary system has traditionally been rejected on the merits that money is not important to God. In the name of spirituality, many followers of Christ have rejected economic awareness. This is staggering, especially when one considers that while Jesus Christ was on the earth, He had more to say about money and possessions than any other topic, including faith, hope, heaven, and hell combined! In fact, over 2,350 verses of the Holy Bible contain a reference to money and possessions. Obviously, money and its effects are an important topic to the God of the Bible.

Considering that the Bible has so much to say about the topic of money, is it possible that it has anything to say about fiat currencies? While this may seem like a strange question, you may be surprised to find that God has a very strong opinion on the topic of fiat currencies. Of course, you will find no reference to the word "fiat" in the Bible. That is because this is a modern word. Instead, when God biblically condemns "unjust weights and balances," this references a concept very similar to the manipulation of fiat money today.

In biblical times, business and commerce were often conducted through the use of scales and measures. However, unscrupulous businessmen in ancient times discovered how to swindle the average consumer through the use of inaccurate scales and balances. By readjusting their scales, merchants could easily cheat and deceive their customers. God obviously took issue with this by calling it thievery. The Bible consistently condemns the use of "unjust weights and balances."

Proverbs 11:1 — *"A false balance is an abomination to the Lord, but a just weight is His delight"* (NASB).

Proverbs 20:10 — *"Diverse weights and diverse measures, they are both alike, an abomination to the Lord."*

In Leviticus 19:35–36, the God of Israel told His people, the Israelites, that all economic transactions (buying and selling) should be conducted with honest weights. *"You shall do no wrong in judgment, in measurement of weight, or capacity. You shall have just balances, just weights. . . ."* (NASB).

Of course, today it is rare to find someone using scales and balances in their business. However, this biblical principle still remains.

So, what would a false balance look like in today's world? One example of a "false balance" would be an automotive mechanic who repairs your vehicle and charges you for a new part but secretly uses an old used part. That would be considered a "false balance" in God's sight according to the biblical definition. Another example could be if you purchased a used automobile from an auto dealer and they secretly manipulated the odometer to display fewer miles than the car actually had. Again, this would be an example of an "unjust weight and balance."

And likewise, a false balance would include our current fiat-based monetary system where our currency is backed by nothing but debt and can be printed at will. In fact, each of the cases of hyperinflation that we discussed earlier are examples of "false balances." *The governments of each of these countries had violated God's Word regarding just weights and balances when they began destroying the purchasing power and life savings of their citizens.*

Fiat currency systems, where the currency is backed by nothing and its value can be manipulated at will, is by definition an unjust weight. *And so therefore, by biblical definition, fiat currency systems are clearly unjust systems.*

What a tragedy then that modern Christianity's de-emphasis of economic literacy has allowed its adherents to misunderstand one of the most basic principles in God's Word. Worse yet, it is amazing how many followers of Jesus Christ insist that the U.S. dollar maintain its idolatrous statement, "In God We Trust," upon the currency. Based upon a proper biblical understanding of the fiat currency, *it is highly unlikely that God is interested in having His name plastered on such an abomination as the fiat U.S. dollar.*

The ignorance pervading the American Church regarding these matters is frightening because it seems more like deception than simple ignorance. Ignorance can be quickly resolved when confronted with knowledge. However, the American Church's ignorance on this topic appears to be more rooted in deception for several reasons.

During His most famous sermon, the Sermon on the Mount, Jesus Christ made a profound observation about mankind's love for money by stating that man "cannot serve both God and money" (Matt. 6:24; Luke 16:13). Christ points out that man's desire to live a life that is spent serving and loving money will always strive to be the chief competitor for the hearts of His followers. The apostle Paul later calls the love of money "the root of all kinds of evil" (1 Tim. 6:10).

For this reason alone, those who choose to follow the teachings of Christ must be all the more diligent in their finances. This is because money is always vying for first place in their hearts.

America's currency system of "unjust weights and balances" can be clearly seen by examining these two very different dollar bills.

1923 One Dollar
Bill (Silver Certificate)

Notice what the 1923 U.S. dollar says at the top of the bill: "Silver Certificate: This certifies that there has been deposited in the treasury of the United States of America." Then notice toward the bottom of the bill it states: "One silver dollar payable to the bearer on demand."

ONE SILVER DOLLAR
PAYABLE TO THE BEARER ON DEMAND

What exactly does all of that language mean? It simply means that the owner of this dollar bill could trade it at any time for one dollar's worth of silver. The reason for this is because in the past, the U.S. dollar was a receipt that could be redeemed in a fixed rate of gold or silver.

Compare that to a modern U.S. dollar as seen below:

Modern U.S. Dollar Bill (Federal Reserve Note)

Notice that the language on the front of this U.S. dollar bill has changed. At the top, it simply states "Federal Reserve Note." And at the bottom, the language has changed from "One Silver Dollar payable to the bearer on demand" to simply "One Dollar."

ONE DOLLAR

What does all this mean, you may be asking? It simply means that if you take your "Federal Reserve Notes" to the bank and ask the banker for some silver or gold in exchange, you will be laughed out of the bank.

The truth is, today's U.S. dollar is completely worthless in and of itself. It is a piece of worthless paper whose value is strictly determined through your government's discretion.

Isn't it amazing that after all of the fiat failures throughout history, we are standing at the cliff of disaster again?

Something inside you may be saying: *Sure, other nations have failed in their attempts at a fiat currency. But this is America. We are different. We are exceptional, and besides, God would never allow this nation to fail.*

I will bite my tongue at this juncture and instead will point you to our next chapter, entitled: "Why the Dollar Is Doomed."

Endnotes

1. John Maynard Keynes, *The Economic Consequences of the Peace* (Charleston, SC: BiblioBazaar, LLC, 2008), p. 168.
2. Mark Watterson, *Don't Weep for Me, America: How Democracy in America Became the Prince* (Pittsburgh, PA: Dorrance Publishing, 2008), p. 68.
3. *Saturday Review*, editorial, April 15, 1978.
4. Bob Davis, *Whatever Happened to High School History?* (Ontario: James Lorimer & Company, 1995).
5. Addison Wiggin, *The Demise of the Dollar — And Why It's Even Better for Your Investments*, Chuck Butler, contributor (England: John Wiley and Sons, 2008), p. 59.
6. Moriah Saul, *Plantation Earth: The Cross of Iron and the Chains of Debt* (Canada: Trafford Publishing, 2003), p. 24.
7. Herbert G. Grubel, *World Monetary Reform: Plans and Issues* (Stanford, CA: Stanford University Press, 1963), p. 333.
8. Ludwig von Mises, Percy L. Greaves, trans., *On the Manipulation of Money and Credit* (Dobbs Ferry, NY: Free Market Books, 1978), p. 279.
9. Michael Foot and Isaac Kramnick, editors, *Thomas Paine Reader* (New York: Penguin Classics, 1987), p. 197.
10. Ludwig von Mises, *Economic Policy: Thoughts for Today and Tomorrow* (Auburn, AL: Ludwig von Mises Institute, 2006), p. 66.
11. *The Works of Daniel Webster* (Boston, MA: Little, Brown, 1890), p. 413.
12. Ludwig von Mises, *Human Action: A Treatise on Economics* (Chicago, IL: Contemporary Books, 1949), p. 448.
13. Forrest Capie, *Major Inflations in History* (Brookfield, VT: E. Elgar Pub., 1991), p. 304.

Chapter 4
Why the Dollar Is Doomed

"Without the confidence factor, many believe a paper money system is liable to collapse eventually."[1]

— Federal Reserve Bank of Philadelphia

"You earn wages, only to put them in a purse with holes in it."

— Haggai 1:6; NIV

OVERVIEW: In 1971, Richard Nixon detached the U.S. dollar from the gold standard. Since then, the amount of currency within the American financial system has skyrocketed to unprecedented amounts. Smart investors like Jim Rogers, Warren Buffett, Bill Gates, George Soros, and Alan Greenspan have stated on numerous occasions that the dollar will continue to drop in value. As more investors (i.e., foreign central banks) awake to this reality and move their investments away from the falling fiat dollar, the dollar will become further devalued, which will have devastating effects upon those who continue to hold them and use them.

Bretton Woods — The Changing of the Guard

At the end of the 19th century, London was the capital of a global superpower. Through its aggressive and systematic colonization efforts, the British Empire had been able to dominate and control more geography than any previous empire before it. At the zenith of its rule, it was accurately stated that "the sun never set" on the British Empire. Put simply, the British Empire was the largest economic empire the world had ever seen. And by default, the British Empire's currency, the British sterling pound, was the most sought-after currency on the planet. However, like most empires before it, military overextension and economic arrogance left Great Britain ripe for replacement by a leaner and more nimble competitor. This was especially true in the aftermath of two World Wars, that spread the British Empire thin. The competitor that would rise to the occasion was none other than the United States of America.

By the end of World War II, Britain's excesses had nearly sealed its fate. Along with the rest of the European community, the British Empire was left economically devastated. In an effort to restore strength and order to the global markets, an important economic conference was held at the Mount Washington Hotel in Bretton Woods, New Hampshire, in July 1944. Under the banner of the United Nations Monetary and Financial Conference, this groundbreaking international gathering included 730 delegates from over 40 Allied nations. In the midst of a world war, the attendees sought to bring financial stability to the international community through the creation of a regulated system. However, the United States knew an opportunity when they saw one. With Europe in shambles, Bretton Woods provided immense power to the emerging American economic empire. One senior official at the Bank of England described the deal reached at Bretton Woods as "the greatest blow to Britain next to the war." This, of course, was due to the transfer of economic power from Britain to the United States.

This historic conference also established a number of government institutions, including the World Bank, the International Monetary Fund (IMF), and General Agreement on Trades and Tariffs (GATT), to be later known as the World Trade Organization (WTO.)

In addition, the United States agreed to link the U.S. dollar to gold at a fixed rate of $35.00 per ounce. The dollar was immediately convertible into a fixed amount of gold, which brought much-needed economic relief and helped to restore confidence in the global financial markets. In response, all other global currencies were then linked to the U.S. dollar, as it was viewed as being as "good as gold." Without doubt, America emerged as the lone economic victor in the post–World War II era.

The monetary and political leverage achieved by the Bretton Woods Agreement gave America the position of economic supremacy on the global stage. From 1944 through the 1960s became an era of great prosperity for the American economy.

Soon, however, this "dollars-for-gold" system began to weigh heavily on the United States. Once again, war was the culprit. This time, it was an American war in East Asia, namely Vietnam. By the late 1960s and early 1970s, America had suffered large numbers of casualties. Additionally, the war was placing a severe strain upon the nation's economy. Inflation became a growing threat and the United States faced its first trade deficit in the 20th century. As economic and political turmoil heated up in America and around the world, many nations that had been dependent upon an economically strong United States began to lose faith in America's ability to responsibly maintain its economy. This lack of faith led to massive pressure upon the "gold for dollars" system. As nations lined up to trade their U.S. dollars for gold, America's gold reserves began to drop as dollars came flooding back into the U.S. economy. By 1971, Washington knew that the Bretton Woods system was neither viable nor sustainable. On August 15 of that same year, President Richard Nixon "closed the gold window," thus ending the practice of exchanging dollars for gold, as directed under the Bretton Woods agreement. It was in this year, 1971, that the U.S. dollar was officially detached from the gold standard and declared a purely fiat currency.

Washington was quick to recognize, however, that this shift in economic policy could eventually lead to a declining demand for the U.S. dollar around the globe. This previous global demand for the U.S. dollar was what, in large part, fueled America's prosperity. After all, strong global demand for a nation's currency is the stuff that empires are made of. Trust and respect for the U.S. economy and its currency had been established in part by the Bretton Woods system. However, with dollars no longer convertible into gold, how long would it be before global demand waned? The United States was not interested in learning the answer. Instead, they quickly moved into action in an attempt to ensure that global demand for the dollar would not be permanently affected by its new "fiat" status.

The Petrodollar System — "Oil for Dollars"

With the protection of global demand for the dollar as the highest priority, the United States would soon unleash its craftiest ploy yet: The petrodollar system. (For full details on the petrodollar system, see chapter 9.) Fully aware that global demand for oil was increasing, the United States held a series of high-level talks with the leaders of the Oil Producing and Exporting Countries (also known as OPEC). By 1973, the United States had cut its first deal with Saudi Arabia. What the United States offered to Saudi Arabia was weapons and vigilant military protection of their precious oil fields. In exchange, the United States asked that all future Saudi oil production be priced exclusively in U.S. dollars.

> **DID YOU KNOW?**
> Not too long ago, it was reported that several members of the U.S. Congressional Banking Committee still believed that the U.S. dollar is backed by gold. The truth, however, is that the U.S. dollar is not backed by gold. Instead, the U.S. dollar is a fiat currency. It is backed by nothing and is intrinsically worthless.

This event marked the inception of the petrodollar system. Soon, this *"oil for dollars"* system grew to the point that all oil produced anywhere on the planet could be purchased only in U.S. dollars. This system forced nations that lacked sufficient natural resources to accumulate U.S. dollars. In response to this "oil for dollars" system, resource-poor nations, such as Japan and Korea, gravitated toward an export-led growth strategy in order to accumulate U.S. dollars for their energy resource needs. For example, to acquire the dollars necessary to purchase its energy supplies, resource-poor Japan would need to sell a Honda to the United States.

Obviously, the petrodollar system has served the United States phenomenally well since the 1970s. But it is also America's Achilles' heel. (Only recently has this system begun to break down, which is discussed at length in chapter 9.) Even though the dollar can be converted into oil, it does not mean that the U.S. dollar is not a fiat currency. Let's be clear on this point: the U.S. dollar, which at one time was backed by gold, is now not backed by anything. It is a purely fiat currency.

The Death of the Dollar

Today, the mighty U.S. dollar is still the world's reserve currency. But its days are numbered. *I firmly believe that we will witness the downfall of the U.S. dollar system within the next decade.* As the old saying goes: "If something is unsustainable, then it can't last forever." Simply put, the dollar system, in its current form, is unsustainable. The reasons behind the unsustainability of the dollar system are numerous. In the remaining pages of this chapter, I want to outline the reasons why the dollar must collapse. While the signs that the dollar is doomed are plentiful, let us focus on *three specific threats* to the endangered U.S. currency:

- The declining purchasing power of the U.S. dollar due to excessive printing

- The U.S. government's lack of a "strong dollar" policy (interest rates). (The Greenspan Doctrine: capital flows to the rate of highest return)

- A growing aversion by foreign nations to hold U.S. dollars

The Declining Purchasing Power of the U.S. Dollar Due to Excessive Printing

As a kid, I used to enjoy hearing stories from my parents and grandparents about how much cheaper things used to be in their "day." For example, a movie ticket today costs on average $7.00. But the average price for that same ticket in 1968 was a mere $1.31! Or a McDonald's hamburger, which costs around $1.00 today, cost only 15 cents in 1966! Those stories of how much things "used to cost" always fascinated me. Perhaps it was this fascination with prices that led me to a professional study of economics. However, it was not until I began studying the inner workings of the economy that I realized how drastic the prices of goods and services in America have increased over the last several decades. The prices of goods and services are certainly affected by a wide variety of factors, including technological advancements and the costs of doing business, among others. However, one of the primary determining factors of prices is related to the purchasing power of a nation's currency. In America, the purchasing power of the U.S. dollar has been declining, rather

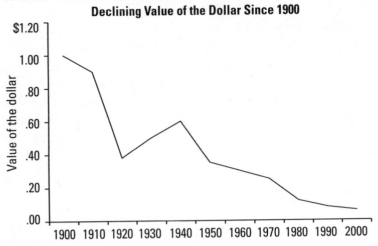

Declining Value of the Dollar Since 1900

Source: Bureau of the Census

dramatically, for decades. In fact, the U.S. dollar is now worth less than 10 percent of what it was in 1945!

The declining value of the U.S. dollar has been, in part, caused by poor U.S. monetary policies, which give the government the ability to print money as often as they wish. Of course, *this is precisely the problem with fiat currencies: the government can print them, as often as they like, with no accountability.*

This decline in the purchasing power of the U.S. dollar has been felt greatly outside of our own borders. Open any newspaper and you will see nearly every week that your hard-earned dollars are hitting all-time lows against other global currencies. Consider the comparisons of the value of the U.S. dollar to other foreign currencies on the following page.

The U.S. dollar is in a long-term downward trend against other currencies. Of course, average everyday Americans may not notice these massive currency fluctuations, especially if they do not travel outside the country. However, one thing everyone notices is gasoline prices and food prices. Have you noticed the price of groceries lately? They are going up rather quickly.

The price of gold is hitting an all-time high as is the price of oil. Gasoline is going up. Food prices are rising. It appears that the price of everything is going up. Of course, the U.S. federal government has told us that inflation is steady. But the prices of gold, oil, and food don't lie.

DID YOU KNOW?

- U.S. dollar vs. euro — U.S. dollar has lost 65%
- U.S. dollar vs. Swiss franc — U.S. dollar has lost 18.2%
- U.S. dollar vs. British pound — U.S. dollar has lost 42.6%
- U.S. dollar vs. Australian dollar — U.S. dollar has lost 75.6%
- U.S. dollar vs. Japanese yen — U.S. dollar has lost 18.2%

In chapter 2 we discussed how money is measured in the U.S. economy using M1, M2, and M3 money supply figures. The broadest measure of the U.S. money supply is the M3 figure. Because the U.S. dollar is a fiat currency, economists pay very close attention to the money supply numbers as reported by the Federal Reserve because those numbers will determine future prices. (The higher the money supply, the higher prices will go.)

Since the mid-1990s, the M3 money supply appeared to be trekking ever upward as the money supply reached new levels. Then suddenly, on March 23, 2006, the Federal Reserve made an announcement that it would cease reporting the M3 money supply numbers to the public effective immediately. What was their reason? *Cost.* Consider the irony in that this announcement comes from an organization that prints money! According to the 2004 and 2005 budgets of the Federal Reserve (available on their website at http://www.federalreserve.gov), the annual savings from not producing the M3 numbers would provide a whopping $1.5 million in savings. According to some sources, this would amount to 0.00000699 percent of the Fed's annual net income of last year.

You would think that such a broad economic and inflation indicator would be continually produced, analyzed, and monitored. However, when the announcement came, it fell on deaf ears. This bold new move by the Fed caused some stir among economists, but it never received any real media coverage. You would think that there would have been some public outcry over the lack of transparency. But the average person on the street has no idea what M3 is, and it is probably just as highly likely that they do not care. Sadly, America has become a nation that finds its interests in prime-time television. As I often say, *"If it's not on prime-time TV, it's likely not to be known, or cared about, by the majority."*

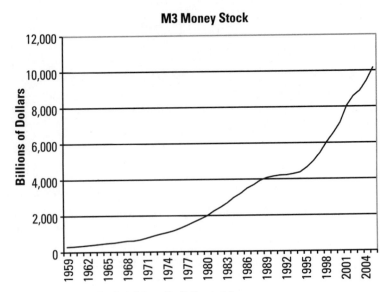

Source: www.research.stlouisfed.org/fred2/data/m3sl.txt

This move by the Federal Reserve to cease public reports of the M3 money supply data demonstrates a concerning lack of transparency. (However, in all fairness, the Federal Reserve has never been known for its transparency. Instead, it is an organization shrouded in secrecy. Read more on the Federal Reserve in chapter 12.) But to understand why the Federal Reserve would cease publishing the M3 money supply numbers, we must simply examine the out-of-control pace at which they have been flooding the economy with their worthless paper dollars. Consider the following:

- From 1776 to 1983, the M3 money supply growth totaled $2.5 trillion (207 years)
- From 1983 to 1997, the M3 money supply growth totaled $2.5 trillion (14 years)
- From 1997 to 2001, the M3 money supply growth totaled $2.5 trillion (4 years)

While the Federal Reserve has become less transparent in its actions than ever, we do know that right now, the printing presses are rolling and that the Federal Reserve is injecting massive amounts of currency into the U.S. economy. So if scarcity of a currency stabilizes

Components of the Money Supply over Time

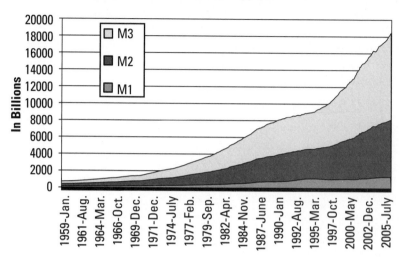

its value, what does an overproduction of that same currency do to its value? Overproduction of the dollar means that its value falls. And if the value of the dollar falls, what does that do to the prices of consumer goods priced in dollars? It drives them up.

But there is another problem with a rising money supply that I have not yet mentioned. *Not only do consumer prices rise when the money supply increases, but investments made in that currency lose value.*

An October 13, 2007, news report by the *International Herald Tribune* entitled "U.S. Stocks Rise, but Fall Behind" tells the shocking reality.

> Five years after the American stock market hit bottom after the bursting of the technology stock bubble and the 2001 recession, share prices as measured by the Standard & Poor's 500 have doubled. That growth amounts to a compound annual increase of 15 percent a year and is the fastest doubling off a market bottom since the 1980s. But in the current world environment, it does not look impressive. Nearly every other stock market in the world has done better. Of the 83 countries for which records of a major stock index were available, *the American share price increase in the five years after Oct. 9, 2002,*

was better than those of only four. All four are small countries, either in the Caribbean or Latin America."[2]

Despite the declining value of the U.S. dollar, millions of Americans continue to believe that the U.S. stock market is making them richer every month.

The U.S. Government's Lack of a "Strong Dollar" Policy

In 2008, a liquidity crisis began to fully rock America and the global financial markets. In response to this crisis, global central bankers decided to treat the crisis with more liquidity. In an effort to delay the inevitable pain of too much liquidity created by a faulty fiat currency system and overleveraging, the central banks have come galloping to the rescue of the fragile global economy with interest rate cuts and massive cash infusions. The credit crisis currently affecting the globe has exposed the reckless lending practices and crafty financial engineering, which has led to a speculative mania.

Unfortunately, these liquidity injections are a short-term solution to a long-term structural problem. The U.S. subprime crisis, which has turned into a global contagion, is serving as a wake-up call to the world's bankers (and global politicians, by default) who have allowed the global fiat systems to spin out of control. The U.S. financial system, built upon a faulty fiat currency system coupled with poor fiscal stewardship, is a house of cards. And it will come crashing down as soon as the global population awakens to the hard realities brought on by the financial excesses of the American lifestyle. *The truth is this: the dollar is worthless paper that is printed at will. No one is working to keep it in limited supply.*

> ### DID YOU KNOW?
>
> *Assume you had placed $10,000 in three-month U.S. Treasury Bills at the beginning of 2002. At the end of five years, the buying power of your money would have decreased by $116.19, or 1.2 percent, when taking inflation into account.*
>
> *If instead you had used $5,000 to purchase gold and silver ($2,500 each) and put the other $5,000 into three-month U.S. Treasury bills, your buying power would have increased by $5,977.28, a gain of 59.8 percent!*

The Greenspan Doctrine

The move to re-inflate through easy monetary policy is now considered by many as the "Greenspan doctrine." During his tenure as Federal Reserve chairman, Alan Greenspan's response to financial crisis was to inflate his way out of them:

- In the stock market crash of 1987, Greenspan inflated the monetary base.
- During the 1994 Mexican peso crisis, Greenspan inflated.
- During the 1997 Asian crisis and LTCM debacle, Greenspan inflated.
- During the 1998 Russian ruble crisis, Greenspan inflated.
- In the wake of the dot-com crash in March 2000, Greenspan inflated.
- After 9/11/01, Greenspan inflated.

And beginning in June 2003, key U.S. interest rate targets were lowered to 1 percent for an entire year under this Greenspan doctrine.

Since Federal Reserve chief Ben Bernanke has been in office, little has changed. Mr. Bernanke is following the same pattern, and recently he lowered short-term interest rates back to the 1 percent level. For the last several years, U.S. inflationary pressures have been building. It has been my mantra that interest rates should be raised and the monetary supply should be tightened to prevent widespread inflation, and even worse, stagflation. Recently, Greenspan has admitted that stagflation appears to be around the corner. By continually lowering interest rates and engaging in the moral hazard of bailouts for U.S. corporations, the United States has shown a great disregard for its stated "strong dollar" policy. Instead of trying to save the fragile currency, it has chosen to allow it to be devalued through extremely poor monetary policies.

The United States continues to enjoy the status of the global economic hegemonic power with the key reserve currency. But the current economic arrangement is unsustainable. I fully anticipated the global central bank coordination to re-inflate their way out of the global credit crunch. However, even if the central bank effort can successfully contain the credit crisis, it will only be a temporary fix.

And it will only serve to delay and enlarge the scope of the impending day of reckoning for the United States.

A Growing Aversion by Foreign Nations to Hold U.S. Dollars

For decades, the U.S. dollar has been considered by most of the world as the safest and most liquid currency. However, over the last several months, foreign central banks have been relying less upon the U.S. dollar due to its perceived instability by selling off many of their dollar holdings. Gone are the days when the U.S. dollar is the only game in town. Many of America's competitors, including Europe and China, have developed their own viable currencies. As the U.S. dollar becomes increasingly difficult to prop up, America's competitors will seek to exploit the U.S. currency weakness.

Currently, foreign nations hold trillions of U.S. dollars in the form of U.S. Treasury bonds. *According to a September 2008 report issued by the U.S. Treasury, China has become America's largest foreign creditor, owning $585 billion of U.S. Treasury bonds.* China's ownership of American debt indicates our nation's growing reliance upon economic subsidies from Beijing. According to this same report, Japan is the second largest holder of U.S. debt at $573.2 billion as of September 2008.

Much of America's consumption-based debt is financed by foreign nations. This means that the American way of life is increasingly dependent upon financial inflows from foreign countries — and their continued willingness to finance our overconsumption. This is a fool's game and is clearly unsustainable. How can the government do all that it has promised if we are dependent upon foreign creditors? And especially if these foreign creditors are beginning to doubt our ability to pay back the debts that we owe.

Foreign governments are acutely aware of America's economic problems. Knowing this, many of them are biding their time by actively looking for alternatives to U.S. dollar-denominated assets for investment purposes. In the months and years ahead, other global currencies, such as the euro and the yuan, will be strong competitors for these same global investment dollars. In recent months, we have already witnessed small-scale changes in investment flows toward Europe and away from the U.S. dollar. These shifts will increase over time until we witness a full-blown collapse of the U.S. dollar. Sadly, when this foreign financing of American debt begins to wane, it will generate great fears within the community of America's creditors (i.e., China, Japan, etc.). If one creditor were to begin massive sell-offs of American debts, it would spark a panic among America's debt holders. *While no nation may want to be the first to sell their dollar holdings, they certainly will not want to be the last!* As the foreign financing of American debt begins to wane, it will be due to the fears surrounding America's ability to control its appetite for debt and to sustain a stable currency. One of the laws of economics is that money always flows to the highest rate of return. Today, the return on the U.S. dollar is not what it once was. The rise of the euro has served to challenge the supremacy of the dollar. Alan Greenspan, the former Federal Reserve chairman, publicly recognized the inevitable decline of the dollar during an interview with the German magazine *Stern.* In the interview Greenspan, who can move financial markets with a single word, confidently declared that the euro could soon replace the U.S. dollar as the global currency of choice.

Meanwhile, America's deficits are hitting all-time highs, the credit crisis continues to worsen, and the U.S. money supply is expanding at a record pace, triggering widespread fears of inflation. And these are just a few of the problems currently facing our economy. Sadly, most Americans remain clueless as to the problems and issues that will inevitably face them and their children. The facts are clear. The current economic situation in the United States is completely unsustainable. A financial day of reckoning awaits this country, and its arrival will serve as a rude awakening to all who are not prepared. If you think that America has seen the worst of the financial crisis, consider yourself forewarned. The real financial crisis awaiting America will begin when the U.S. dollar collapses. Unfortunately for American citizens, the U.S. government is doing little to prevent this impending dollar collapse. As long as the debt-loving, interest-rate cutting, currency-printaholic feds can't seem to find the "off" switch on the printing press, the dollar will continue to decline in value and in purchasing power.

Finally, current global economic arrangements require that foreign nations transact in dollars for purchasing their oil supplies. This arrangement, known as *the petrodollar system,* will eventually collapse under the weight of America's reckless economic stewardship. When the petrodollar system collapses, it will lead to astronomical interest rates and an end of the U.S. dollar. (To learn more about the petro-dollar system, see chapter 9.)

Seeing what lies ahead should make us glad that our true investments are safe in heaven where "neither moth nor rust destroys and where thieves do not break in and steal" (Matt. 6:20).

Endnotes

1. Federal Reserve Bank of Philadelphia, Gold, p. 10.
2. http://www.iht.com/articles/2007/10/13/business/13floyd.php.
3. Peter Schiff, "What Record High?" April 27, 2007, http://www.europac. net/extrenalframeset.asp?from=home&id=8422.

Part II
A Nation of Debt

Chapter 5
America: The Greatest Debtor Nation in World History

"Blessed are the young for they shall inherit the national debt."[1]

— Herbert Hoover

"I place economy among the first and most important virtues, and debt as the greatest of dangers to be feared."[2]

— Thomas Jefferson

OVERVIEW: *In 1980, America was the largest lender nation in world history. Just three short decades later, America now stands as the greatest debtor nation in world history. As of 2008, the United States has a national debt of over $9 trillion. It is projected to cross the $10 trillion mark in 2009. Much of this amount is owed to foreign countries, including China and Japan. Additionally, as the world's largest consumer nation, the United States has seen rapidly increasing trade deficits with its international trading partners. This chapter is filled with jaw-dropping statistics regarding the remarkable fiscal spending and over-consumption of the American government, including how we got here.*

In 1980 the U.S. national debt totaled $900 billion. In 2008, a mere 28 years later, the U.S. national debt had skyrocketed over 1000 percent to a jaw-dropping $9 trillion! This meteoric rise in the public national debt in America has been due to the result of something economists call *deficit spending*. Put simply, deficit spending is an economic term for spending more than you earn. A government that relies upon deficit spending as a perpetual growth model is like a man who pays his grocery bill and his rent with his credit card. It feels good for a while, but eventually the bill comes in. Never in all of recorded history has any government been as good at convincing its constituents of the benefits of deficit spending as America. And never has any constituency been more supportive of a government's out-of-control spending than the American public. In 1980, Ronald Reagan defeated President Jimmy Carter in the race for the White House. Reagan, a major proponent of deficit spending, won in a landslide victory after campaigning on the fact that "government is not the solution to our problem, government is the problem."

It took the country from George Washington until Ronald Reagan to reach a national debt level of $1 trillion. But in just eight years under Reagan, *the debt tripled to nearly $3 trillion!* Reagan later described the new debt as the "greatest disappointment" of his presidency. But the Reagan years of deficit spending were just the warm-up.

The 1990s — The Enchanting Decade

President Bill Clinton. To those who had the joy of following the amusing American political scene during the 1990s, the mere mention of his name evokes a wide variety of responses. Suffice it to say that his image, and his masterful political chicanery, is deeply enshrined in the American political memory and consciousness. One of the more priceless memories from that enchanting decade occurred during a presidential radio address on January 27, 1996. During President Clinton's scripted commentary, he made one of the most absurd statements to be uttered from the lips of a modern U.S. politician. While clamoring about the need to reinvent the U.S. government so that it "serves better and costs less," the first baby boomer president audaciously declared: "The era of big government is over." While this statement provides some brief side-splitting entertainment now, one must remember the context in which the statement was made. During the enchanting decade of the 1990s, the mood among many Americans was one of hope. The hope was that the U.S. government would undergo massive reductions in size and in excessive spending. Much of this hope was rooted in the sweeping changes that occurred in the political landscape in 1994. Dubbed as the Republican Revolution, the Republican Party gained majority control of the House of Representatives after their counterparts, the Democrats, had dominated it for nearly four straight decades. One year later, in 1995, Republicans also regained control of the Senate and were promising to reduce the size and scope of the U.S. government. All of the idealistic details of this seismic feat were codified in a brilliant document written by Larry Hunter, Newt Gingrich, and several other GOP leaders entitled the Contract with America. Through this proposed "Contract," Republicans made promises to demonstrate fiscal restraint and sought to bring the era of "big government" to an end. Ironically, this Republican "revolution" led to an increase, not the promised decrease, in government spending.

Today, not only is the era of "big government" back, it never went away in the first place. To Mr. Clinton's chagrin, 21st century America suffers at the hands of a grossly bloated federal government led by spendthrift politicians who answer only to constituents who have learned that they can vote themselves *entitlements* through their local ballot box. All hopes of reducing the size of the U.S. government have been dashed as Republicans and Democrats appear to be in a race to outspend each other to appease the entitlement-crazed generation. Of course, the few renegade politicians naïve enough to suggest massive spending cuts are quickly schooled by their polished political forerunners that placing a gun into the side of their temple and pulling the trigger may be more comfortable than asking the masses of Americans to give up a single entitlement benefit.

The "Ludicrously Over-Governed"

Caring for the U.S. population in the early 1800s cost the federal government roughly $20 per U.S. citizen per year. Today, that number has increased to over $7,500 per year! Of course, this massive increase in spending requires a much larger number of government employees. In 2003, the Bureau of Labor Statistics estimated that there were 21.5 million federal, state, and local government employees across the nation. This is a remarkable increase from the paltry 4.5 million government employees in the 1940s. At 21.5 million, it means that roughly 7 percent of the American population is employed in the government sector today. That means that *1 out of every 14 Americans is employed by the government,* making it the largest employer of any industry in the national economy. Is that anybody's idea of small government?

Clearly, the U.S. government, whether it is federal, state, or local, is costing taxpayers a fortune. But of course, no one ever accused government of being an efficient manager of capital and human resources. As Tom Peters, a former vice-presidential advisor, once said, "In the public (government) sector we routinely have five people doing the work of one. It's a simple fact. Are we over-governed in the United States? We are wildly, bizarrely, sickeningly, ludicrously over-governed."[3]

Put simply, America has witnessed a very large increase in the size of government since the 1980s and into the 1990s. And this growth has skyrocketed in the 21st century under President George W. Bush. In his first presidential term alone, total government spending grew by a whopping 33 percent! And according to Stephen Moore, president of the Club for Growth, the growth in the size of government is in a perpetual upward trend. "We are now seeing the biggest expansion in government since Lyndon Johnson was in the White House," Mr. Moore said. "It is pretty much an across-the-board mushrooming of government. We have the biggest education, foreign aid, and agriculture bills in history, and bigger expansions are on the agenda."[4]

Mr. Moore is correct in his observation that federal government spending is growing at a record pace. According to a report released by the Cato Institute, total federal spending has increased *twice as fast* under President Bush as under President Bill Clinton. *Today, government spending per household stands at over $20,000.* These outrageous levels have not been witnessed since the height of World War II.

The Fruit of Your Government

It is no secret that America is over-governed. But it is by pointing at this over-governance that we lay the foundation for this short book; for it is in the fruit of this over-governance that we find one of America's most potentially destructive issues. What has been the fruit of this insane amount of over-governance? *Massive debt.* To put it mildly, the U.S. government is in severe debt! To put it more abruptly, **the U.S. government is bankrupt.**

How much debt does the U.S. government have? In 1996, the U.S. national debt totaled over $5,000,000,000,000 (that's $5 trillion). Ten years later (in the post-"big government" era) the U.S. national debt has skyrocketed to a whopping $9 trillion! (That's over $9,000,000,000,000!) To help put all of these zeroes into perspective, let us consider again that it took the United States from George Washington until Ronald Reagan — *almost 200 years* — to reach the first $1 trillion in debt in 1980.

But from 1980 to 1986, the national debt did in six short years what it had taken nearly 200 years to do the first time: it increased by $1 trillion to a total of $2 trillion. From 1986 to 1990, it added another $1 trillion for a total of $3 trillion.

And in the 1990s, the national debt began to balloon in an unprecedented way. From 1990 to 1992, it grew by another $1 trillion for a total of $4 trillion.

From 1992 to 1996, one trillion more dollars were spent, bringing the total to $5 trillion.

From 1996 to 2002, the debt grew by another $1 trillion for a total of $6 trillion.

And as the U.S. entered the 21st century, the national debt spun completely out of control.

From 2002 to 2004, the debt grew by another $1 trillion for a total of $7 trillion.

From 2004 to 2006, the debt grew by another $1 trillion for a total of $8 trillion.

From 2006 to 2007, one trillion more dollars were spent, bringing the total to $9 trillion.

I don't know about you, but I am still getting used to "billions," let alone "trillions." And as any casual observer can see, the national debt is *not* shrinking. In fact, it is estimated that it is actually expanding at a record pace of $2–4 billion *per day* as American lawmakers (and consumers) continue to spend more than they earn and to live beyond their means.

The Magic of Compound Interest . . . in Reverse

As of this writing, the U.S. national debt stands at just under $9.4 trillion and is rising by the billions daily. And these record debt levels are going up every second of every minute of every day, because the miracle of compounding interest is working against us. When

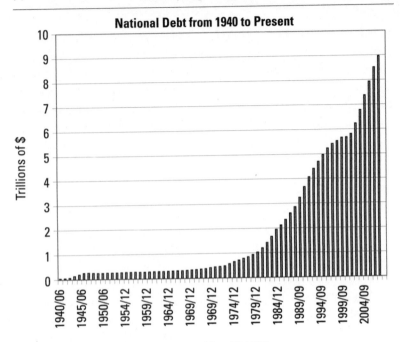

National Debt from 1940 to Present

Source: www.swivel.com/data_columns/spreadsheet/1944692

you are an investor, compound interest is your friend and causes your investments to grow rapidly over time, but when you are a debtor, its tremendous power works against you. *America is the largest debtor nation the world has ever seen.* America is clearly spending more than it can ever pay for. Sadly, compound interest, which Albert Einstein reportedly once called "the most powerful force in the universe," is currently working its magic against the United States citizen, and his government. When my wife and I purchased our first home many years ago, we were stunned when the loan officer explained how much interest

• U.S. NATIONAL DEBT •
DID YOU KNOW?

If 9 trillion U.S. dollar bills were stacked on top of each other, they would create a pile that would reach 2.5 times the distance to the moon from the earth!
If 9 trillion U.S. dollar bills were stretched out end to end, they would stretch from the sun to the orbit of Saturn!

we would end up paying over the course of 30 years. For example, a $100,000 house financed at 6 percent for 30 years could easily cost over $150,000 in interest payments alone. So can you imagine what the payments, plus interest, would be on America's $9.4 trillion debt? Since most of us don't tend to think in terms of billions, or trillions, let me simplify the gravity of this situation by examining the U.S. government's annual budget. In fiscal year 2006, *the U.S. government spent $406 billion of their tax receipts (translation: your tax dollars) on interest payments to the holders of the national debt. That $406 billion is just the interest on our skyrocketing debt!*

To help you understand just how much money $406 billion is, let's compare this amount to other important expenditures by the federal government. Consider the items from the Federal Budget from Fiscal Year 2006 below.

All of these important departments bear a total cost of $266.3 billion per year. But they pale in comparison to the $406 billion interest due on the national debt in 2006. Our mounting debt is a crisis that must be dealt with immediately. However, America's politicians appear oblivious to the fact that they are bankrupting the country through their irresponsible spending. You may be wondering why

---

Federal U.S. Budget — Fiscal Year 2006

- The entire annual budget for the Department of Labor in 2006: **$11.5 billion**
- The entire annual budget for the NASA Space Program in 2006: **$16.5 billion**
- The entire annual budget for the Department of Energy in 2006: **$23.4 billion**
- The entire annual budget for the Department of Homeland Security in 2006: **$34.2 billion**
- The entire annual budget for the Department of Transportation in 2006: **$57.5 billion**
- The entire annual budget for the Department of Education in 2006: **$56 billion**
- The entire annual budget for the Department of Health and Human Services in 2006: **$67.2 billion**

Source: http://www.whitehouse.gov/omb/budget/fy2006/budget.htm

the public does not rise up and demand fiscal restraint on the part of our political leaders. After all, is it not a moral travesty to place the burden of an insurmountable debt upon the yet unborn citizens of this nation? What our government is doing right now is spending more than we make, charging it to a credit card, and asking our children and our grandchildren to pay for it. It is an immoral act. The reason is simple, and it is twofold:

- The public is not interested.

- The majority of U.S. citizens have no idea how large our national debt is, let alone how much is spent in interest annually. If it is not on prime-time television, and if they don't have to write a check for it, then most Americans will not know, and will continue not to care. *The public likes the entitlements afforded by deficit spending.*

We live in an entitlement generation that loves government handouts. The public does not want to hear that it needs to sacrifice for the good of the unborn. We want all we can get, and we want it now. Like it or not, Americans love the entitlement system that they have created, all with the help of their elected spendthrift politicians. All of this becomes more sinister when we discover who our country is in debt to. So, who holds the debt?

The truth is, many people do. But the most important holders for our purposes in this book are foreign countries. A tremendous amount of America's outstanding national debt is owed to foreign creditors like Japan, China, Middle Eastern nations, and Europe. This means that the American way of life is greatly dependent upon foreign countries' continued willingness to finance our over-consumption. We will discuss the importance of this topic in an upcoming book. For now, let's examine what economists call the "twin deficits."

The Twin Deficits

The United States is currently suffering from what economists have termed the "twin deficits." Put simply, the U.S. government's two deficits are: a *fiscal deficit* and a *trade deficit*. The U.S. fiscal deficit occurs when the government spends more money than it takes in through tax revenues. Over time this accumulation of budget deficits has led to a $9.4 trillion national debt.

The *trade deficit* occurs when the U.S. imports more goods and services than it exports to other countries. Unfortunately, America's massive trade deficit has moved from being a matter of convenience to an absolute dependence. It is estimated that the U.S. government requires over $70 billion in monthly capital inflows from foreign countries simply to sustain the current level of U.S. consumption. *America is living far beyond its means and is funding its extravagant lifestyle by exchanging its U.S. dollar for cheap goods and services from abroad.* As America's liabilities to foreigners have grown, the U.S. government has responded by printing more dollars to meet its obligations. This increase in the money supply, as any freshman student of economics knows, may provide some short-term relief, but in the long run it only serves to weaken the purchasing power of the currency. As of this writing, foreigners are still agreeing to accept the U.S. dollar as payment for the goods they send to the U.S., despite the fact that the supply of the currency is increasing at unprecedented levels. *The continued acceptance of the dollar is largely due to the global perception of the United States as an economic powerhouse.* However, as the dollar continues its downward spiral in value on the global financial markets, several important foreign creditors to the United States are beginning to express concern. When, not if, foreigners awake to the fact that the U.S. dollar is a worthless piece of paper that is not backed by any commodity, they will begin to invest their money elsewhere. And when they do, it will lead to a massive spike in interest rates as the U.S. desperately attempts to attract fresh infusions of capital to aid the ailing economy. Of course, a sharp rise in U.S. interest rates, during the largest housing bubble in history, will be like sticking a sharp needle into a balloon.

Unfortunately for many Americans who are not familiar with economic history, all of this talk about a failing economy is hard to believe. Surely the good times will continue in America and the economy will continue to go higher, right? In the short-term, yes. But not in the long term. *This is because the economic excesses that have fueled the American way of life are unsustainable.* There is nothing inherently new about the economic path that America has taken, with the exception of the size of its debts. It has simply gone the way of every glorious economic empire before it. *And while history may not necessarily repeat, it certainly does rhyme.* Historically, nations that have

• U.S. NATIONAL DEBT •
DID YOU KNOW?

There are 100 billion stars in our galaxy. While that number used to be considered large, it now represents only around 1% of the U.S. national debt!

slid into economic disaster have done so progressively — and they all tend to follow the same pattern.

First, the government officials determine that to "properly" care for the growing needs of the nation, the governing institutions must exert a greater influence over the population. This expansion of governmental influence comes in the form of greater entitlement spending, social welfare, and a variety of other state-endorsed programs designed to create a state-dependent population. These added programs are all made possible through the extraction of money from the governed public, typically in the form of forced taxes, and at other times through more subtle means. Amidst all of this newfound tax revenue, the government excitedly embarks on an even larger spending spree with the people's money.

DID YOU KNOW?

When politicians increase or decrease federal government spending in an effort to influence the direction of the U.S. economy, it is known as fiscal policy. Conversely, attempts to influence the U.S. economy through the manipulation of interest rates by the Federal Reserve is known as monetary policy.

At this point, the euphoria of engaging in the "work of the people" with few budgetary constraints slowly takes hold of the governing body. With the taxing authorities running at full throttle, the "work of the people" eventually leads the government into the red, as they begin accumulating large amounts of debt. Eventually, the government begins spending considerably more than it is taking in through tax revenues, making the debt completely unmanageable. The crushing weight of the debt ultimately overwhelms the government's ability to pay back its creditors. After exhausting all other options, the government begins defaulting on its promises and thereby ruins its credibility among its creditors. Thus begins the total destruction of the nation and its currency.

Saints of God, understand this: *America is not the light of the world.* The sun shone long before the red, white, and blue. And it will continue to shine when this nation is gone. But the hubris-fueled delusion manufactured inside a declining empire is thick and intoxicating. And few are able to avoid its deceptions.

Endnotes

1. Francis X. Cavanaugh, *The Truth about the National Debt: Five Myths and One Reality* (Boston, MA: Harvard Business School Press, 1996), p. 25.
2. *The American Journal of Economics and Sociology*, Robert Schalkenback Foundation, v. 20 (1960/1961): p. 231.
3. "Grandfather State & Local Government Spending Report," http://mwhodges.home.att.net/state_local.htm.
4. Tom Hamburger, "Despite Bush's Credo, Government Grows," *Wall Street Journal*, http://online.wsj.com/article/SB106262519812480700.html?apl=y, published Sept. 4, 2003.

Chapter 6
The 2040 Crisis

"They who have been bred in the school of politics fail now and always to face the facts. Their measures are half measures and make-shifts, merely. They put off the day of settlement indefinitely, and meanwhile, the debt accumulates."[1]

— Henry David Thoreau

"In our every deliberation, we must consider the impact of our decisions on the next seven generations."[2]

— From the great law of the Iroquois confederacy

OVERVIEW: While the current U.S. national debt stands at $9.4 trillion, this amount does not reflect what the federal government has promised to pay millions of Americans in entitlement benefits down the road. Those future obligations put our real debt figure at nearly $60 trillion — a staggering sum that is about as large as the total household net worth of the entire United States. According to the U.S. Government Accountability Office, if present trends continue in the form of reckless fiscal spending, the entire federal budget will be consumed by Social Security and Medicare payments alone by 2040. Are you prepared for the 2040 crisis?

It was a day like any other as 61 year-old Kathleen Casey-Kirschling logged onto a computer in Washington, DC, on the morning of October 15, 2007. However, that day also marked the end of an era. Reporters from the national and the international media had arrived in Washington to record this monumental moment in history. Who is Kathleen Casey-Kirschling and why was she important enough to demand the attention of the global media? Is she a famous actress, a noteworthy scholar, or a determined politician? Well, not quite. And if you don't recognize her name, you are not alone. Ms. Casey-Kirschling is a recently retired school teacher living in New Jersey. And the reason behind her global debut was quite simple. She was the very first "baby boomer" *to file for U.S. Social Security benefits. The first of over 78 million baby boomers*, to be more exact.

Her filing, which was performed online at an event hosted by Michael J. Astrue, the commissioner of Social Security, sparked immediate national and international media coverage. In a speech given that day, Ms. Casey-Kirschling, who was born one second after midnight on January 1, 1946, thus gaining her recognition as the first baby boomer, had this to say: "I think I'm just lucky to be at the top of the boom. I'm just one of many, many millions and am really blessed . . . to take my Social Security now."

If you were not aware of the U.S. government's enormous spending problem, the importance of this story would make no sense. Why should an unknown retiring teacher from New Jersey be front page news for the entire world?

The answer is simple. However, before providing you with it, the publisher of this book has recommended a disclaimer for this chapter. It is highly recommended that you find a comfortable couch or a chair to recline in as you peruse the next several pages. Are you seated? Okay. You might even want to take a few deep breaths. Deep breaths have a tendency to lower blood pressure and pulse rates, which you will need for the remainder of this chapter. *Are you ready?*

The "Silver Tsunami"

It is only fitting that if the answer is deserving of a disclaimer, it is also deserving of a title. "America's silver tsunami" has recently been proposed, so let us continue this brief diatribe under that banner.

The answer begins with a couple of brief definitions. First, what is a baby boomer? Demographers define a baby boomer as a U.S. citizen

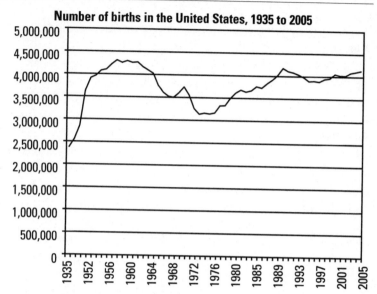

Number of births in the United States, 1935 to 2005

Source: www.infoplease.com/ipa/a0005067

born between 1946 and 1964. It was the era of rock 'n' roll, TV dinners, and Dr. Spock. Elvis was the king and the Beatles took the nation by storm with their unique blend of vocal harmonies and driving rhythms. In addition, this era saw the decline of racial desegregation with the likes of Rosa Parks, Martin Luther King, Jr., and Brown vs. the Board of Education.

But this era was also marked by an explosion, or a "boom," in the national birth rate. Beginning in the post–World War II era, birth rates skyrocketed across the country as the U.S. economy fully recovered from the depression of the previous decade. An article from *Time* magazine dated February 9, 1948, demonstrates the early awareness of the seismic demographic shift. "The U.S. had been expected to reach its population peak of 155–165 million by the end of the century. But the 'present surge of births'... indicates that the peak will actually be from 10 to 25 million higher and the crest of the growth curve has now been pushed beyond the year 2000."

The *Time* magazine prediction on the future U.S. population was a little off. Instead of ending the century with just fewer than 200 million, the United States Census Bureau estimated the number was closer to 300 million — *281,421,906* to be exact. This explosion in U.S. birth rates has caused massive upheaval in demographic trends that will create large economic ripples as we dive headlong into the 21st century.

According to U.S. government birth records, which began being officially recorded in 1910, there are nearly 80 million baby boomers alive today. Each of these 80 million Americans has paid large amounts into government entitlement programs, most often through payroll deductions. Until now, these 80 million baby boomers have been funding the entitlement system for the current retirees. But in 2008, the story began changing. For it was in that year that the first wave of 3.2 million boomers turned 62 years of age. Each of them, like Ms. Casey-Kirschling, is now eligible under the current government standards to apply for early retirement benefits and to receive a monthly Social Security check for the rest of their lives. Instead of paying into the system, they can begin taking from the system.

Later, in 2011, as this first wave begins turning 65, they will become eligible for subsidized healthcare benefits under the Medicare system. Finally, in 2012, those of the 3.2 million early boomers who opted not to take early retirement benefits will reach age 66 and will qualify for their full share of Social Security benefits. *It is highly likely that a large majority of retiring boomers will take the early retirement option due to the perceived weakness in the Social Security system.* And this first wave is just the beginning.

Over the course of the next two decades, the remainder of the 78+ million baby boomers — or 10,000 people every single day — will retire and become financial and medical dependents of the current U.S. taxpayers. They will all retire, and they will certainly all demand their fair share of the entitlement pie, which includes an assortment of elderly benefits, including Social Security, Medicare, and Medicaid. *These three entitlement programs currently make up over 40 percent of the federal government's annual budget.* And this percentage is expected to increase dramatically as the baby boomers begin taking from the system instead of giving into it. If all this sounds like it is going to cost the U.S. government a lot of money, you would be wrong. *The enormous bill created by this entitlement crisis is going to fall squarely upon the U.S. taxpayer.* Hard-working, tax-paying citizens are going to foot the bill for the retirement and medical benefits for the largest group of senior citizens in American history.

How much money will this crisis cost? (Put this book down and grab the Tums.) *Nearly $60 trillion.* You might be thinking, didn't we just learn in the last chapter that America's total national public debt is just over $9 trillion? You have probably forgotten that we are dealing with the government. And the government approaches fiscal accounting in, let's say, it's own "special" way. According to the federal government's methods of accounting, promised unfunded liabilities to future citizens are not required to be included in the accounting process. (Of course, if *you* do not claim future obligations on your books in your business, you would find yourself reading this book behind bars. Go figure.)

So what does this all mean exactly, you may ask. Well, the truth is that the official national debt figure of $9 trillion, as defined in our last chapter, only includes what the government owes on money that it has *already* borrowed. *The current $9 trillion national debt does not include the promises made by the federal government to millions of retiring Americans in the future through entitlement benefits.* If those future obligations are calculated (as normal business accounting requires), the real U.S. debt figure jumps from $9 trillion to a whopping $59.1 trillion! To help put this mammoth number in perspective, $59.1 trillion is larger than the total household net worth of the entire United States, as of this writing.

Since the purpose of this book is to provide you with strategies on how you can protect yourself and your family from this whole mess, let's quickly translate what this means for your wallet. If the repayment of this $59 trillion debt were to be spread out evenly over all of the 300 million citizens of the U.S., it would mean that your individual share of this debt would be around $197,000. That is similar to being responsible for a $200,000 mortgage, but having no house to back it up. *If you are married with one child, your household's share of this debt currently stands at nearly $600,000!*

Is it any surprise that the conservative think tank, the Heritage Foundation, has called this looming entitlement crisis *"the single greatest economic challenge of our era"*?

To put all of this into even more stark terms, consider that the annual GDP of the *entire world* in 2006 was $65 trillion. Therefore, to pay off the entire reported accrued U.S. debt of $59.1 trillion would be similar to paying off the amount of the GDP of every nation on earth combined!

Now for the Bad News . . .

You would think that with all of these obvious problems facing U.S. entitlement programs, the federal government would be scurrying around the Beltway attempting to salvage the system that they have created. But have they? No. Here's the hard, honest truth: the U.S. government has no plan on how to ensure that the entitlement crisis does not destroy the U.S. economy.

Consider these words from Newt Gingrich in 1994 upon becoming the Speaker of the House: "I think Social Security is off the table for the foreseeable future. We have so many other, more pressing and more immediate problems, and we ought to focus on the ones that are immediate, not the one that are 20 years out."[3] If a $59 trillion problem that begins "20 years out" is not a problem worthy of current consideration by our nation's leaders, we have more problems than we could ever imagine.

It is not that our nation's leaders do not want stable and secure retirement benefits for the country. Efforts have been made to rescue the failing entitlement systems. For example, over the last few decades lawmakers passed a series of increases in Medicare and FICA taxes. But placing money in the hands of America's spendthrift politicians is about as safe as placing your crawling infant in the middle of a busy street. The dollars are gone and in their place are worthless IOU's that will more than likely never be repaid. Put simply, the system is overburdened. It demands too much from too little for too many.

On March 3, 2001, a freshly minted President George W. Bush optimistically stated: "We're going to keep the promise of Social Security and keep the government from raiding the Social Security surplus."[4] But just a few short years later, Bush's idealism had morphed into reality: "Some in our country think that Social Security is a trust fund — in other words, there's a pile of money being accumulated. That's just simply not true. The money — payroll taxes going into the Social Security are spent. They're spent on benefits and they're spent on government programs. There is no trust."[5]

> • THE REAL NATIONAL DEBT •
> DID YOU KNOW?
>
> *If 60 trillion U.S. dollar bills were stretched out end to end, they would stretch from the sun to Pluto!*

As the saying goes, *the Social Security Trust Fund is*

a double oxymoron: it is not "funded" and it should not be "trusted." It is simply mind-boggling that the United States has become so fiscally reckless in its responsibilities to American citizens. And all of this in the course of just one generation . . . the baby boom generation.

Despite being poorly prepared for the long-term future obligations of the Social Security system, what really keeps economists, actuaries, and demographers awake at night are the unrealistic promises made by the federal government to 80 million retirees concerning the Medicare and Medicaid systems. *According to most projections, Social Security will remain solvent until around 2040.* Current projections for the Medicare system, which was established in 1965, show a much more grim picture. *It is estimated that the funds for the Medicare system will be depleted by 2018.*

Here is how it all breaks down if current trends continue:

- In its 2006 annual report to Congress, the Social Security Board of Trustees projected that incoming tax revenues will fall below program costs in 2017. And in 2040, the Social Security Trust Fund will be completely exhausted.

- In its 2006 annual report to Congress, the Medicare Board of Trustees reported that the program's hospital insurance trust fund could run out of money by 2018.

When the U.S. Congress passed the Social Security Act in 1935 as a part of the New Deal, an estimated 42 workers paid into the system for every retiree. By 1950, this ratio had decreased to 16.5 workers for every retiree. Today, it has decreased dramatically to three workers for every retiree. By the year 2030, the ratio will drop to a dismal two workers for every retiree.

Today, around 50 million U.S. citizens draw a monthly Social Security check. That number will increase dramatically to an estimated 84 million by the year 2030. Today, there are 44 million Medicare recipients. But in 2030, that number will nearly double to 79 million. And by 2040, the entire entitlement system will be in a state of disrepair unless something is done quickly.

Just the Facts

Enter David M. Walker. Mr. Walker was the comptroller general of the Government Accountability Office (GAO) from 1998 to 2008.

During his tenure, he was the chief auditor of U.S. government spending. (If you think that there are problems with fiscal immorality in corporate America and in the non-profit sector, imagine viewing the bloated expenses of government bureaucracies for a living.)

Mr. Walker became disgusted with government wasteful spending and lack of stewardship, and in 2006 he gathered his findings and began visiting a host of U.S. cities in an effort to raise awareness about the insurmountable debts facing the U.S. government. The effort was billed as the *Fiscal Wake-Up Tour* and sought to bring the shocking economic realities directly to the sleeping U.S. taxpaying citizenry.

Walker's presentations are visual and include charts and graphs to paint the picture that America is going bankrupt. In alluding to the similarities to the end of the Roman Empire and modern-day U.S. policies, Walker states: "The Roman Empire lasted 1,000 years, but only about half that time as a republic. The Roman Republic fell for many reasons, but three reasons are worth remembering: declining moral and political civility at home, an overconfident and overextended military in foreign lands, and fiscal irresponsibility by the central government."

Mr. Walker has since resigned from his post at the GAO, and now serves as CEO/president of the Peter G. Petersen Foundation. This foundation is committed to informing and warning the public of the looming economic disaster due to America's "fiscal irresponsibility." This "fiscal irresponsibility" is clearly displayed through the $59 trillion debt, much of which has been promised in future liabilities to millions of retiring Americans over the coming decades. *Our country is spinning uncontrollably toward the precipice of economic destruction. And little is being done to stop it.*

In the 2006 *Financial Report of the United States Government*, released in December of that year, Mr. Walker states the following:

> Despite improvement in both the fiscal year 2006 reported net operating cost and the cash-based budget deficit, the U.S. government's total reported liabilities, net social insurance commitments, and other fiscal exposures continue to grow and now total approximately $50 trillion [it is now $59 trillion], representing approximately four times the Nation's total output (GDP) in fiscal year 2006, up from about $20 trillion, or two times GDP in fiscal year 2000. As this

long-term fiscal imbalance continues to grow, the retirement of the "baby boom" generation is closer to becoming a reality with the first wave of boomers eligible for early retirement under Social Security in 2008. Given these and other factors, it seems clear that the nation's current fiscal path is unsustainable and that tough choices by the president and the Congress are necessary in order to address the nation's large and growing long-term fiscal imbalance.

Walker is correct in saying that the entitlement crisis will demand tough choices. But tough choices demand tough political leaders, leaders who are not afraid of uttering words like "sacrifice" in public. But even if the nation's leaders could collectively muster that type of courage without destroying each other in the process, it would not be likely to avoid a head-on collision with a disastrous fiscal future. And if recent history is any indicator, it is highly probable that the crisis will have to generate complete economic havoc and chaos before the politicians will even begin to discuss it seriously, let alone confront it. If this is indeed the case, Mr. Walker predicts the following: "*If present trends continue, by 2040 the entire federal budget will be consumed by Social Security and Medicare alone.*"

While it appears that Mr. Walker is great at pointing out the problems with our economy, does he offer any solutions? Yes, but solutions only serve to demonstrate the severity of our economic dilemma. To avoid this impending fiscal nightmare Mr. Walker states that "the U.S. economy would need to grow by double digits every year for the next 75 years." Basically, all America needs to do to avoid its rendezvous with the modern-day debtor's prison is to grow the economy by at least 10 percent every year for the next 75 years. The problem with that solution is that since 1970, U.S. GDP growth has averaged 3.16 percent per year, after inflation. This is far below Walker's required 10+ percent annual growth rate.

Mr. Walker continues, "In order to pay for the promises that we have made to Americans through Social Security, Medicare, and Medicaid, the U.S. government would need to have $8 trillion invested at Treasury interest rates. We currently have nothing invested."

Clearly, the U.S. economy is headed for a major crisis, barring any massive economic intervention. To make matters worse, many in the government, and in the media, are proposing that we should solve this problem with more spending. The logic goes something like this: by spending more money, we can grow our economic productivity and output to levels that will help us pay off our massive debts. *Anyone who thinks that the solution to a massive debt crisis is to go more into debt is utterly deceived. Consuming more and saving less will only aggravate our current problems and delay the inevitable pain that awaits us.* It is like giving a bottle of wine to a drunk with a hangover. Sure, more alcohol may make his headache go away; but only temporarily. Eventually, the pain will have to be dealt with and it will be even worse than before.

Put simply, America is not going to grow its way out of this problem. Or as Mr. Walker is fond of saying: "Anyone who believes that we can grow our way out of this problem either does not know economic history, or is bad at math."

Endnotes:

1. Henry David Thoreau, "Slavery in Massachusetts," http://www.thoreau-online.org/slavery-in-massachusetts.html.
2. www.solarhaven.org/Quotes.htm.
3. Laurence J. Kotlikoff and Scott Burns, *The Coming Generational Storm: What You Need to Know about America's Economic Future* (Cambridge, MA: MIT Press, 2005), p. 87.
4. Radio address of the president to the nation, March 3, 2001, http://www.ssa.gov/history/gwbushstmts.html#radio030301.
5. Max B. Sawicky, "Debt and Taxes," *The American Prospect* (Feb. 11, 2005), http://www.prospect.org/cs/articles?article=debt_and_taxes.

Chapter 7
Why Inflation Is Coming

"History teaches us that men and nations behave wisely once they have exhausted all other alternatives."[1]
— Abba Eban

"The budget should be balanced; the treasury should be refilled; national debt should be reduced; and the arrogance of public officials should be controlled."[2]
— Cicero 106–43 B.C.

Before progressing any further into our assessment of America's unrestrained fiscal spending, it is wise to stop and reconsider the true amount of money that your government actually owes. With the total national debt at around $59 trillion — when future liabilities are factored in — it is vital that we do not pull a Dick Cheney and say that "deficits don't matter." To trivialize these massive numbers by ignoring them will be done at our own peril — $59 trillion is an enormous amount of money. But to fully grasp just how large this amount is, let us consider a simple illustration.

You have heard the old saying, "Time is money." According to our traditional measurement of time, one million seconds is roughly equivalent to 12 days. That makes 59 *million* seconds equal to 708 days. How does that compare to 59 *billion* seconds? Fifty-nine billion seconds is equal to 1,870 years! If 59 billion seconds is equal to 1,870 years, how many years is 59 *trillion* seconds? Almost 1.9 million years!

> 59 million seconds = 708 days
> 59 billion seconds = 1,870 years
> 59 trillion seconds = 1,888,000 years

As you can see, the increases from one to the other are exponential. One letter can make a huge difference.

To illustrate this point further, let's employ another illustration. This time the example will include you and the government. (Relax, the IRS is not involved.) Suppose that today you were to receive a letter from the United States government addressed directly to you. Inside the letter you find this message:

Dear Mr. Reader,

We, the United States government, have selected your name at random and will begin paying you $1.00 per second beginning tonight at midnight for our own undisclosed purposes.

Sincerely,
The Federal Government

Upon reading this you would probably leap with joy thinking about how much money you would begin receiving for doing absolutely nothing at all. (Sort of like being a politician, except you get to maintain your reputation.) Now assuming you were to live another 20 years after receiving this incredible notice, your inheritance would equal *approximately $630 million*. Not too bad, until you consider that the federal government spends that amount alone every 13 hours to simply service the interest on the growing national debt.

That's right: every 13 hours your government spends over $600 million on INTEREST on the national debt.

Now suppose that the federal government collectively decided one day to begin paying off the $59 trillion it owes at this same rate of $1.00 per second. Assuming that this $59 trillion was not compounding with interest daily (which it is, by the billions), how long would it take our government to pay off $59 trillion dollars at this imaginary rate of $1.00 per second? *Only 1,888,000 years.* Which means that according to this repayment plan, America could be completely debt-free in the year A.D. 1,882,007. *Are you beginning to see how large these numbers truly are?* Think about that the next time you hear some slick-haired, shiny-shoed politician utter the word "trillion."

And remember, these 1.88 million years do not even take into account that the $59 trillion debt is getting larger every minute due to compounding interest.

A few years ago, in an effort to place the immense number "one billion" into perspective for the American public, an advertising agency stated the following:

A billion seconds ago it was 1959.

A billion minutes ago Jesus was alive.

A billion hours ago our ancestors were living in the Stone Age.

A billion dollars ago was only 8 hours and 20 minutes, at the rate Washington spends it.

While those numbers are obviously incorrect now, their impact has not changed.

The Certainty of Uncertainty

As 78 million baby boomers prepare to launch into the realm of retirement villages, entitlement benefits, and subsidized healthcare, no one can say with certainty how things will fare. But the one thing that is certain is that the concept of retirement has changed and will continue to change. Gone are the days of working for the same corporation for 40 years, retiring with a nice watch, and then going home to collect a healthy pension. In today's era of hyper cost-consciousness and global competitiveness, many businesses are in a fight of survival simply to afford the most basic of employee benefits. In sharp contrast to the corporate America of yesteryear, the modern employee will likely be employed by a host of companies throughout his working lifetime. This will mostly be due to corporate downsizing, mergers, and more often then not, employee dissatisfaction.

Today, the financial risk and burden that once fell upon the corporation now falls onto the individual worker. *Those under 40 years old who are planning on the federal government taking care of them financially in their old age are living in absolute ignorance.* Barring a strong dose of fiscal discipline, coupled with political vision and intestinal fortitude, the American social safety net of government entitlements will falter before our eyes. Its impending collapse will be under the immense weight of inadequate planning, unrealistic promises, dreadful demographics, and skyrocketing medical costs. Or as the first baby boomer, Ms. Casey-Kirschling, puts it: "I can't imagine what's going to happen with our children and our grandchildren. They're not going to be able to retire."[3]

During a 2005 speech in Colorado, President George W. Bush expressed his growing concerns about the looming entitlement crisis by stating: *"Some of you may think there's what they call a Social Security trust: the government collects the money for you, we hold it for you, and when you retire, we pay it to you. But that's not how it works. You pay your payroll tax; we pay for the people who have retired, and if there's any money left over, we spend it on government. That's how it works. And what's left is an empty IOU, a piece of paper."*

If your desire is to live free from deception, it is vital that you wake up to the economic realities facing our nation. The truth is, the Social Security system is broken, as is the Medicare system. The entitlement crisis is real and there are no easy answers. But there are answers. Two that immediately come to mind are:

1. cutting benefits
2. raising taxes

Both of these are easier said than done. This is because our current generation is notoriously known for its intolerance for any — and all — types of economic pain. There is also a third option that will prove much less painful in the short-term, but it is the most disastrous in the long run. What is the third option? To answer this stumper, think: *What is the typical American response to a financial dilemma?* While they sometimes get a second job or cut their spending, more often than not, they borrow money. When Americans wish that they had the largest flat-screen television or the nicest lawn on their block, most of them turn to their favorite money lender. And America's favorite money lenders are the credit card companies.

Satisfying one's immediate desires by borrowing money has not been restricted to the U.S. consumer. To the contrary, a $59 trillion national debt testifies to the obsession our federal government has with credit.

Therefore, the third option for the U.S. federal government, and its pain-averse citizenry, in confronting the entitlement crisis will be to simply borrow the money. We borrow for everything else in this country, so why not just borrow the money we need to pay for the entitlement crisis from foreign countries? Besides, the international community would probably love to loan us even more of their hard-earned money in exchange for our debts, right? Borrowing from others will allow Americans to keep their financial house of cards propped up long enough to continue their lives of self-indulgence without having to bother with things like tax hikes and spending cuts. Don't think the federal government would stoop that low?

Consider the words from former Treasury Secretary Paul O'Neill regarding the three options facing us: "... *because the Social Security trust fund does not consist of real economic assets, we are left to rely on the federal government's future decisions to either raise taxes, reduce spending, or increase borrowing from the public to finance fully Social Security's promised benefits.*"[4]

Let's briefly examine each of these three options one at a time.

Option #1 — Raise Money by Increasing Tax Revenues

In America today, it is becoming nearly impossible for families to get ahead financially on one income. This has forced many women into the workforce, and some spouses even work two jobs just to make ends meet. Unlike the family, the government can't make more money by delivering pizzas on the weekend. Instead, the way it raises extra money is by exacting higher tax rates on the tax-paying public. The problem with this option is obvious. Taxpayers are rational creatures who naturally do not like giving up more of their income in the form of taxes. In fact, not only does the public not have a favorable view of tax hikes, they tend to resist them at all costs — *especially our current entitlement generation.* Raising taxes has become risky business in modern politics, and there are few politicians who are interested in risk, especially when it could cost them a re-election.

Summary: *Taxpayers vote for politicians who do not raise taxes.*

Option #2 — Raise Money by Cutting Spending and Entitlement Benefits

The New York subway system is a modern marvel. The intricate transit system covers a total of 842 track miles, which if laid end to end would stretch from New York City to Chicago! In between, or just outside the subway tracks, lies something known as *the third rail.* The third rail provides 625 volts of electrical power, which powers the entire transit system. Without the third rail, the trains go nowhere. Occasionally, a news story comes out about some poor fellow who accidentally touches the third rail. The result is usually the same: instant death by electrocution.

Similarly, politicians have recognized "third rails" that they try to avoid touching at all costs. A political third rail is usually defined as an idea or a topic that is so highly charged that one's political career is jeopardized simply by "touching" it. One of the most notorious "third rails" in American politics is the topic of entitlement benefits. Just ask the late U.S. Senator Barry Goldwater, who, while running for president against Lyndon B. Johnson in 1964, had the audacity to question whether the Social Security system should be a voluntary program. Goldwater lost the election in a landslide, undoubtedly due in part to the voting public's perception that Goldwater was hostile to entitlements. *Those who dare to venture into the forbidden forest of cutting entitlement spending do so at their own risk.* Asking the baby boom generation to sacrifice any part of their promised entitlement benefits, even for a humanitarian cause, will likely be met by formidable resistance.

But even if a politician could successfully dodge the many political hazardous obstacles that encircle the third rail of entitlement spending, there are still other practical reasons why cutting entitlement benefits would be extremely difficult. One of the chief concerns in cutting benefits is the lack of savings of the boomer generation. In his book *Boomer Century*, Richard Croker reveals that only one-third of baby boomers think they will have enough money to live comfortably once they retire. Could this be because four out of ten boomers currently have less than $10,000 in retirement savings?

And since boomers have failed to save for their golden years, is it any wonder that they will resist any and all attempts to cut their promised retirement benefits?

But even if some boomers are prepared for the financial demands of retirement, are they prepared to finance a *long* retirement? Thanks to medical advances, Americans are living longer than ever. According to Croker, boomers who reach age 65 in the year 2011 can expect to live at least another 18 years on average. And some will even live longer. Maintaining the lifestyle that millions of retiring boomers have become accustomed to during their working years will be a very expensive proposition. *Today's "entitlement generation" believes that it is owed a good life at the taxpayer's expense. This belief has become deeply ingrained in the nation's psyche.* Anyone foolish enough to suggest spending cuts for millions of boomers would be better off placing his wet hand on the third rail of the New York City subway system.

Summary: *Baby Boomers will continue to demand more benefits, not less, and any suggestions to cut spending for entitlements will be met by a formidable boomer voting bloc.*

Option #3 — Raise Money by Borrowing

The third option given by Mr. Paul O'Neill is to "increase borrowing from the public to finance fully Social Security's promised benefits." At last, you say, a reasonable option has been laid on the table that doesn't involve economic pain. You are right, at least temporarily. It is a near certainty that America will attempt to delay the economic pain caused by the entitlement crisis for as long as possible. And the most obvious way to postpone the day of reckoning will be to export the debt to anyone who will buy it through the issuance of treasury securities. According to Alan Greenspan, the former head of the Federal Reserve, this is exactly what the federal government plans to do. In a speech given on April 27, 2001, Greenspan stated the following: "When the baby boom generation retires, and as the population subsequently ages further, these contingent liabilities [Social Security] will come due and — barring an offsetting surplus in the remainder of the government's budget — *will be met by the issuance of Treasury securities,* shifting much of total federal liabilities from contingent liability to *debt to the public.* At that point, of course, the unified budget will be in deficit."

In other words, the government will take the political low road by borrowing the money it needs to pay for the entitlements that it has promised to millions of Americans. In keeping with our national obsession of avoiding sacrifice at all costs, the path of least resistance will be all too appealing to desperate politicians. If you are shaking your head wondering how all of this could be happening in America, it is an indication that you now fully understand the 2040 crisis and the other looming economic challenges facing the country that we all know and love. At one time in this nation's history it would have been considered implausible that the government would do something so reckless as to fund incredible amounts of entitlement spending with domestic *and* foreign capital. How would you feel about a man who walks into the finest restaurant in town, spends exorbitant amounts of money on a lavish dinner and then tells the waiter to mail the bill to his son? Or even worse, to his unborn grandson? Yet this is exactly what America is likely to do by selling future debt obligations to fund current expenses. Sadly, to an entitlement-crazed generation who blindly refuses to embrace the concept of short-term sacrifice for longer-term security, there is no other alternative.

Summary: Creating debt is what Americans do best. Why would it apply any other logic to the looming entitlement crisis?

Why Inflation Is Coming

Understanding the Federal Reserve's role as the lender of last resort is vitally important to our current discussion of why inflation is going to strike America's shores relentlessly as we move into the uncertain future. The Federal Reserve has been a controversial institution since its creation by an act of Congress in 1913. Much has been written about the Fed, both good and bad. (My feelings on the Federal Reserve are disclosed in a forthcoming book. There I express my view that the Fed exerts more negative pressures on the U.S. economy than positive ones and is unnecessary.) However, one of the most important functions of the Federal Reserve is its role as the "lender of last resort" to the federal government. What this means is that the U.S. government *always* has a buyer for its debt. This is because the Federal Reserve is obligated to step in and buy government debt when public interest in that debt wanes. As of this writing, the Federal Reserve holds approximately 45 percent of the $9 trillion national debt. You may wonder how the Federal Reserve can afford to be the "lender of last resort" since it means purchasing trillions of dollars of U.S. debt. *Quite simply, the Federal Reserve creates the money out of thin air.* Put simply, when the U.S. government borrows money from the Federal Reserve, it simply means that that amount of money is printed. *It is the beauty of the fiat currency system.* When times get tough, you can always print more money! Obviously, when the printing presses begin spitting out new currency, it works to devalue the current dollars in circulation. Just as the discovery of a viable new source of oil puts downward pressure on the price of petroleum, creating money "out of thin air" with the printing presses only serves to devalue the existing currency base. Printing new money today makes every dollar worth less tomorrow.

But the real money printing will not begin as long as we are able to borrow money from foreign countries. America has become far too dependent upon foreign capital to prop up its economy. *Today our economy is subsidized by foreign capital inflows to the tune of $70 billion a month.* This means that the "buy now, pay later" way of life, so creatively exhibited by America, is entirely dependent upon the continued willingness of foreign countries to finance our over-consumption by purchasing our debt. Among the most voracious of U.S. debt purchasers are several Asian and European countries. As of this writing, foreign countries own nearly 25 percent of America's $9 trillion national debt. That means that *one out of every four dollars that we have borrowed is owed to foreign creditors!* According to a June 2007 official report issued by the Federal Reserve, the total amount of all U.S. dollars in circulation is equal to $755 billion. This means that *America owes foreign creditors nearly three times the total amount of U.S. currency in circulation!*

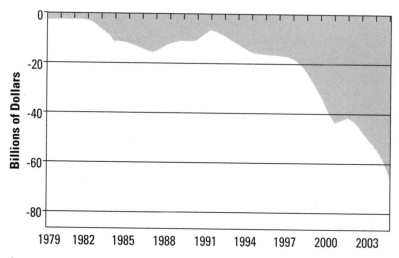

U.S. Trade Balance

Source: www.census.gov

It should be no surprise that foreign creditors are beginning to express concern regarding the U.S. government's ability to make good on their future debt payments. America's credibility as a good credit risk is becoming more suspect by the day. The obvious structural problems facing the American economy, including a falling dollar, a soft economy, an entitlement crisis, a housing bubble, and a credit crisis, are far from minor issues. *To the contrary, they are enormous problems.* And because investment capital tends to flow to the rate of highest return for the least amount of risk, many foreign investors are beginning to perceive U.S. debt as possibly a "bad bet."

According to a report issued by the U.S. Treasury, $163 billion of foreign capital reportedly flowed out of all forms of U.S. investments in just one month during the summer of 2007. According to the detailed report, released by the *London Telegraph* newspaper (Oct. 18, 2007), "Asian investors dumped $52 billion worth of U.S. Treasury bonds alone, led by Japan ($23bn), China ($14.2bn) and Taiwan ($5bn)." This major sell-off marked the first time that foreigners had collectively sold more U.S. Treasuries than they had purchased since 1998. The *Telegraph* report added: "Central banks in Singapore, Korea, Taiwan, and Vietnam have all begun to cut purchases of U.S. bonds, or signaled an intent to do so."

What this means is that foreign countries are beginning to question the wisdom of holding and hoarding U.S. debt instruments. As foreign countries begin to wise up to the deep financial challenges facing the United States, they are likely to begin looking to invest their funds in other, more stable, assets. Because the economic problems facing the United States are structural, it means that long-term prospects for the debt-laden U.S. economy are dismal at best. The idea that America can forever spend and borrow its way into prosperity is a delusion that is promoted by the government and the media. It is a lie and its effects are going to harm millions of unsuspecting Americans who continue to believe the deception.

The mounting domestic and international fears surrounding the growing U.S. government debt will mean one thing: *fewer borrowers.* And fewer borrowers will mean less money for the federal government to use in shoring up the entitlement crisis that it has created. With its back against the wall, the federal government will be forced to borrow from its "lender of last resort": the Federal Reserve. And how will the

Federal Reserve go about purchasing the debt? Through the creation of freshly printed paper money. And printing more money only *dilutes the value of the currency, leading to massive inflation.*

Admittedly, this is a gloomy scenario. But it is based upon fact. And facts are stubborn things. The truth can be found in the numbers. If the United States does nothing to stem the tide of this entitlement crisis, the U.S. Government Accountability Office (GAO) has projected that by the year 2040, the entire U.S. federal budget will be spent on paying for its promised entitlements. *This means that no money will be left over to pay for public education, national defense, and homeland security, or anything else for that matter.*

The ugly truth that no one is telling you is that America is preparing to enter the greatest financial crisis in world history. To be forewarned is to be forearmed.

So now that we have clearly stated the problem, what can you do to protect yourself and your family? We'll present some strategies in the next chapter.

Endnotes:

1. David Wiedemer, Robert Wiedemer, Cindy Spitzer, and Eric Janszen, *America's Bubble Economy: Profit When It Pops* (Wiley-Interscience, 2007), p. 234.

2. Kathleen Hall Jamieson, *Packaging the Presidency: A History and Criticism of Presidential Campaign Advertising* (Oxford: Oxford University Press, 1996), p. 509.

3. Richard Wolf, "Social Security Hits First Wave of Boomers," *USA Today*, http://www.usatoday.com/news/washington/2007-10-08-boomers_N.htm.

4. Jeannine Aversa, "Treasury Secretary: 'Social Security Has "No Assets,"'" *Augusta Chronicle*, July 10, 2001, http://chronicle.augusta.com/stories/2001/07/16/bus_318998.shtml.

Part III
The Energy Crisis

Chaper 8
Hubbert's Peak: Our Greatest Fears Confirmed

"I'd put my money on the sun and solar energy. What a source of power! I hope we don't have to wait until oil and coal run out before we tackle that."[1]

— Thomas Edison, 1931

"We are not good at recognizing distant threats even if their probability is 100 percent. Society ignoring [peak oil] is like the people of Pompeii ignoring the rumblings below Vesuvius."[2]

— James Schlesinger, former U.S. Energy Secretary

OVERVIEW: There is nothing we know of now that carries so much energy per unit volume or per unit weight as oil. Oil has become largely irreplaceable in today's exploding global economy. Yet, as the global economy continues to grow, credible sources are telling us that global oil supplies have peaked. The truth is, we have entered an era where global oil demand will consistently outstrip the global oil supply. This means one thing for oil prices: they will continue to climb higher. In Saudi Arabia there is a saying: "My father rode a camel. I drive a car. My son flies a jet airplane. His son will ride a camel." In our oil-dependent world, it is vital that we invest in alternative energy sources. However, little investment has occurred. This lack of foresight is positioning oil-producing nations (e.g., OPEC) in a place of tremendous advantage as we march forward into the uncertain future.

*"The end-of-the-fossil-hydrocarbons scenario is not
therefore a doom-and-gloom picture painted
by pessimistic end-of-the-world prophets,
but a view of scarcity in the coming years
and decades that must be taken seriously."*[3]

— *Deutsche Bank*

Energy is the lifeblood of a nation's economy. And today, oil has become the primary source of energy that fuels the world economy. Nowhere is this dependence upon petroleum-based energy products more clearly seen than in the United States. According to the U.S. Department of Energy, oil represents over 50 percent of America's total energy use. That number rises to 75 percent when oil and natural gas usage are both considered.

As we will see in this chapter, over the last several decades the world's oil supplies have been marked by two important characteristics. Oil supplies have been (1) cheap and (2) plentiful. These two factors have led to an increase in America's demand for oil and to America's crippling dependency upon imports of oil from foreign nations. *Unfortunately for America, and the world, petroleum is a form of energy that scientists refer to as a "non-renewable energy source."* This term is somewhat self-explanatory. Basically, there is a finite, or limited, supply of oil within the earth. Since the world's oil supplies are finite, this means that at some point in the future the extraction of petroleum from the earth will become too expensive for oil producers to retrieve. We will discuss this point in more detail in our discussion on peak oil.

But before we delve into the details of the energy concerns that are plaguing America, let us first gain some perspective on our place in the history of energy sources.

The Evolution of Energy Since 1700

Despite its increasing global demand, oil has not always been the world's most important energy source as it is today. In his book *American Theocracy*, author Kevin Phillips provides an illuminating look at the evolution of energy supplies over the last several centuries.[4] Phillips writes about the world's various energy leaders of recent memory and begins in the 17th century with Holland. Thanks to Dutch ingenuity, they were able to harness enormous amounts of energy supplies from three basic sources: wood, water, and wind. As the global leader of energy, Amsterdam soon became the center of commerce and finance and boasted the largest share of world trade. And their navy fleets dominated the sea lanes from Holland to Asia.

By the mid-18th century, Great Britain began rising in energy dominance, thanks to the discovery of coal-fired energy. As Britain began to harness the power of refined coal, it soon led to the creation of steam power (which would later give rise to the internal combustion engine). These early discoveries, including the development of iron-making, gave rise to what historians refer to as the Industrial Revolution. During this same time, Holland's energy influence began to wane as the new center of global power began to shift toward Great Britain. Put simply, the Dutch windmills could not compete with the efficiency of British coal-fired energy.

As the British continued their massive investment in coal, a second industrial revolution began occurring near the end of the 19th century. During this new era, the focus moved from the steam engine, iron, and coal to the internal combustion engine, steel, and petroleum-based energy. Leading the charge of this new energy source was none other than the United States.

As the global hegemonic power of the 19th century, Britain entered the 20th century with all of the wounds of an empire in decline: an overextended military, a failing currency, and an aging national infrastructure. Their massive investment in coal-based energy meant that converting to a new energy source would mean starting over. The British remained one step behind the United States moving into the 20th century and would eventually give way to total American dominance halfway through the 20th century.

The impact that this second phase of the Industrial Revolution had upon the world is indescribable. The introduction of petroleum as a viable energy source transformed industry and commerce the world over. It revolutionized the way wars were fought. And the influence that it would have upon the American economy and culture is too widespread to mention in this book. (I have included book recommendations on these topics in our recommended reading section at the end of this book.) America's energy leadership during this newfound era meant that our nation stood to gain the great prosperity that would come from harnessing oil. Today, the energy produced by oil has made life extremely comfortable. Thanks to the many innovations it has made possible, the average middle class family in America lives a life that would have been the envy of monarchs in centuries past.

Peak Oil 101

One of the greatest — and most imminent — challenges looming on America's economic horizon is the threat of global peak oil production. You may have heard of the phrase "peak oil" from television,

---

DID YOU KNOW?

All of the following products are made from oil: heart valves, crayons, parachutes, telephones, transparent tape, antiseptics, deodorant, pantyhose, rubbing alcohol, carpets and upholstery, hearing aids, cassettes, motorcycle helmets, pillows, shoes, refrigerator linings, electrical tape, safety glass, awnings, rubber cement, nylon rope, ice buckets, fertilizers, hair coloring, toilet seats, denture adhesive, movie film, fishing boots, candles, water pipes, car enamel, shower curtains, credit cards, aspirin, golf balls, detergents, sunglasses, glue, fishing rods, linoleum, plastic wood, soft contact lenses, trash bags, hand lotion, shampoo, shaving cream, footballs, paint brushes, balloons, fan belts, umbrellas, paint rollers, luggage, antifreeze, model cars, floor wax, sports car bodies, tires, dishwashing liquids, unbreakable dishes, toothbrushes, toothpaste, combs, tents, hair curlers, lipstick, ice cube trays, electric blankets, tennis rackets, drinking cups, house paint, roller skate wheels, guitar strings, ammonia, eyeglasses, ice chests, life jackets, TV cabinets, car battery cases, insect repellent , refrigerants, typewriter ribbons, cold cream, glycerin, plywood adhesive, cameras, anesthetics, artificial turf, artificial limbs, bandages, dentures, mops, beach umbrellas, ballpoint pens, boats, nail polish, golf bags, caulking, tape recorders, curtains, vitamin capsules, dashboards, putty, percolators, skis, insecticides, fishing lures, perfumes, shoe polish, petroleum jelly, faucet washers, food preservatives, antihistamines, cortisone, dyes, LP records, solvents, roofing.[5]

newspapers, or other media sources. But what exactly does the phrase "peak oil" mean? Well, just like everything else, there is a simple answer and a more complex answer. Let's begin with the simple answer. "Peak oil" is a theory that basically goes something like this:

"PEAK OIL" DEFINED: The oil trapped beneath the surface of the earth exists in a limited supply. It is non-renewable, and therefore its supply is finite. Because the amount of oil under the earth is limited, eventually readily available oil supplies will decrease. As it decreases, it also becomes more expensive to extract from the earth. As the amount of oil available to humanity becomes harder to extract, it will lead to declining oil production. Declining oil production will make each barrel of oil more expensive due to increasing global demand for oil. Higher prices will hurt the global economy and will eventually require the globe to discover and implement alternative energy sources.

Many people have mistakenly thought that "peak oil" is the theory that the world is running out of oil. Let me be the first to say that the world is not running out of oil. The world has tremendous amounts of remaining oil supplies to be tapped. In fact, it is highly probably that the earth will *never* completely be sucked dry of its petroleum (oil) reserves. So let me emphasize this point: *The problem is not that the world is running out of oil; rather, the world is running out of cheap oil.*

Peak Oil vs. Cheap Oil

There is a huge difference between peak oil and "cheap" oil. What America and, indeed, the world has built their economic infrastructures upon is cheap oil. Let me quickly define what I mean by cheap oil. To give a proper definition, I need to first explain another term, something known in the petroleum industry as Energy Return on Energy Invested (EROEI).

++
NOTE: Now, I know what you are thinking. You are thinking that I am going to get all technical on you and that this is going to be a boring chapter. But if you are thinking of skipping this chapter, I warn you, this section on the energy crisis facing America may be one of the most important concepts in this entire book. Skip it — at your own peril.

++

EROEI is simply a petroleum industry term for determining the return on investment, also known in the financial industry as ROI (return on investment.) In financial terms, if you invested one dollar into a company and it provided you with an annualized return of 25 percent, you would get back $1.25 for your one dollar invested. This is similar to the EROEI concept, except with EROEI we are measuring *the amount of energy spent as compared to the amount of energy extracted from the earth.* This ratio is used by petroleum companies to determine whether a particular oil field is worth drilling in. If the amount of energy an oil company will have to use will end up costing less than the energy that they will obtain, they are likely to proceed with the project. However, if the amount of energy required to drill will cost more than the oil company could potentially extract, this is an example of negative EROEI. Just a few decades ago, when several new oil discoveries were being made, some of these new oil fields could produce an EROEI of 200.[6] This means every dollar of energy invested could provide a return of $200 in energy. That is a great return on investment and explains much of the enormous oil wealth that we have seen throughout history. Oil that can be explored and produced with a high EROEI has the potential to provide a high rate of return to oil companies. This potential for high profits is a powerful motivating factor to continue exploring and producing. And continue they did as we will see shortly.

When EROEI is at a high level, this traditionally leads to "cheap oil" supplies. However, when energy extracted from the ground begins to require more energy than can be produced by the extraction, this is referred to as "peak oil."

Over the last several decades, global oil supplies, for the most part, have been plentiful, readily accessible and, therefore, relatively inexpensive — or "cheap." Oil companies love "cheap" oil sources because they increase their profits due to high EROEI by decreasing their exploration and production costs. Businesses love "cheap" oil because it stabilizes their costs of doing business, drives down transportation costs, can allow them to create or employ innovative technologies, and can generally increase their bottom line. Finally, consumers love cheap oil because it lowers their monthly costs, thereby freeing up more money for other types of consumption.

What the "peak oil" theory proposes is that the globe is nearing the end of "cheap oil" supplies. Currently, we are living in a time when EROEI is declining at a fairly steady rate around the globe. According to the "peak oil" theorists, the energy supplies under the ground will eventually become too expensive to extract — that is, their EROEI will become too low, or even negative! And that is why I say that the earth will never "run out of oil." It will simply run out of "cheap oil" because energy companies will not extract at an unreasonably low rate of EROEI.

DID YOU KNOW?

The energy produced by one barrel of oil is the equivalent of 20,000 hours of human labor.

However, this topic of declining oil production is one that has been generally ignored by the American public. Because there is such a lack of understanding on this potentially catastrophic problem, I have committed the rest of this chapter to helping you gain a basic understanding of what peak oil means to America and the world by organizing it into a series of questions and answers. And because the questions on this topic are too numerous to answer in one chapter, I have included a recommended reading list at the conclusion of this chapter.

Questions and Answers Regarding Peak Oil

Q: What proof exists that the peak oil theory is indeed true?

A: The "peak oil" theory was first advanced by an American geophysicist named Marion King Hubbert. Hubbert was a Shell Oil employee in the oil heyday of the 1950s. During this era, American oil production was growing rapidly and EROEI was high. In many ways, these were the glory days of the American oil business. But on March 8, 1956, a shock wave would strike the calm and prosperous waters of America's oil industry. That day, in a small ballroom at the Plaza Hotel in San Antonio, Texas, M. King Hubbert delivered a speech, entitled, "Nuclear Energy and the Fossil Fuels." In his speech, Hubbert demonstrated that graphs of oil discoveries over time tended to follow a bell-shaped curve similar to the chart on the following page.

According to Hubbert, all energy production naturally moved through three distinct phases:

- The first stage of a newly discovered energy source is a period of increasing energy production with a high rate of EROEI.

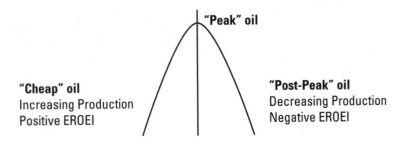

- The second stage occurs when production from the energy source begins to flatten out. It is at this point that production is said to have "peaked."

- The third stage occurs shortly after production has peaked. This period is marked by a declining production and a declining rate of EROEI.

But Hubbert did not stop at simply explaining his findings. Hubbert also boldly dared to make predictions as to when the United States would collectively reach its own period of peak production. (He did this despite pressure from his employer, Shell Oil. History tells us that the status quo is fiercely defended until the majority demands change.) To the shock and dismay of the American oil industry, M. King Hubbert declared in 1956 that America, as a whole, would reach their peak oil production sometime between 1965 and 1971. It was during this time period that Hubbert expected America's oil production to stop increasing and instead to hit a ceiling, or a "peak." From that point on, Hubbert's research indicated that America would enter the third stage of declining production and lower rates of EROEI. Hubbert was the first scientist in the oil industry to publicly warn of the threat posed to America by "peak oil." His research and theories became known as Hubbert's Peak. (Google "Hubbert's peak" for more information.) As you can imagine, both Hubbert's findings and his predictions were greeted by a large amount of controversy in his day. For the most part, Hubbert's analysis was dismissed as sensational and was quickly forgotten. It was not until the 1970s that Hubbert's research would be revived by a concerned public.

"Peak Oil" Strikes the United States

Despite being marginalized by his peers and facing ridicule from the media, Hubbert's prediction came true in 1970. After decades of increasing oil production and high rates of EROEI, the United States began to enter a period of peak production in the year 1970. In that year, oil production peaked at a rate of 9.6 million barrels per day. One decade later, despite massive efforts to increase production, American oil output declined to 8.6 million barrels per day. Today, U.S. oil production stands at around 5 million barrels per day — about half of what it was back in 1970. Did Hubbert accurately predict America's energy crisis nearly 15 years *before* it happened? Examine the following graph of America's daily oil production to confirm Hubbert's Peak for yourself.

Q: If America's oil production peaked in 1970 and has been declining ever since, how has America been able to feed its own growing demand?

A: Imports from foreign nations.

It is no secret that America is addicted to oil. Our nation's appetite for oil has been steadily increasing over the last several decades. In 1970, the year of America's peak oil production, we imported only 24 percent of our oil from foreign nations. *Today, that number has increased to 70 percent.* And it is growing. *In fact, each and every day America consumes around 25 percent of the world's available oil production.* That's about 21 million barrels a day! What makes this

U.S Crude Oil Field Production (Thousand Barrels per Day)

Decade	Year-0	Year-1	Year-2	Year-3	Year-4	Year-5	Year-6	Year-7	Year-8	Year-9
1850s										0
1860s	1	6	8	7	6	7	10	9	10	12
1870s	14	14	17	24	30	33	25	37	42	55
1880s	72	76	83	64	66	60	77	77	75	96
1890s	126	149	138	133	135	145	167	166	152	156
1900s	074	190	243	275	320	369	347	455	488	502
1910s	574	604	609	681	728	770	822	919	920	1,037
1920s	1,210	1,294	1,527	2,007	1,951	1,700	2,112	2,469	2,463	2,760
1930s	2,460	2,332	2,145	2,481	2,488	2,723	3,001	3,500	3,324	3,464
1940s	4,107	3,847	3,796	4,125	4,584	4,695	4,749	5,088	5,520	5,046
1950s	5,407	6,158	6,256	6,458	6,342	6,807	7,151	7,170	6,710	7,054
1960s	7,035	7,183	7,332	7,542	7,614	7,804	8,295	8,810	9,096	9,238
1970s	9,637	9,463	9,441	9,208	8,774	8,375	8,132	8,245	8,707	8,552
1980s	8,597	8,572	8,649	8,688	8,879	8,971	8,680	8,349	8,140	7,613
1990s	7,355	7,417	7,171	6,847	6,662	6,560	6,465	6,452	6,252	5,881
2000s	5,822	5,801	5,746	5,681	5,419	5,178	5,102	5,103		

Source: tonto.eia.doe.gov/dnav/pet/hist/mcrfpus1a.htm.

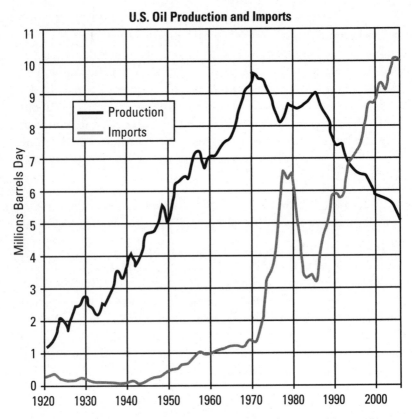

U.S. Oil Production and Imports

Source: http://en.wikipedia.org/wiki/File:US_Oil_Production_and_Imports_1920_to_2005.png

number even more staggering is that America only makes up 5 percent of the global population. Of course, this means that the remaining 95 percent of the world's population must grow and maintain their economies with only 75 percent of the world's oil supplies. Sadly, America's dependency upon foreign oil has exposed our nation's obsession with overconsumption. Never before in history has one nation been as dependent upon foreign nations for its own supply of energy as America is today.

You will notice from the above chart that U.S. oil production peaked in 1970 and then began to decline (just like Hubbert predicted). Also, notice how sharply imports rose just after 1970. By the mid-1990s, imports began to outpace domestic production. And

> ## DID YOU KNOW?
>
> According to a July 2008 estimate, the U.S. population was just over 300 million. With the entire world's population at 6.7 billion, this means the United States represents less than 5 percent of the entire world's population.
> The world currently produces 86 million barrels of oil per day. America consumes 21 million barrels of that production every single day. That means that only 5 percent of the world's population consumes over 25 percent of the world's daily oil production. This leaves the remaining 95 percent of the world's population with only 75 percent of the world's daily oil production for their consumption.

by 2005, imports from foreign nations were about twice as great as America's own oil production.

Based upon this chart, do you think that America's imports are going to go up or down in the future? Where do you think American oil production is heading, up or down? This chart makes it clear that some tough choices lie ahead for America.

Q: Okay, this "peak oil" deal seems like really bad news for America. But I am sure that the U.S. government has been working on a way to fix this problem soon, right?

A: Wrong.

Despite being warned for decades that the United States would eventually face peak production, the U.S. government has done nothing to date to solve the energy crisis that is about to strike America's shores with a fury.

You read that correctly: the American government has no plan.

And not only has America become dependent upon foreign nations for the majority of its energy supplies, it has also become dependent upon a national infrastructure that is almost completely dependent on cheap and abundant oil. Today, a large part of American government and commerce operate under the assumption that our nation will have limitless supplies of "cheap" oil. The perilous ramifications of these assumptions are discussed later in chapter 10.

Q: I have heard that America still has large amounts of oil reserves that have not been tapped for production. Won't America be fine if it just uses its own untapped reserves?

A: One of the major factors contributing to America's decreasing oil production has been a decline in new domestic oil discoveries. The last major U.S. oil discovery occurred in the late 1960s. The only way to increase our oil production is to strike new, currently undiscovered sources of oil, or to extract more from our existing reserves. Until this happens, America's oil supplies will continue to dwindle.

Some have pointed to places like ANWR as holding the answer to America's energy crisis. Well, what about ANWR?

Known as the Arctic National Wildlife Refuge, ANWR is a hotly debated topic among politicians. This region has pitted environmentalists against the big oil lobbyists in a political struggle over a relatively small amount of oil. According to the USGS (United States Geological Survey), ANWR is estimated to hold somewhere between 6 and 16 billion barrels of oil. The U.S. Department of Energy has stated that based upon their research, ANWR could potentially produce between 1.0 and 1.3 million barrels of oil per day. According to the DOE, to reach these production levels would take around 20 years. Currently, America consumes 21 million barrels of oil per day. And that number is set to increase to 26 million barrels per day by 2020. *Are one million barrels per day really worth the current political debate?* Could we not find some better use of our time, to find *real* solutions that could actually make a big impact on our problem?[7]

Others have pointed to the oil trapped in the Canadian oil sands as being the solution. In 2003, Canada reported a huge discovery of oil trapped inside of Alberta tar sands. Unfortunately, extracting oil from these sands is extremely labor-intensive and requires an immense amount of water and an enormous amount of energy. In addition, the extraction is extremely slow, not to mention a low EROEI of 1.5. This is not a likely candidate for solving America's energy crisis.

Q: All right, peak oil may be a reality for America, but we are just one country. There are plenty of other nations with lots of oil that America can import from. Are you saying that every single one of those nations is facing peak oil, too?

So far we have limited our discussion to the effect that "peak oil" has had on U.S. domestic oil production. But what about global oil production? Does Hubbert's Peak theory apply to world oil production, too?

A: The U.S. Department of Energy has beat us to the punch because it has already asked these same questions. (I guess 1970 really spooked them.) In an effort to gain answers, they commissioned and sponsored an in-depth report detailing the likelihood of short-term global peak oil production. The report, entitled "Peaking of World Oil Production: Impacts, Mitigation, and Risk Management," is also known as *the Hirsch Report.* Released in 2005 by energy expert Robert Hirsch, the 67-page report drew several important conclusions. They include the following:

- The era of plentiful, low-cost petroleum is approaching an end.

- World oil supplies will peak, and in fact already are beginning to in several areas.

- Without massive intervention, the problem will be pervasive and long lasting.

- Oil peaking will adversely affect global economies, particularly those most dependent on oil. World oil demand is forecast to grow by 50 percent by 2025.

- Oil production is in decline in 33 of the world's 48 largest oil-producing countries.

- It is highly probable that when global oil supplies collectively peak, the world will have less than one year's warning.

- The world has never confronted a problem like this.

The release of the Hirsch Report further legitimized and solidified the imminent threat posed by "peak oil." In addition, the Hirsch Report surveyed a number of energy experts regarding what year they expected the world's oil supplies to reach a peak. Interestingly, an overwhelming number of responses pointed to the year 2010 as the general time frame for global peak oil to begin.

Today, however, there is very little debate about the reality of peak oil. The question is not *if* peak oil is coming, but *when.* Even the

U.S. government has confirmed the validity of Hubbert's Peak in a February 2007 report entitled "Uncertainty about Future Oil Supply Makes It Important to Develop a Strategy for Addressing a Peak and Decline in Oil Production." The report, issued by the Government Accountability Office (GAO), admits that the world will reach peak oil production sometime between now and 2040.

In its World Energy Outlook 2004, the International Energy Agency (IEA) forecasts global peak oil production by 2040.

Among oil companies, Exxon Mobil's "The Outlook for Energy: A View to 2030" predicts peak production after 2030; Total's "Sharing Our Energies: Corporate Social Responsibility Report 2004" forecasts the peak around 2030; Shell's "Energy Needs: Choices and Possibilities. Scenarios to 2050" estimates the date to be prior to 2050.[8]

Today, total global oil production is roughly 86 million barrels per day. But that number will have to rise due to increasing demand from around the globe. In a news report from Bloomberg entitled "Total, Shell Chief Executives Say 'Easy Oil' Is Gone," the International Energy Agency estimates that the global oil production will have to rise 39 percent from today's 86 million barrels to 116 million barrels of oil a day by 2030.[9] The report quotes the CEOs of Total and Shell as saying that the days of easy oil are over.

The ugly truth that few are telling you is that the world is preparing to be plunged into an era of declining oil production that will lead to enormous energy price increases. Much of the problem stems from decreasing global supplies due to a simultaneous occurrence of peak energy production around the globe. But what is exacerbating the global energy problem is the increasing demand from both developed and developing nations. And despite having foreknowledge of the issues we are facing today, the American government has done little or nothing to prevent such a predicament.

Today, the world is facing an energy crisis of immense proportions that few nations have prepared for — and even fewer people are even aware of.

In chapter 10 we will discover major players behind the increasing demand for energy. But first, we turn to what may be the most important chapter in this book: "The Coming Breakdown of the Petrodollar System."

Endnotes

1. William H. Calvin, *Global Fever* (Chicago, IL: University of Chicago Press, 2008), p. 213.
2. "Your Future — Challenges, Opportunitites, and Transition," http://www.grinningplanet.com/articles/peak-oak/peak-oil-resources.pdf.
3. Heinz Duthel, *The Big Bang Financial Crash . . . and How to Plan on a Limited Budget* (lulu.com, 2008), p. 39.
4. Kevin Phillips, *American Theocracy* (New York: Penguin Group, 2007), p. 3–30.
5. Arctic National Wildlife Refuge, http://www.anwr.org/features/oiluses.htm.
6. William Clark, *Petrodollar Warfare* (Gabriola Island, B.C.: New Society Publishers, 2005), p. 79.
7. Ibid., p. 79.
8. "U.S. Report Predicts Peak Oil by 2040"; http://www.resourceinvestor.com/pebble.asp?relid=30858.
9. "Total, Shell Chief Executives Say 'Easy Oil' Is Gone"; http://www.bloomberg.com/apps/news?pid=20601072&sid=aH57.uZe.sAI&refer=energy.

Chapter 9
The Coming Breakdown of the Petrodollar System

"I am saddened that it is politically inconvenient to acknowledge what everyone knows: the Iraq war is largely about oil."[1]

— Alan Greenspan

"I hereby find that the defense of Saudi Arabia is vital to the defense of the United States."[2]

— Franklin D. Roosevelt, U.S. president 1933–1945

OVERVIEW: In 1971, a deal was struck between OPEC and the United States in which every barrel of oil purchased in the global marketplace would be purchased in U.S. dollars. Therefore, any country desiring to purchase oil must first exchange their national currency into U.S. dollars. This "petrodollar" system has created an artificial demand for U.S. dollars as global oil demand has increased. Today, several countries are moving, or already have moved, their oil sales or purchases into other currencies in spite of the dollar. Examples include pre-war Iraq, Iran, Syria, North Korea, and Venezuela ... or the "axis of evil," if you prefer. (What is happening in our world today makes a whole lot of sense if you simply read between the lines and ignore the "official" reasons.) When OPEC decides to denominate its oil sales in another currency than the dollar, the artificial demand for the dollar will decrease rapidly, leading to massive inflationary pressures on the U.S. economy.

By 1945, around 80 percent of the world's gold was sitting in U.S. vaults. And as the saying goes, "He who holds the gold makes the rules." This statement has never been more true than in the case of America in the post–World War II era. By the end of the war, the dollar had officially become the world's undisputed reserve currency. In the devastating wake of a world war, the nations of the world sought comfort in the perceived stability and growth of the United States. As a result of the Bretton Woods arrangement, the dollar was considered to be "safer than gold."

Fast forward a few decades to 1971. In that year, the "stability" of Washington was being challenged as America was faced with severe economic turmoil. An expensive and unpopular war in Vietnam coupled with record deficits led some nations to question the economic underpinnings of America. While Europe and Japan were fully on the mend from the devastation of World War II, the continuation of their economic growth was largely dependent upon a financially stable American economy. Foreign nations could sense the economic difficulties mounting in Washington as the United States was under pressure at home and abroad. According to most estimates, the Vietnam War had a price tag in excess of $200 billion. This mounting debt, plus other debts incurred through poor fiscal policies, was highly problematic. The problems stemmed from the imbalance of the U.S. gold reserves to debt levels. Basically, the United States had created a huge mountain of new debts but did not have the money to pay for it. Making matters worse, U.S. gold reserves were at all-time lows as nation upon nation began requesting gold in exchange for their dollar holdings. It was almost as if foreign nations could see the writing on the wall for the "gold for dollars" system created by the Bretton Woods arrangement.

As 1971 progressed, so did foreign demand for U.S. gold. Foreign central banks began cashing in their excess dollars in exchange for the newfound "safety" of gold. As you may recall from chapter 4, the Bretton Woods arrangement created a new international monetary system with a fixed exchange rate on the U.S. dollar. In essence, an ounce of gold could be purchased on the global markets for the artificially low fixed price of $35. However, Washington's motives were not to be a gold supply warehouse. Instead, the dollar convertibility into gold was meant to generate a global trust in U.S. paper money. Simply knowing that the U.S. dollar could be converted into gold if necessary was good enough for some — but not for everyone. Those who began to doubt America's ability to manage a severe global crisis — in the event one were on the horizon — gravitated toward the recognized safety of gold. Historically, gold has been, and will likely remain, the beneficiary of poor fiscal and monetary policies, and 1971 was no different. As Washington continued racking up enormous debts to fund its imperial pursuits and its over-consumption, foreign nations sped up their demand for more U.S. gold and less U.S. dollars. Washington was caught in its own trap and was required to supply *real money* (gold) in return for the inflows of their *fake paper money* (U.S. dollar). They had been hamstrung by their own imperialistic policies. Soon the United States was bleeding gold. Washington knew that the system was no longer viable and certainly not sustainable. But what could they do to stem the crisis? There were really only two options. The first option would require that Washington immediately reduce its massive spending and dramatically reduce its existing debts. This option could possibly restore confidence in the long-term viability of the U.S. economy. The second option would be to increase the dollar price of gold to accurately reflect the new economic realities. There was an inherent flaw in both of these options that made them unacceptable to the United States at the time — *they both required fiscal restraint and economic responsibility.* Then, as now, there was very little appetite for reducing consumption in the beleaguered name of "sacrifice" or "responsibility."

Goodbye, Yellow Brick Road

The Bretton Woods system created an international gold standard with the U.S. dollar as the ultimate beneficiary. But in an ironic twist of fate, the system that was designed to bring stability to a war-torn global economy was threatening to plunge the world back into financial chaos. The gold standard created by Bretton Woods simply could not bear the financial excesses, coupled with the imperialistic pursuits, of the American economic empire. On August 15, 1971, under the leadership of President Richard M. Nixon, Washington chose to maintain its reckless consumption and debt patterns by detaching the dollar from its convertibility into gold. By "closing the gold window," Nixon destroyed the final vestiges of the gold standard. Nixon's decision effectively ended the practice of exchanging dollars for gold, as directed under the Bretton Woods agreement. It was in this year, 1971, that the U.S. dollar officially abandoned the gold standard and was declared a purely fiat currency.

As all other fiat empires before it, Washington had come to view gold as a constraint to their colossal spending urges. A gold standard, as provided by the Bretton Woods system, meant that America had to demonstrate fiscal restraint by maintaining holistic economic balance. By "closing the gold window," Washington had affected not only American economic policy — it also affected global economic policy. Under the international gold standard of Bretton Woods, all currencies derived their value from the value of the dollar. And the dollar derived its value from the fixed price of its gold reserves. But when the dollar's value was detached from gold, it became what economists call a "floating" currency. By "floating," economists mean that the currency is not attached, nor does it derive its value, from anything externally. Put simply, a "floating" currency is a currency that is not fixed in value. Like any commodity, the dollar could be affected by the market forces of supply and demand. When the dollar became a "floating" currency, the rest of the world's currencies, which had been previously fixed to the dollar, suddenly became "floating" currencies as well. (Note: It did not take long for this new system of floating currencies with floating exchange rates to attract manipulation by speculators and hedge funds. Currency speculation is, and remains, a threat to floating currencies. As we will see in chapter 14, proponents of a single global currency use the current manipulation of currency speculators to promote their agenda.)

In this new era of floating currencies, the U.S. Federal Reserve, America's central bank, had finally freed itself from the constraint of a gold standard. Now, the U.S. dollar could be printed at will — without the fear of having enough gold reserves to back up new currency production. And while this new-found monetary freedom would alleviate pressure on America's gold reserves, there were other concerns.

One concern that Washington had was regarding the potential shift in global demand for the U.S. dollar. With the dollar no longer convertible into gold, would demand for the dollar by foreign nations remain the same, or would it fall?

The second concern had to do with America's extravagant spending habits. Under the international gold standard of Bretton Woods, foreign nations gladly held U.S. debt securities, as they were denominated in gold-backed U.S. dollars. *Would foreign nations still be eager to hold America's debts despite the fact that these debts were denominated in a fiat debt-based currency that was backed by nothing?*

The Rise of the Petrodollar System: "Dollars for Oil"

In the early 1970s, the international gold standard had collapsed, and America was beginning to live far beyond its means. And despite facing unemployment and inflation, America displayed few signs of the kind of fiscal discipline that could prevent future complications. But fixing the root of the problem was not the concern of Washington. Instead, the primary concern of those governing America was how to maintain its position of economic dominance on the global stage. In order to ensure continued hegemonic power and thereby preserve an increasing demand for the dollar, Washington needed a plan. According to John Perkins, author of *Confessions of an Economic Hit Man: The Shocking Story of How America Really Took Over the World*, that plan came in the form of the petrodollar system.[3]

But what exactly is the petrodollar system? First, let's define the petrodollar. A petrodollar is a U.S. dollar that is received by an oil producer in exchange for selling oil. It's really that simple: money — in our case, U.S. dollars — received in exchange for oil.

Despite the seeming simplicity of this arrangement of "dollars for oil," the petrodollar system is actually highly complex and one with many moving parts. It is this complexity that prevents the petrodollar system from being properly understood by the American public. Allow me to provide a very basic overview regarding the history and the mechanics of the petrodollar system. Once you understand this "dollars for oil" arrangement, I believe that it will provide you with a more accurate understanding of what motivates America's foreign policy. Let's take a closer look.

The petrodollar system originated in the early 1970s in the wake of the Bretton Woods collapse. In a series of highly secret meetings, the United States — represented by then U.S. Secretary of State Henry Kissinger, according to many commentators — and the Saudi royal family made a powerful agreement. According to the agreement, the United States offered military protection for Saudi Arabia's oil fields. What did the United States want in exchange? For Saudi Arabia to agree to price all of their oil sales in U.S. dollars *and* to then invest their surplus oil proceeds into U.S. Treasury bills. This system was later referred to as "petrodollar recycling" by Henry Kissinger. The Saudis agreed and the petrodollar system was born. By 1975, all of the oil-producing nations of OPEC had agreed to price their oil in dollars and to hold their surplus oil proceeds in U.S. government debt securities as well. Today, the United States maintains a major military presence in much of the Persian Gulf region, including the following countries: Bahrain, Iraq, Kuwait, Oman, Qatar, Saudi Arabia, United Arab Emirates, Egypt, Israel, Jordan, and Yemen.

Today, virtually all oil transactions are made in U.S. dollars. *This means that if you want to buy a barrel of oil anywhere in this world, you must pay for it with U.S. dollars.* If you do not have U.S. dollars, you must obtain them somehow. One way is to simply convert your currency for U.S. dollars on the exchange markets. Or products can be exported to the United States in exchange for U.S. dollars. If you are a small business owner in Japan, you must first convert your yen into dollars to purchase oil. Mexico must convert its pesos to dollars to buy oil, and so on. This should help partially explain much of East Asia's export-led strategy. Japan, for example, has very few natural resources, including oil. It must import large amounts of oil and to do this requires that they have U.S. dollars. So Japan manufactures a Honda and ships it to the United States and immediately receives payment in U.S. dollars.

The petrodollar system has proven very beneficial to the U.S. economy. In essence, America receives a double loan out of every oil transaction. First, oil consumers are required to purchase oil in U.S. dollars. Second, the excess profits from the oil-producing nations are transferred to U.S. government debt securities. This arrangement provides two large benefits to the United States. It increases global demand for U.S. dollars and for U.S. debt securities.

Additionally, having oil priced in dollars means that the United States can print money to buy oil and then have the oil producers hold the debt that was created by printing the money in the first place. *What other nation, besides America, can print money to buy oil and then have the oil producers hold the debt for the printed money?*

Obviously, the petrodollar system was a brilliant political and economic move on the part of U.S. strategists. Washington, knowing that the demand curve for oil would increase dramatically with time, positioned the dollar as the primary medium of exchange for all oil transactions. This single move created a growing international demand for both the U.S. dollar and U.S. debt — all at the expense of oil-producing nations.

Growing Threats to the Petrodollar System?

Currently, the world consumes more than 80 billion barrels of oil a day. And with each barrel of oil sold, more demand for U.S. dollars is created. What kind of effect do you think that this perpetual demand for the U.S. dollar has on the U.S. economy? Based upon the benefits I have described above, we can agree that the effect is much more positive than negative. The increased demand for the U.S. dollar provided by the petrodollar system means that the Federal Reserve must keep the dollar in a plentiful supply. This means that the U.S. dollar must be printed regularly. More money in circulation leads to an expansion of the monetary base. And a larger monetary base typically means a higher standard of living — *assuming that the demand for the currency and for the debt securities remains strong.* This last point is extremely important. For if the petrodollar system were ever to crumble, *America would be stuck with a whole lot of extra U.S. dollars that would no longer be in demand.* Those dollars would then naturally find their way back to America, which would ultimately lead to massive inflation.

But Is the Petrodollar System Endangered?

Since 1980, America has devolved from being the world's greatest creditor nation to the world's greatest debtor nation. But thanks to the massive global demand for U.S. dollars and government debt made possible by the petrodollar system, America is able to continue its spending binges, imperial pursuits, and record deficits. In America today we are living proof that having the world's most important currency translates into a higher standard of living than most nations.

At one point in America's history, our nation's largest export was a variety of consumer goods. *Today, America's largest export is the U.S. dollar.* And the dollar costs us practically nothing to create. *How long before the nations of the world figure out the dollar fiasco is a fraud?* Instead of viewing U.S. dollars as worthless paper backed by nothing (as they should), foreign oil producers and consumers were convinced — *and required* — to hold U.S. dollars in order to purchase oil. However, this demand is not genuine. It is purely artificial, and over the next several years, it will become obvious to all that it is unsustainable.

Dr. Bulent Gukay of Keele University puts it this way: "This system of the U.S. dollar acting as global reserve currency in oil trade keeps the demand for the dollar 'artificially' high. This enables the U.S. to carry out printing dollars at the price of next to nothing to fund increased military spending and consumer spending on imports. There is no theoretical limit to the amount of dollars that can be printed. As long as the U.S. has no serious challengers, and the other states have confidence in the U.S. dollar, the system functions."[4]

Pay particular attention to Dr. Gukay's comment regarding "serious challengers" to the United States. Are there no serious challengers to America's current position as holder of the world's reserve currency? The answer to this question will be saved for our next chapter. For now, let us turn our attention to the darker side of the petrodollar system.

+++

Warning: The remainder of this chapter is going to be difficult to read for those who are thoroughly indoctrinated by their particular political persuasions. If you believe human governments are inherently good, that politicians do not lie, and that global leaders have your best interests in mind, please immediately move on to the next chapter. However, if you have already come to terms with the fact that men are incapable of ruling themselves, and that this world is wicked and is in desperate need of divine redemption, then read on. Nothing that lies in the remainder of this chapter will offend you because you are not easily surprised at man's folly. In fact, I think there will be some "connecting of the dots" in store for you. Are you ready?

+++

Petrodollar Warfare?

The petrodollar system created in the 1970s has served America well. It has enriched our nation at the expense of other's potential prosperity. And it helped solidify the U.S. dollar as the global currency of choice. Of course, the petrodollar system is directly connected to America's relations with the Middle East.

On September 11, 2001, America's relations with the Middle East would be altered forever. The tragic events of that day live on in the memory of every American. The dreadful carnage in New York City, Washington, and Pennsylvania was heart-rending to the billions who watched the terror unfold before their eyes on television sets around the world.

Six days after the attacks, President George W. Bush named Osama bin Laden as the "prime suspect." Washington's response was swift. On October 7, 2001, Operation Enduring Freedom was launched, sending thousands of U.S. troops into Afghanistan. Washington's goal was to capture bin Laden and wipe out two groups connected to bin Laden: al-Qaeda and the Taliban.

Soon after, Washington began building a case for a full-scale invasion of Iraq. While bin Laden appeared to have no legitimate connection to Iraq, U.S. officials claimed that Iraq presented an entirely separate set of national security threats. These threats included Iraq's alleged development and possession of weapons of mass destruction, and their intimate ties to international terrorist groups. America became sharply divided on Washington's hasty insistence to launch another war. While a majority of the American public supported a full-scale invasion of Iraq, others urged a more diplomatic approach. But in the wake of the devastation of 9/11, few were in the mood for diplomacy.

As the war drums over Iraq beat ever so loudly, legitimate questions concerning the merits of the war led Washington to provide specific answers to a confused and terror-weary public. Such questions included: is there proof that Iraq actually had weapons of mass destruction? And was there evidence linking Iraqi president Saddam Hussein to the terror of 9/11?

Then there were others who questioned America's motives on the invasion of Iraq. In his book *Petrodollar Warfare*, author William R. Clark makes an audacious claim that the 2003 U.S.-led invasion of Iraq was not based upon "violence or terrorism, but something very different, yet not altogether surprising — declining economic power and depleting hydrocarbons."[5]

Clark's work is heavily influenced by another author named F. William Engdahl and his book, *The Century of War: Anglo-American Oil Politics and the New World Order.*

According to Clark and Engdahl, the U.S.-led invasion of Iraq was not motivated by Iraq's connection to terror. Nor was it out of sympathy for the Iraqi people's lack of a democratic process. Instead, Clark and Engdahl claim that it was Iraq's 2002 decision to refuse to sell its oil in dollars that led to the conflict. These efforts to "protect the dollar" began taking shape in the fall of 2000. According to page 28 of Clark's book, "On September 24, 2000, Saddam Hussein allegedly emerged from a meeting of his government and proclaimed that Iraq would soon transition its oil export transactions to the euro currency." As renegade and newsworthy as this action was, it was sparsely reported on in the American media. On page 31, Clark adds: "CNN ran a very short article on its website on October 30, 2000, but after this one-day news cycle, the issue of Iraq's switch to a petroeuro essentially disappeared from all five of the corporate-owned media outlets."

Not long after this meeting in 2000, Saddam began making the switch from dollar-based transactions to requiring euros for all future oil sales. By 2002, Saddam began converting all of his excess petrodollars into petroeuros — in essence dumping the dollar. A few months later, on March 19, 2003, a full-scale U.S.-led invasion of Iraq had begun. According to Clark and Engdahl, Saddam's bold threat to the petrodollar system had brought the full force and fury of the U.S. military onto his front lawn. Was the Iraq war really about weapons of mass destruction, al-Qaeda, and fighting terrorism? Or was America's goal to bring democracy to Iraq a guise for making an example of Iraq for threatening the petrodollar system? I don't claim to know. However, the more that you consider the data, the more compelling the argument becomes.

What's "Our" Oil Doing under "Their" Sand?

Of course, Washington's stance was clear. This war was not, nor was it ever, about Iraq's oil supplies.

Consider a small sampling of quotes from U.S. officials:[6]

The idea that the United States covets Iraqi oil fields is a wrong impression. I have a deep desire for peace. That's what I have a desire for. And freedom for the Iraqi people. See, I don't like a system where people are repressed through torture and murder in order to keep a dictator in place. It troubles me deeply. And so the Iraqi people must hear this loud and clear, that this country never has any intention to conquer anybody (U.S. President George W. Bush).

This is not about oil; this is about a tyrant, a dictator, who is developing weapons of mass destruction to use against the Arab populations (U.S. Secretary of State Colin Powell).

It's not about oil and it's not about religion (U.S. Secretary of Defense Donald Rumsfeld).

I have heard that allegation [of oil motives] and I simply reject it (Coalition Provisional Authority Paul Bremer).

It's not about oil (General John Abizaid, Combatant Commander, Central Command).

It was not about oil (Energy Secretary Spencer Abraham).

It's not about the oil, the *Financial Times* reported Richard Perle shouting at a parking attendant in frustration.

This is not about oil (Australian Treasurer Peter Costello).

The only thing I can tell you is *this war is not about oil* (Former Secretary of State Lawrence Eagleburger).

This is not about oil. This is about international peace and security (Jack Straw, British Foreign Secretary).

This is not about oil. That was very clear. This is about America, and America's position in the world, as the upholder of liberty for the oppressed (Utah Republican Senator Bob Bennett).

White House spokesperson Ari Fleischer on the United States' desire to access Iraqi oil fields: "There's just nothing to it."

Condoleeza Rice, in response to the proposition, "If Saddam's primary export or natural resource was olive oil rather than oil, we would not be going through this situation," said: "This cannot be further from the truth. He is a threat to his neighbors. He's a threat to American security interest. That is what the president has in mind." She continued: *"This is not about oil."*

Clearly, the government line was loud and clear: this war was not about oil. But despite this seemingly impenetrable defense of Washington's intentions, it did not take long for the dissenters to emerge. And as the war with Iraq raged on, even those within Washington began to make revealing comments on the U.S.-Iraq oil connection.

In January 2003, British Foreign Secretary Jack Straw admitted that oil was a key priority to the West's involvement in Iraq.[7]

In June 2003, Deputy Defense Secretary Paul Wolfowitz made the following comments after being asked why Iraq was being treated differently than North Korea on the question of a nuclear threat while speaking to an Asian security summit in Singapore: "Let's look at it simply. The most important difference between North Korea and Iraq is that economically, we just had no choice in Iraq. The country swims on a sea of oil."[8]

In an August 2008 *BusinessWeek* interview, Republican vice-presidential candidate Sarah Palin, stated: "We are a nation at war and in many [ways] the reasons for war are fights over energy sources, which is nonsensical when you consider that domestically we have the supplies ready to go."[9]

During a 2008 Townhall campaign meeting, presidential hopeful Senator John McCain made the following statement: "My friends, I will have an energy policy which will eliminate our dependence on oil from the Middle East that will then prevent us from having ever to send our young men and women into conflict again in the Middle East."[10]

Former Chairman of the Federal Reserve Alan Greenspan recently stated the following in his latest book: "I am saddened that it is politically inconvenient to acknowledge what everyone knows: the Iraq war is largely about oil."[11]

In a televised interview with the History Channel regarding global energy policy, former Secretary of State James A. Baker III said: "I worked for four administrations under three presidents. And in every one of those, our policy was that we would go to war to protect the energy reserves in the Persian Gulf."[12]

General John Abizaid, who was formerly the commander of the United States Central Command during the Iraq war, stated during an October 2007 round-table discussion entitled "Courting Disaster:

The Fight for Oil, Water and a Healthy Planet," at Stanford University: "Of course [the Iraq war] is about oil, we can't deny that."[13]

While it is clear that Iraq's oil supplies played some role in the 2003 U.S.-led invasion of that nation, there are even more questions regarding the change in the political logic used prior to the invasion. Vice President Dick Cheney was one of the architects behind the 2003 Iraq war. However, nine years prior to this war, in 1994, Cheney was interviewed about the 1991 Gulf War in a C-Span interview:

> Q: Do you think the U.S., or U.N. forces, should have moved into Baghdad?
>
> A: No.
>
> Q: Why not?
>
> A: Because if we'd gone to Baghdad we would have been all alone. There wouldn't have been anybody else with us. There would have been a U.S. occupation of Iraq. None of the Arab forces that were willing to fight with us in Kuwait were willing to invade Iraq.
>
> Once you got to Iraq and took it over, took down Saddam Hussein's government, then what are you going to put in its place? That's a very volatile part of the world, and if you take down the central government of Iraq, you could very easily end up seeing pieces of Iraq fly off: part of it, the Syrians would like to have to the west, part of it — eastern Iraq — the Iranians would like to claim, they fought over it for eight years. In the north you've got the Kurds, and if the Kurds spin loose and join with the Kurds in Turkey, then you threaten the territorial integrity of Turkey.
>
> It's a quagmire if you go that far and try to take over Iraq.
>
> The other thing was casualties. Everyone was impressed with the fact we were able to do our job with as few casualties as we had. But for the 146 Americans killed in action, and for their families — it wasn't a cheap war. And the question for the president, in terms of whether or not we went on to Baghdad, took additional casualties in an effort to get Saddam Hussein, was how many additional dead Americans is Saddam worth?
>
> Our judgment was, not very many, and I think we got it right.[14]

Saddam's move to switch Iraq's oil sales from dollars to euros may have been enough to change Cheney's mind. Based upon the quotes above, it is obvious that oil had played some role in the U.S.-led Iraq invasion. Let's take a look at what has transpired in the aftermath of the U.S.-led invasion of Iraq to see if the words and the actions line up.

The Rush for Post-War Iraqi Oil

In late 2002 and early 2003, the preparations for the Iraq war were well under way. As the United States sought international support for the war, several nations expressed opposition to the invasion. China, Russia, and France were among these nations. Many in the American media portrayed these nations as sympathizers, and even supporters, of terrorism due to their hesitancy to invade Iraq. However, what the media failed to mention was that these nations had existing oil contracts with Iraq that would be endangered in the event that the West gained control of Iraq. In an October 2002 interview with the *Observer UK*, a Russian official at the United Nations stated: "The concern of my government is that the concessions agreed between Baghdad and numerous enterprises will be reneged upon, and that U.S. companies will enter to take the greatest share of those existing contracts. . . . Yes, if you could say it that way — an oil grab by Washington."[15]

Prior to the invasion of Iraq, Russia was owed billions of dollars by Iraq and had billions more in contracts. Together with France and China, Russia stood to gain billions in future oil contracts when, and if, sanctions were lifted against Iraq.

In a separate 2002 news article entitled, "Oil After Saddam: All Bets Are In," Samer Shehata, a Middle East expert at the Center for Contemporary Arab Studies in Washington, was interviewed regarding the situation. "Russia, China, France have the highest stakes in the Iraqi oil industry. Once Saddam is out, everything becomes null and void and there is no legal authority to enforce those claims." Then she said, "The U.S. oil industry will post a major challenge to Saudi Arabia's position as market leader."[16]

Iraqi Oil for the West?

Since the Iraq invasion of 2003, much has transpired. Obviously, this chapter is not about the Iraq war but, rather, about the petrodollar system that the Iraq war may have been waged to protect. *It is interesting to note that within weeks of the invasion of Iraq, all Iraqi oil sales were switched from the euro — back to the U.S. dollar.*[17] Was this war, as Clark and Engdahl suggest, the first oil currency war? It is difficult to know for sure.

However, another development in 2007 gave this view more credence. In that year, a newly proposed *Iraqi Oil and Gas Law* made headlines in the media. Together with the Iraqi government, Washington and Western oil companies had carefully drafted a new law that would give foreign oil companies access to Iraq's oil fields for a period of ten years. After the ten years are up, the foreign oil companies have the option of extending their lucrative oil contracts for another 20 years. This newly drafted Iraqi Oil Law would convert Iraq's most precious national resource into a privatized industry dominated by foreign oil companies. In addition, the Oil Law would require the creation of an unelected body of oil officials known as the Federal Oil and Gas Council. This council, which could include heads of foreign oil companies, would have authority to award future Iraqi oil contracts. This newly formed council would naturally require Iraq to withdraw its membership from OPEC and would leave the Iraqi Parliament with little control over its own national oil reserves. Additionally, this new law, heavily promoted by the West, would not require foreign oil companies to hire Iraqi citizens as employees, nor would it require any reinvestment by the oil companies back into Iraq. As of the writing of this book, the verdict is still out on whether Iraq can agree to pass this new Oil Law. Getting the fractured country to agree on such a massive plan will require a strong majority from all in the Iraqi Parliament.

But regardless of whether this new Oil Law passes, what is more telling is the fact that the West is promoting it so ambitiously. After all, didn't our elected officials swear up and down to the American people that the invasion of Iraq was not about oil?

But if Iraq was not ultimately about oil, then how ridiculous is it that a nearly bankrupt nation like America is spending hundreds of billions of dollars on "spreading democracy" to foreign nations like Iraq, when our own nation is in a steep economic decline.

How are the American people able to afford such an altruistic foreign policy? And since when have the two oilmen in the White House — President George W. Bush and Vice President Dick Cheney — who have been motivated by profit all their lives as good businessmen, become so interested in giving American lives and dollars for the benefit of foreign nations with nothing in return?

And speaking of return, what could Iraq possibly offer in return to America? Perhaps Vice President Cheney answered that question best when he said in a 1999 speech at the Institute of Petroleum: "The Middle East, with two-thirds of the world's oil and the lowest cost, is still where the prize ultimately lies; even though companies are anxious for greater access there, progress continues to be slow." It is obvious to any casual observer that the United States is in desperate need of secure sources of foreign oil that it can depend on in the future. President Bush has admitted that: "What people need to hear, loud and clear, is that we're running out of energy in America." Bush is correct. Interruptions to America's oil supply could be devastating in the coming years as global oil supplies tighten due to growing demand and declining supplies.

Finally, consider Republican Senator Charles Hagel's rather blunt statement given in a 2007 speech at the Catholic University of America regarding the true purposes behind the Iraq War: "People say we're not fighting for oil. Of course we are," said Hagel. "They talk about America's national interest. What the hell do you think they're talking about? We're not there for figs."[18]

A Growing Move from Petrodollars to Petroeuros

As the petrodollar system begins to break down, there will be a shift away from the U.S. dollar and toward another stable currency, or basket of currencies. Based upon recent events, the new currency of choice for many oil-producing nations is the euro.

In 2002, Iran began making plans to move its oil sales away from dollars and into euros. Iran was soon listed on Washington's "axis of evil" list. By 2007, Iran had completely moved all of its oil sales from dollars to euros — and some yen. Washington has remained silent on this issue and instead has begun to seriously question Iran's nuclear capabilities. *This is almost an exact mirror of Washington's approach to pre-stages of the Iraq war.*

In 2002, North Korea decided it would begin using the euro instead of the dollar for all of its purchases.[19] North Korea is also a proud member of Washington's "axis of evil."

OPEC producer Venezuela has been making preparations to move all of its oil sales to the euro and away from the dollar. Venezuela and its leader, Hugo Chavez, has been a consistent point of frustration to Washington. Venezuela is now leading the charge to move all OPEC nations off the dollar and to the euro.

And as of 2008, OPEC appears to be seriously considering moving all its oil sales from the dollar to the euro.[20] Of course, this would be devastating to U.S. attempts to maintain their grip upon global hegemony. But how realistic is it that the dollar could lose its crown to the euro? And if it were to happen, how close are we to such an event?

Endnotes

1. Alan Greenspan, *The Age of Turbulence: Adventures in a New World* (New York: Penguin Group, 2007), p. 463.
2. From a letter written to Stettinius, February 18, 1943.
3. John Perkins, *Confessions of an Economic Hit Man: The Shocking Story of How America Really Took Over the World* (Ebury Press, 2006).
4. Sylvia L. Mayuga, "Crisis, Oil and the U.S. Dollar," 07/27/2008, http://opinion.inquirer.net/viewpoints/columns/view/20080727-150943/Crisis-Oil-and-the-US-Dollar.
5. William R. Clark, *Petrodollar Warfare* (Gabriola Island, BC: New Society Publishers, 2005), p. 15.
6. Robert Weissman, "From Greenspan to Kissinger," *Counterpunch Magazine,* Sept. 19, 2007, http://www.counterpunch.org/weissman09192007.html.
7. "Straw Admits Oil Is Key Priority," http://www.guardian.co.uk/politics/2003/jan/07/uk.iraq.
8. "Update: Iraq War 'Was about Oil'"; http://www.news24.com/News24/World/Iraq/0,,2-10-1460_1369424,00.html.
9. "Bartiromo Talks with Sarah Palin," http://www.businessweek.com/bwdaily/dnflash/content/aug2008/db20080829_272692_page_2.htm.
10. mediamatters.org/items/200805060004.
11. Greenspan, *The Age of Turbulence: Adventures in a New World,* p. 463.
12. http://www.pbs.org/wgbh/pages/frontline/shows/saudi/interviews/baker.html.
13. "Roundtable Debates Energy Issues," http://daily.stanford.edu/article/2007/10/15/roundtableDebatesEnergyIssues.
14. http://www.metacafe.com/watch/1193195/cheney_admits_in_1994_that_an_iraq_invasion_would_be_a_disaster/.
15. "Scramble to Carve Up Iraqi Oil Reserves Lies behind US Diplomacy," http://www.guardian.co.uk/world/2002/oct/06/russia.oil.

16. Michael Moran and Alex Johnson, "Oil after Saddam: All Bets Are In," Nov. 7, 2002, http://www.msnbc.msn.com/id/3071521/.

17. "Iraq Returns to International Oil Market," http://www.thedossier. ukonline.co.uk/Web%20Pages/FINANCIAL%20TIMES_Iraq%20 returns%20to%20international%20oil%20market.htm.

18. www.inteldaily.com/?c=144&a=3684.

19. "North Korea Embraces the Euro," http://news.bbc.co.uk/2/hi/asia-pacific/2531833.stm.

20. http://uk.reuters.com/article/businessNews/ idUKL0882239220080208.

Chapter 10
The Future of Oil and the End of Dollar Hegemony

"The glory of the twentieth century is now the burden."[1]
— Kevin Phillips

"We can evade reality, but we cannot evade the consequences of evading reality."[2]
— Ayn Rand

OVERVIEW: Insatiable demand from emerging markets coupled with uncertain oil supplies will lead to higher oil prices in the near future. Middle Eastern countries who dominate the majority of global oil reserves have become "the prize" of oil-dependent Western nations. Due to the lack of consistent investment in long-term non-oil energy solutions, oil prices could potentially reach jaw-dropping prices over the long term. For America's weakening economy and volatile currency, this global focus upon oil brings another challenge in the form of a crumbling petrodollar system. Will oil-producing nations soon move away from accepting dollars for their oil in favor of the more stable euro?

In the preceding chapters on the global energy crisis, two issues have been discussed: the threat of global peak oil production and the impending demise of the petrodollar system.

Most Americans have no clue how potentially devastating these two threats will be to their way of life. Peak oil marks the beginning of the end of the oil age. And once it is in full effect, it will lead to rapidly decreasing energy supplies and skyrocketing energy prices. And *when*, not *if*, the petrodollar system breaks down, it could potentially lead to massive hyperinflation followed by double-digit interest rates.

Let's first consider the implications facing America in the event that peak oil occurs sooner rather than later.

As the world's largest consumer of oil, the United States will be particularly vulnerable to the effects of peak oil. Because oil is a non-renewable resource, the reality of peak oil cannot be averted. At best, peak oil can be delayed. Because America currently consumes 25 percent of all global energy production annually, they might have the ability to delay global peak oil by adjusting their production and/ or their consumption of energy. Whether it is now or later, America will eventually have to do one of three things in the face of declining global oil production:

- Discover and produce more oil domestically
- Dramatically cut back on domestic oil consumption
- Go to war with other nations in an effort to maintain its current oil import levels

These are the tough choices that must be made by a nation that has valued consumption over production. While a case could be made that America could produce more energy, it is doubtful that any new sources could sustain both current and future consumption levels. And short of some new energy source becoming available within the next several years, it is highly improbable that America will cut back on its energy consumption. That leaves the one choice that most empires throughout history have chosen: *resource wars*.

The second largest importer of oil, China, will also face the same choices when confronted with global peak oil. There is little doubt that the United States and China could end up in a struggle over declining resources (and not just energy) in the future. When the continued growth and prosperity of both countries becomes endangered by a lack of energy and other natural resources, war will increasingly appear to be a viable short-term solution.

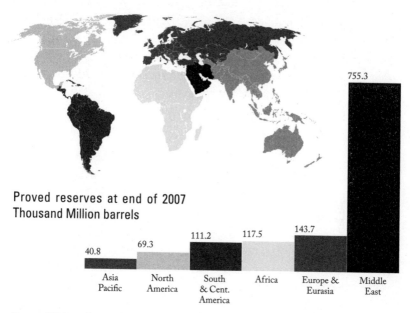

Proved reserves at end of 2007
Thousand Million barrels

Asia Pacific	North America	South & Cent. America	Africa	Europe & Eurasia	Middle East
40.8	69.3	111.2	117.5	143.7	755.3

Source: BP http://www.bp.com/sectiongenericarticle.do?categoryId=9023769&contentId=7044915

According to industry statistics on current global oil reserves, 80 percent of the world's remaining 1.1 trillion barrels of oil reserves are controlled by OPEC countries. *The United States holds only 2 percent while the Middle East holds 62 percent.* And since he who holds the gold makes the rules (black gold in this instance), this would present the Middle East, with their vast oil reserves, with a seismic increase in political and economic power over other nations. In essence, the Middle East will become "the prize."

The Times They Are a-Changing

In 1940, seven major oil companies had gained dominance over international oil production, which exceeded two billion barrels annually. Five of these oil companies were American.

Known as the "Seven Sisters," this list of oil companies included the following:

- **Standard Oil of New Jersey (Esso),** which merged with Mobil to form ExxonMobil.

- **Royal Dutch Shell (Dutch/British)**

- **Anglo-Persian Oil Company (APOC) (British).** This later became Anglo-Iranian Oil Company (AIOC), then British Petroleum, and then BP Amoco following a merger with Amoco (which in turn was formerly Standard Oil of Indiana). It is now known solely by the initials BP.

- **Standard Oil Co. of New York ("Socony").** This later became Mobil, which merged with Exxon to form ExxonMobil.

- **Standard Oil of California ("Socal").** This became Chevron, then, upon merging with Texaco, ChevronTexaco. It has since dropped the "Texaco" suffix, returning to Chevron.

- **Gulf Oil.** In 1985, most of Gulf became part of Chevron, with smaller parts becoming part of BP and Cumberland Farms, in what was, at that time, the largest merger in world history. A network of stations in the northeastern United States still bears this name.

- **Texaco.** Merged with Chevron in 2001. The merged company was known for a time as ChevronTexaco, but in 2005 changed its name back to Chevron. Texaco remains a Chevron brand name.[3]

However, just a few short decades later, the shift of global energy dominance has been swift and profound. On March 11, 2007, the *Financial Times* released a report detailing the changing face of the oil industry.[4] Based on proven global oil reserves, the report concluded that the new "Seven Sisters" were as follows:

- Saudi Aramco (Saudi Arabia)
- Gazprom (Russia)
- CNPC (China)
- NIOC (Iran)
- PDVSA (Venezuela)
- Petrobras (Brazil)
- Petronas (Malaysia)

According to the report, these new Seven Sisters "control almost one-third of the world's oil and gas production and more than one-third of its total oil and gas reserves. In contrast, the old seven sisters — which shrank to four in the industry consolidation of the 1990s

— produce about 10 percent of the world's oil and gas and hold just 3 percent of reserves."

The report continues: "Robin West, chairman of PFC Energy, an industry consultancy, says: 'The reason the original seven sisters were so important was that they were the rule makers; they controlled the industry and the markets. Now, *these new seven sisters are the rule makers* and the international oil companies are the rule takers.'"

The *Financial Times* article also cites a separate report by the International Energy Agency, which estimates that *over the next 40 years, 90 percent of all new oil supplies will come from developing countries — including the Middle East.* This dramatic shift in oil production and reserves — from West to East — will leave Western nations completely dependent upon OPEC, and primarily the Middle East, for the majority of their energy supplies — both now and in the future.

Considering America's increasing dependence upon foreign oil, this shift of oil dominance from West to East is politically and economically awkward, at best. As domestic oil supplies continue to decline in the West, the stranglehold that Middle Eastern nations have upon future oil production will become evident and potentially explosive as nations engage in resource wars in an effort to maintain their consumption levels. If energy is a non-renewable resource, which it is, and if domestic production is declining at a rapid rate, which it is, then this is the bleak future facing America. However, reality is hard and few are interested in it on the inside of a declining empire. The one economic link to the Middle East that America cannot afford to lose, both politically and economically, is the petrodollar system.

The Real U.S. Energy Crisis: Emerging Nations Converted by the "Consumption Gospel"

As these chapters on oil have demonstrated, America is consuming far too much oil for a nation that does not have a "plan B." Many Americans feel they have a God-given right to large, gas-guzzling vehicles (SUVs) and expect no limitations to be placed upon their energy consumption. I would agree wholeheartedly with them if there was a contingency plan in place for what to do when conventional oil supplies become an unviable source of American energy. But the truth is, the West is blindly (and rapidly) moving toward the edge of the "energy" cliff. Expectations of energy supplies have been unrealistic and quite frankly, irresponsible. But the West does not like to be lectured.

Instead, they like to evangelize the world with their "consumption gospel." And to their credit, they have been effective ministers of this "consumption gospel." The world (namely the East) has become dissatisfied with both their past and current consumption levels. As new converts, the East desires to emulate the West by drastically increasing its oil consumption. This drive toward Westernized consumption levels in the East is giving birth to billions of brand-new insatiable inhabitants of planet Earth. The flaunting of American wealth has awoken the rest of the poverty-stricken world to realize their "potential."

China: The Sleeping Dragon Awakens

Most economists and international strategists agree, China will be the world's next great economy. In fact, the numbers are staggering.

- China has a population of 1.3 billion — and growing.
- China has 320 million people under the age of 14, *more than the entire population of the United States.*
- China's economy has been growing at an astounding average rate of 9 percent per year.
- The average Chinese family saves and invests upward of 40 percent of their income.
- China has more speakers of English as a second language than America has native English speakers.

Every U.S. citizen consumes
25 barrels of oil per year

Every Chinese citizen consumes
just under 2 barrels
of oil per year

DID YOU KNOW?

America's population of 300 million people consumes 21 million barrels of the world's oil each and every day. That equals about 25 barrels per person every year.

China's population of 1.3 billion people consumes 7 million barrels of the world's oil each day. That equals about 2 barrels per person, per year.

What if China's entire population of 1.3 billion people each consumed 25 barrels of oil a year just as America does? Their oil demand would be 32.5 billion barrels per year. That is more than the 31.4 billion barrels that the entire world currently produces today!

Translation: If Chinese demand for oil matched that of U.S. demand, China would require all of the world's current oil production, leaving no extra for any other nation!

What if the world's entire population consumed the world's oil production at the same rate that America does?

If the entire world consumed oil at the same rate as the United States, it would require a minimum of 167.5 billion barrels of oil to be produced, per year.

Translation: If every country consumed oil at the same rate the United States currently does, it would require five times the world's current daily oil production. *That is equivalent to the oil production of five planet earths!*

China's rapid economic growth has led to its tremendous demand for massive amounts of commodities. In fact, China is currently the number-one importer of many of the world's raw materials (i.e., concrete, iron, steel, etc.) and will only demand more as their economy continues to grow exponentially. In addition to these commodities, China has a strong demand for one other raw material that is vital for economic growth in any modern-day economy: oil.

Until very recently, China relied primarily upon coal for heating fuel. But with international pressures on reducing worldwide pollution, China has begun to move away from coal and is turning to oil. And along with China's recent economic growth comes a new and growing middle class. This new Chinese middle class wants, and can afford, the conveniences that oil can provide. In particular, the demand for automobiles in China has been growing steadily. *As of 2008, 14,000 new automobiles are produced in China each and every day.* As this newfound Chinese demand for automobiles firmly takes hold, *massive amounts of oil will be required for the automobile fuel that will be needed.* Imagine tens — if not hundreds — of millions of new cars flooding the Chinese market over the next several years. And these new cars do not run on water or electricity. They run on good old-fashioned oil. Can you imagine the future Chinese demand for oil? It will be staggering.

Since 1985, the demand for oil in China has been doubling *every decade.* With a new middle class rising in China, oil demand should begin to increase even faster.

India: The Rise of a Growing Middle Class

While China is the world's fastest-growing auto market, India is second. India's government has been actively promoting car ownership among its citizens and hopes to quadruple automotive sales by 2016.[5]

Tata Motors is one company that is leading the charge in India to make cars more affordable for the growing Indian population. Tata made American news headlines in 2008 when they publicly acquired the high-class Jaguar and Land Rover brands from Ford Motor Company for $2.3 billion. The story made news as many Americans were stunned that a relatively unknown automaker from India would be the top bidder for Ford's premiere auto brands.[6]

In an effort to make cars more affordable in India, Tata unveiled its latest car, the Tata Nano, in 2008. The Nano, which gets around 50 mpg, is now the world's least expensive automobile at a low price of $2,300. This low-price strategy is enabling many of India's 1.1 billion citizens to be able to purchase their first vehicle. And thanks to their bustling economy, many Indians have been able to rise to the ranks of India's growing middle class. According to some estimates, India's middle class is expected to increase tenfold by 2025. Even if India's growth is a fraction of these expectations, the nation's demand for oil will increase exponentially in the coming years as the Tata Nano, and other similar vehicles, begin to fill the streets of India.

Unfortunately, due to a lack of proven oil reserves, India currently imports 70 percent of its daily oil requirement. As the burgeoning Indian middle class grows in number, and as more automobiles hit

India's roads, Indian oil demand is going to skyrocket. And you thought 2008 gas prices were high?

Global Oil Production in Decline

Exacerbating the increasing global demand for oil are concerns about dwindling production numbers from oil-exporting nations.

Mexico

Mexico is currently the third largest exporter of oil to the United States. However, like other developing nations, Mexico has increasing internal oil demand for its own economy. This, coupled with the fact that Mexico's production numbers have been shrinking annually, have led experts to project that by 2012 it will have no oil left to export.

Indonesia

In 2008, Indonesia announced that due to declining oil reserves, it would be forced to leave OPEC. After decades of being a net exporter of oil, Indonesia's dwindling supplies have reduced the nation to become a net oil importer. The nation's oil production recently reached it lowest levels in 30 years.

North Sea

Hailed as the solution to Europe's dependence upon Middle East oil when it was discovered in 1971, the North Sea reached its peak production in 1999. Since then, production has been decreasing rapidly.

Russia

According to a report by the International Energy Agency (IEA), Russian oil production fell for the first time in a decade in the first quarter of 2008. It has been feared for some time that Russia was nearing peak oil production. Russia is one of the largest oil producers and the second largest oil exporting country in the world, and the world has grown very dependent upon healthy amounts of exports from Russia. Is Russia nearing its peak production? If so, Russia will not be able to increase its production as oil demand goes higher in the future.

Peak Oil Could Affect Food Supplies

Since the dawn of petroleum, the world's food supplies have grown increasingly dependent upon oil and gas. For example, fertilizers, herbicides, pesticides, and farm machinery are needed to maintain the global food supply. And each of these require vast amounts of oil. Although many of us never stop to think about it, modern agriculture would be nearly impossible without large amounts of oil. Without oil, agriculture would become far more laborious and inefficient. Inefficiency in agriculture would lead to less food production. And less food production would lead to global famine.

Studies have been conducted to demonstrate the global population's dependency upon oil production. Consider the chart below. The world's population and global oil production are compared from 1960 to 2007. Notice the dependency that the world's population growth appears to have on global oil production.

The connection between these two seemingly unrelated factors is undeniable. The world's population explosion occurred after the discovery of oil. How could the discovery of oil have impacted population so directly? There are several answers:

- the massive worldwide increase in food production made possible by oil

- mass transportation, making reproduction more possible

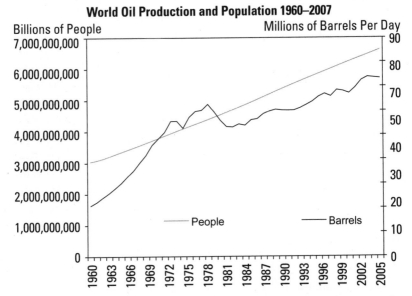

World Oil Production and Population 1960–2007

Source: www.geohive.com/earth/his_history3.aspx, www.eia.doe.gov/aer/txt/ptb1105.html

- the industrialization made possible by oil leading more people from the rural areas to more urban communities

Under the peak oil scenario, limits to growth would mean that declining oil production would, in turn, lead to declining food production. Therefore, a fair question to ask here is: "If oil production declines dramatically in the coming years, will the world be able to sustain a population of nearly seven billion people?" And, "If growth in oil production led to a direct increase in the world's population, will a decline in oil production lead to a direct decrease in the world's population?"

My desire is for the peak oil theory to be wrong. I hope the world discovers vast new supplies of oil and is able to sustain its current consumption levels for centuries to come. However, facts are stubborn things. The evidence suggests that the world is nearing the end of cheap oil. If this is true, maintaining the petrodollar system is absolutely imperative for America. Can America afford to cede control over global oil resources by allowing the petrodollar system to collapse? How can America maintain control of the supply of global oil?

Let us now turn our attention to examine the petrodollar system more in-depth.

The End of Dollar Hegemony

The threat posed by peak oil to the United States is real and potentially devastating. However, the threat posed by our second issue, the coming breakdown of the petrodollar system, will be just as real and is probably more imminent. In the preceding chapter, we explored the possible connection between the 2003 Iraq war and U.S. protection of the petrodollar system. Our basic contention was that the U.S.-led invasion of Iraq had less to with spreading democracy and more to do with securing strategic Middle East oil reserves. Because America has built its entire financial house atop a massive debt-based system, all made possible by being able to print the world's reserve currency, it is in America's *national interest* to protect the international position of the dollar. *And if that means war, so be it.* But regardless of your views on the motives behind the Iraq war, one thing is for certain: the U.S. dollar is in a massive decline and this is severely threatening the existence of the petrodollar system.

So what would happen if the petrodollar system were to break down? Here are a few likely scenarios.

- The American debt-based fiat monetary system would break down because such a system requires perpetual growth.

- The United States would be forced to create a currency reserve of the new currency in which oil could be traded. This means that the United States would need to run a trade-surplus with this nation through exporting goods to obtain their currency.

- Foreign central banks would no longer have a strong incentive to hold U.S. dollars. These dollars could come flooding back to America's shores, causing massive inflation.

- In an effort to control the hyperinflation created by this flood of dollars, the Federal Reserve would be required to drastically increase interest rates, quite possibly to double digits.

- In the end, the U.S. dollar would lose its position as the key reserve currency, which would bring our debt-based monetary system to a final day of reckoning.

But some may object: "How is this even possible? The dollar is irreplaceable on the global markets, isn't it?" It is true that the dollar has reigned supreme as the world's reserve currency for decades, and that it has gained the trust of central banks around the world. However, unlike in decades past, the dollar is no longer the only possible currency that could hold the title as the key reserve currency. But what other currency could possibly challenge the power of the almighty U.S. dollar?

The Euro: A Threat to the Petrodollar System?

Since its grand introduction in 1999, the euro, the European Union's single currency, has been the second most widely held international reserve currency after the U.S. dollar. The intricacies involved in the currency conversion made the switch the largest in history. Surprisingly, very few problems were reported as the new currency was established and soon surged in value past the dollar. As recently as 2008, the euro's value has climbed to a record-breaking $1.60 (as compared to the dollar), raising eyebrows among world markets. Translating this into laymen's terms is simple: *As the U.S. dollar is getting weaker, the euro is getting stronger.*

Despite some of the recent bad news coming out of Europe — such as increasing deficits and rising unemployment — a few things should be considered:

- **From day one, the euro has had more daily users than any other currency.** This is no surprise, as the European Union is the single largest trade market on earth.

- **The European Union is the top investor in the United States.** As of 2006, European firms account for 70 percent of all direct investment in the United States. With billions of euros flowing into the U.S. economy, one analyst has correctly remarked that *not since the colonial days has so much of the United States been under the control of the Europeans.*

- **Immediately upon its adoption, the euro became the second most important currency in the world.** Interestingly, those who study the European Union will tell you that Europe is not shooting for second best. They will only be satisfied when they have become equal to (or greater than) the United States.

Since coming onto the world scene, many so-called experts have stated that the euro would not succeed in its efforts to be a stable currency. Despite its critics, the euro has performed rather well over the handful of years that it has existed. (And it has proven to be far more stable than the U.S. dollar.) What the critics had failed to consider was that planning for such an economic and political alliance in Europe was not a sudden idea hatched in an afternoon. Instead, the idea for the European Union and their burgeoning currency was conceived in the aftermath of World War II.

A Brief History of the European Union

Europe, a region ravaged by more wars than any other in history, began its search for a lasting peace in 1950–1951 with the formation of the European Coal and Steel Community (ECSC) with six members: Belgium, West Germany, Luxembourg, France, Italy, and the Netherlands. After the devastation of World War II, European leaders had come to the conclusion that the only way to avoid future wars was to create *a single Europe.* This single Europe would need to be so economically coordinated and politically integrated that war would be unthinkable. Ironically, America helped lead the charge to heal and unify Europe through the Marshall Plan, which provided upward of $12 billion dollars in aid money to the war-torn countries of Europe. (Note: It should be added that the U.S. aid money was more than simply a gracious gift. The United States felt a strong Europe could help hold back the growing Soviet threat.) The Bretton Woods meetings of July 1944 led to the creation of the World Bank, which was initially set up to help rebuild Europe and to provide economic development for the former European colonies (much of the Middle East, Africa, and Latin America) whose economies had become extremely disarticulated and extraverted through the effects of colonialism. It was around this same time period that the Middle Eastern nations (modern-day Iraq, Iran, Syria, Lebanon, Israel, etc.) became self-ruled nations, after years of domination by various empires.

The rapid rise of the EU is a fascinating study that deserves more attention than will be discussed in this book. For our purposes, consider this brief time-line detailing the evolution of the European super state.

- 1950–1951: Modern Europe began as a six-nation steel and coal trading bloc.

- 1957: The signing of the Treaty of Rome forms the European Economic Community (also known as the Common Market).

- 1979: The European Monetary Systems (EMS) is introduced, paving the way for a single European currency.

- 1992: The Maastricht Treaty changes collective Europe's name to the European Union.

- 1995: The EU increases in size from 6 to 15 nations.

- 1999: Europe adopts plans for a single currency (euro) in 11 member states.

- 2002: The euro becomes the sole national currency in 12 member states on January 1.

- 2004: Ten new member states enter the EU, bringing the total to 25 nations.

The European Union's rise as a global power, along with its powerful currency, has provided a tremendous political and economic challenge to America. In fact, the European Union has publicly stated its desire to be a major international economic and political player on par with, if not greater than, the United States.

America's recent economic meltdown is further proof to many that its days of global hegemony are numbered.

While the European Union's rise to power has been impressive, so too has its currency's sustainability and usage. And it is not only economists and historians who have been surprised and impressed by the euro ... *so have a majority of the oil-producing nations.*

A list of nations that have recently been diversifying into the euro, or who have seriously considered such a move, include China, Russia, Iran, Venezuela, pre-war Iraq, Syria, North Korea, South Korea, and Malaysia — just to name a few.

Some doubt that the euro is a potential threat to the U.S. dollar. However, there are few convincing arguments that the dollar will not be replaced as the world's key reserve currency in the next several years.

Even former Federal Reserve Chairman Alan Greenspan stated in a September 2008 interview with the German magazine *Stern* that it is *"absolutely conceivable that the euro will replace the dollar as reserve currency, or will be traded as an equally important reserve currency."* Greenspan added that the European Central Bank had *"developed into a global economic force to be taken seriously."* Greenspan is obviously not a monetary novice, having run the world's most powerful central bank for the last two decades. It is clear that the euro is rapidly moving toward equality with the dollar. As the nations continue to get comfortable with the euro and witness the further breaking down of the dollar, the potential for the euro to eclipse the dollar as the new global reserve currency will become highly plausible in the coming years.

Praying for the Best, Preparing for the Worst

Just as quickly as I made this last prediction, I am reminded of the futility of such efforts. *No one can really know for certain when any of this will occur.* While I am sure that it will happen, *when* it will happen is the million-dollar question. And quite frankly, my hope is that it happens centuries from now. The calamity that peak oil and the breakdown of the petrodollar system will bring to America is not something that any sane person would desire. However, the data is clear and as I have said before, facts are stubborn things. Wishing that these facts will go away will not make them disappear.

Can peak oil be averted? Yes ... and no.

No, peak oil is inevitable due to the finite supply of petroleum within the earth.

However, the answer is yes in that *the effects of peak oil* can be averted if America, and the world, can develop a viable energy strategy to wean the public off of petroleum-based energy supplies. So far, the alternative energy sources to petroleum have not been impressive. The hard reality is that America has built an extremely advanced economy that requires cheap and plentiful petroleum supplies. The problem remains that as global oil supplies continue to decline, these supplies will neither be cheap nor plentiful. Instead, global oil supplies will become increasingly expensive and in limited supply. Faced with the threat, many have sought an easy answer by pointing to America's continental shelf, ANWR, and even oil shale and oil sands. While all of these are good ideas, the real problem lies in the required costs and lead time that is needed to make these strategies viable long-term strategies.

And finally, what can be done concerning the U.S. dollar system attached to oil? Is it possible that the petrodollar system can be salvaged so that a massive dollar crisis can be averted? Here the answer is a clear no. As a fiat debt-based monetary system, the U.S. dollar is doomed to the dust bin of history just like every fiat currency before it. Because the dollar is debt-based, it simply cannot survive in a period of declining production and limited growth. This fatal flaw in America's economy will be examined and exposed in the next section. Topics will include America's addiction to consumer debt, the sub-prime mortgage crisis, America's recent bailout efforts, and finally, how the creation of the Federal Reserve has led to the demise of the American experiment.

Endnotes

1. Kevin Phillips, *American Theocracy* (New York: Penguin Group, 2007), p. 31.
2. http://www.working-minds.com/ARquotes.htm.
3. Seven Sisters (Oil Companies); Wikipedia. http://en.wikipedia.org/wiki/Seven_Sisters_(oil_companies).
4. "The New Seven Sisters: Oil and Gas Giants Dwarf Western Rivals," *Financial Times*, http://us.ft.com/ftgateway/superpage.ft?news_id=fto 031220071410487854&page=2.
5. "Crude Oil $200 — Smart Investors Stand to Make a Fortune," http://www.marketoracle.co.uk/Article3393.html.
6. "Tata Motors to Buy Jaguar, Land Rover for $2.3B," http://www.usatoday.com/money/autos/2008-03-25-ford-sells-jaguar-land-rover-tata_N.htm.

Part IV

The Federal Reserve Fraud

Chapter 11

How America Lost the Revolutionary War

"From the Great Depression, to the stagflation of the seventies, to the burst of the dotcom bubble in 2001, every economic downturn suffered by the country over the last 80 years can be traced to Federal Reserve policy."[1]

— U.S. Congressman Ron Paul

OVERVIEW: There is an old saying that goes, "Follow the money." In order to come to a complete and full understanding of what is really happening in America's economy, and what will happen in the near future, we have one final task: to "follow the money" throughout America's history of central banking.

During the last couple of centuries, private international banking interests have aggressively sought favor with the governments of Western nations. At times, this favor by government has allowed the private banking system to control the issuance of the nation's specified currency. Historically, this hybrid system of government and banking follows a predictable pattern that eventually leads to a devaluation of the nation's currency system. These government-banking alliances, referred to as central banks in this chapter, ultimately lead to the destruction of the underlying nation's wealth — leading to the bankruptcy of the nation itself.

On December 23, 1923, President Woodrow Wilson signed into law the Federal Reserve Act. With the stroke of a single pen, Wilson created a government-run banking cartel — otherwise known as a central bank. During the 18th century, America had experimented with the central banking concept, as we will see momentarily. But these prior attempts would pale in comparison to the total monetary control that the Federal Reserve would be given a century later. In this section on the Federal Reserve, we will witness the financial carnage caused in one single century by the marriage of government and banking. And its effect upon America's collective wealth has been devastating.

It is interesting to note that, despite the vast economic control wielded by the Federal Reserve over consumers, most Americans are not aware of the true purpose of the institution — let alone its sordid history. While this chapter cannot treat the topic of the Federal Reserve Bank exhaustively, I point you to the recommended reading sources at the end of this chapter for more information. My goal in this chapter is to familiarize you with a very brief history of America's attempts at central banking. Some readers will already know much of what is written. Others will learn more than they may expect. But ultimately, my goal is to expose the fatal flaws in America's central banking system. This section will reveal how the corruption of sound monetary principles in our nation's banking sector has contributed greatly to America's financial excess. The financial prosperity that Americans believe to be real is, instead, fueled by debt. The corrupt policies of the American federal government, along with those of the Federal Reserve Bank, have converted our nation's monetary system into a system that is dependent upon debt to survive. Together, they have plundered our nation's wealth and have replaced it with debt. We have been shepherded to the cliff of bankruptcy by the very ones entrusted with our nation's economic protection.

All the perplexities, confusions, and distresses in America arise, not from defects in their constitution or confederation, not from a want of honor or virtue, so much as from downright ignorance of the nature of coin, credit, and circulation.[2] — John Adams

Reasons for the Revolutionary War

Since grade school, Americans have been taught that one the primary reasons that America's founding fathers fled their British homeland in search of the New World was to escape religious persecution. While this is true, there was another very important reason behind the move to the new world. This reason had less to do with religion and more to do with money.

The British Empire's tyrannical rule over its numerous colonies around the world is well-documented. America's 13 new colonies were no exception, as they were subject to many of the same unfair rules as other British colonies of their day. The Americans, however, sought freedom from the religious and economic persecution of their British oppressors. The British crown could hardly impose strict religious adherence to their subjects across the Atlantic Ocean. But the British were not nearly as interested in the religious behavior of their colonies as much as they were with the taxes that could be exacted from the colonies. Religion was simply a tool the British used to demand submission to the Crown. And part of that submission came in the form of extreme taxation on those over whom it reigned.

Up until the mid-18th century, early Americans were predominantly faithful to the wishes of the British Crown. This was true even in spite of America's theological disagreements with the Church of England. Americans were also experiencing great prosperity in the absence of strict income taxes and unemployment. The Americans had begun using paper money, but unlike Britain, America's paper money was not being issued by central bankers for obscene profits. It was regarding this American era that Benjamin Franklin wrote: "There was abundance in the Colonies, and peace was reigning on every border. It was difficult, and even impossible, to find a happier and more prosperous nation on all the surface of the globe. Comfort was prevailing in every home. The people, in general, kept the highest moral standards, and education was widely spread."[3]

On a later diplomatic trip to England in 1763, Franklin witnessed the squalid conditions of England. Franklin claimed that the streets of London were "covered with beggars and tramps." After probing for answers, a shocked Franklin discovered that England was suffering from massive unemployment. And because the high income earners were faced with high taxes, they were unable to provide aid to the poor. British officials, acutely aware of America's growing economic prosperity, quizzed Franklin about the financial structure of America. Franklin replied, "That is simple. In the Colonies, we issue our own paper money. It is called Colonial Scrip. We issue it in proper proportion to make the goods and pass easily from the producers to the consumers. In this manner, creating ourselves our own paper money, we control its purchasing power, and we have no interest to pay to no one."[4]

Never one to miss an opportunity for economic gain, the British sought to outlaw America's Colonial Scrip by forcing the American colonies to use British money. This came in the form of the Currency Act of 1764. Within a year, according to Franklin, America's streets began to resemble London's, as America's money supply plummeted and unemployment rose dramatically. More taxes targeting the American colonies included the Sugar Act, the Stamp Act, the Townshend Acts, and the infamous Tea Act, which ultimately led to the Boston Tea Party. In response to America's growing acts of economic defiance, Britain next passed the Intolerable Acts, which further damaged the fragile relationship between the two nations. To justify the taxes upon the American colonies, the British declared that America should help shoulder the economic burden of keeping the new country in the Empire. America, however, defied Britain's attempts to confiscate its wealth through heavy taxes with the cry of "taxation without representation." Finally, after much deliberation, the tensions between the two nations sparked the American Revolutionary War. The Americans succeeded in gaining independence from the British tyranny that they so greatly despised. Or so they thought.

Alexander Hamilton's Central Banking Scheme

Having escaped the economically diseased European continent, which had become dominated by destructive central bankers, America's founding fathers knew the importance of laying a sound economic foundation for their new nation. It did not take long, however, for the central banking community to come knocking at America's door. The First Bank of the United States, a proposed central bank similar to that in England, came at the suggestion of Alexander Hamilton, who argued for a strong centralized government. With England's economic machinations fresh in the minds of the

American public, Hamilton's idea for a central bank quickly found numerous opponents. Few Americans were in the mood for a new private banking cartel that would loan newly printed money to the U.S. government at interest. Many early Americans were intimately aware of the dangers and potential devastation that these central banking systems could have upon their new nation. One such opponent was U.S. Secretary of State Thomas Jefferson. Jefferson, who also authored the Declaration of Independence, believed that a central bank, such as the proposed First Bank of the United States, was forbidden by the Constitution. According to Jefferson, and the Constitution, the creation and issuance of a nation's currency was the sole privilege of the government. In defense of his argument, Jefferson wrote: "I believe that banking institutions are more dangerous to our liberties than standing armies. . . . If the American people ever allow private banks to control the issue of their currency, first by inflation, then by deflation, the banks and corporations that will grow up around them will deprive the people of all property until their children wake up homeless on the continent their fathers conquered. . . . The issuing power should be taken from the banks and restored to the people, to whom it properly belongs."[5]

Jefferson's quote is not prophetic. He was not predicting what he thought would happen. Instead, he was speaking from experience. Jefferson knew the failed history of the central banking schemes. And he passionately warned of their effects upon a nation: *"first by inflation, then by deflation. . . ."* This is precisely how central banks manipulate the economies that they leach on. First, they encourage borrowing by creating "cheap" money by lowering interest rates, which increases the overall money supply. Then, the central bank raises interest rates, which leads to credit defaults, foreclosures, and bankruptcies. This allows the bankers to purchase properties and businesses and smaller banks for "pennies on the dollar." Sound familiar?

Opponents of the proposed First Bank referred to the U.S. Constitution in an effort to prevent private central banks from gaining control over their own government's monetary activities. Constitutional support for this opposition is taken from Article I, Section 8 of the Constitution where it states that the U.S. federal government is authorized ". . . to coin money, regulate the value thereof, and of foreign coin, and fix the standard of weights and measures." But while the

Constitution may not give express permission to print paper money, Hamilton reasoned, it also certainly did not restrict it.

Is the U.S. Dollar Unconstitutional?

Notice in the Constitution that the U.S. Congress is only authorized to create *coins* with fixed "weights and measures" — *not paper money*. Based upon this section of the Constitution, many Americans today believe that America's creation of paper money is forbidden by the U.S. Constitution!

And while the Constitution *does* give Congress express permission to coin money, it *does not* give them permission to outsource this responsibility to an outside institution. According to some monetary experts, this means that the Federal Reserve Bank is an unconstitutional institution — despite being passed into law by Congress!

Despite vehement opposition to the First Bank of the United States, President Washington signed the First Bank of the United States into law on April 25, 1791, along with a 20-year charter, set to expire in 1811. During its first five years of operation, the American government borrowed more than $8 million from the First Bank and prices rose by an average of 72 percent.[6] Just two years prior to the passage of the First Bank, President Washington had warned his countrymen: "No generation has a right to contract debts greater than can be paid off during the course of its existence."

Jefferson would later lament in 1798, "I wish it were possible to obtain a single amendment to our Constitution — taking from the federal government their power of borrowing."[7]

As the 20-year charter for the First Bank came up for renewal in 1811, Congress began to debate whether to renew the First Bank's charter for another 20 years or to let it expire. Pressure to not renew the bank's charter became strong as it was discovered that 70 percent of the First Bank's ownership was held by foreigners — namely England. Nathan Rothschild, a powerful European central banker, was one foreign banker who had a strong, vested interest in the continuation of the First Bank of the United States. Gustavus Myers, in his 1936 book entitled *The History of the Great American Fortunes*, further confirms the Rothschild connection to the First Bank when he wrote: "Under the surface, the Rothschilds long had a powerful influence in dictating American financial laws. The law records show that they were the power of the old Bank of the United States."

It is reported that Rothschild — eager for the renewal of the First Bank charter — issued a bold threat to the U.S. Congress: "Either the application for renewal of the charter is granted, or the United States will find itself involved in a most disastrous war."[8] But on March 3, 1811, after the bank's 20-year charter had expired, the Congress voted against renewing it.

In the following year, the British invaded the United States in the War of 1812. The British war efforts were funded by none other than the Rothschild family. Four years later, in the wake of the war, the United States was crippled by inflation and rising unemployment. Seeking economic stability, Congress moved to charter the Second Bank of the United States.

This second attempt at a U.S. central bank occurred under the administration of President James Madison. Despite being deeply opposed to the idea of private central banking, Madison had little choice but to support the creation of the Second Bank of the United States in the face of growing economic instability. The Second Bank included the same mandates as First Bank: to issue currency and purchase government debt. It, too, was passed with a 20-year charter, set to expire in 1836.

Like the First Bank, 80 percent of the Second Bank was privately owned by banks. One-third of these were foreign. True to form, the Second Bank quickly led the United States into massive inflation. Within the first 18 months, the Bank had injected nearly $20 million into the U.S. money supply. As prices soared due to the increase in money supply, inflationary pressures began to harm American business. The bank reacted by quickly cutting the money supply in half — from over $20 million to just $11.5 million.[9] This manipulation of the money supply led to the infamous "boom and bust" cycle brought on by central banks.

As the central banking scheme continued, Americans became wise to the Second Bank's attempts to loot the nation of its hard-earned wealth through crafty monetary policies that encouraged inflationary periods followed by deflationary periods.

President Madison, aware of pitfalls of the Second Bank, warned: "History records that the money changers have used every form of abuse, intrigue, deceit, and violent means possible to maintain their control over governments by controlling the money and its issuance."[10]

Andrew Jackson — "I Killed the Bank"

Twelve years after the inception of the Second Bank of the United States, Andrew Jackson was elected president in 1828. President Jackson came into office with one mission: *to kill the Second Bank of the United States.* However, the bank's charter would not be up for renewal until 1836 — another eight years. This meant that Jackson would need two full terms in office to accomplish his goal. During his first term, he fired nearly 20 percent of the employees of the federal government — many with ties to the Second Bank.

In 1832, with his re-election approaching, the bank struck an early blow, hoping that Jackson would not want to stir up controversy. They asked Congress to pass their renewal bill four years early.[11]

Jackson swiftly vetoed the bill and stated: "It is not our own citizens only who are to receive the bounty of our government. More than eight millions of the stock of this bank are held by foreigners. . . . Is there no danger to our liberty and independence in a bank that in its nature has so little to bind it to our country?. . . Controlling our currency, receiving our public moneys, and holding thousands of our citizens in dependence . . . would be more formidable and dangerous than a military power of the enemy."[12]

Jackson's lengthy veto message goes on to explain why the Second Bank of the United States should be abolished. Jackson's reasons included the following:

- It concentrated the nation's financial strength in a single institution.
- It exposed the government to control by foreign interests.
- It served mainly to make the rich richer.
- It exercised too much control over members of Congress.
- It favored northeastern states over southern and western states.[13]

After his successful 1832 re-election bid against his opponent, Henry Clay (who received $3 million in campaign contributions from the banks), Jackson continued his tireless campaign to permanently dissolve the Second Bank. He began removing funds from the Second Bank to render it ineffective, provoking strong opposition from the bankers. The president of the Second Bank, Nicholas Biddle, lashed out at President Jackson, saying, "This worthy President thinks that because he has scalped Indians and imprisoned judges, he is to have his way with the bank. He is mistaken."

Jackson responded: "Gentlemen, I have had men watching you for a long time and I am convinced that you have used the funds of the bank to speculate in the breadstuffs of the country. When you won, you divided the profits amongst you, and when you lost, you charged it to the bank. You tell me that if I take the deposits from the bank and annul its charter I shall ruin ten thousand families. That may be true, gentlemen, but that is your sin! Should I let you go on you will ruin fifty thousand families, and that would be my sin! You are a den of vipers and thieves. I have determined to rout you out, and by the Eternal God, I will rout you out!"

Jackson's courageous and controversial act of pulling funds from the government-controlled banking cartel, known as the Second Bank of the United States, led to the final demise of the bank. It also led to Jackon's. When later asked what his greatest accomplishment had been during his two terms as president, Andrew Jackson replied, "I killed the bank."

The National Banking Act

After the death of the Second Bank of the United States, America soon began experimenting with various types of monetary systems. The period from 1837 to 1862 was known as the Free Bank Era. While the central bankers were still at bay, their influence was ever present in America's political system — and was threatening to creep back in.

As America entered the 1860s, the nation's economy was fractured and the political climate between the North and the South reached a boiling point. Eleven Southern slave states declared their secession from the United States to form the Confederate States of America in 1861. On April 12, the Confederates led an attack upon a U.S. military installation in Fort Sumter, South Carolina. Thus, the first shots had been fired on what would become known as the American Civil War — the deadliest war in American history.

War is an expensive proposition for a nation. In search of an effective way to fund the costs of the war, President Abraham Lincoln authorized the National Banking Act. This act was similar in structure to the First and Second Bank of the United States. However, instead of vesting power into just one central bank, this new act made provisions

DID YOU KNOW?

On January 8, 1835, President Andrew Jackson became the first — and only — president to ever pay off the U.S. national debt.

"If the American people only understood the rank injustice of our money and banking system — there would be a revolution by morning." — President Andrew Jackson, in a speech to Congress in 1829

for the federal government to control a number of national banks. These national banks were then responsible for purchasing federal government bonds with their own created bank notes.[14] The importance of this act should be noted, as it helped establish our current debt-based monetary system, which allows our federal government to create money out of thin air with the help of the Federal Reserve Banking system. Despite its sophistication and complexities, in the end our modern system is unfortunately just a flawed concept that in essence bankrupts our nation of its true wealth. The full realization of this "smoke and mirrors" approach to monetary policy will be discussed in full detail in our next chapter.

> The few who can understand the system will either be so interested in its profits, or so dependent on its favors, that there will be no opposition from that class, while on the other hand, the great body of the people, mentally incapable of comprehending the tremendous advantages that capital derives from the system, will bear its burdens without complaint and perhaps without even suspecting that the system is inimical to their interests. (John Sherman in a letter sent in 1863 to New York Bankers in support of the 1863 National Banking Act)

Just before the passage of the National Banking Act, President Abraham Lincoln wrote a letter to William Elkin stating: "I see in the near future a crisis approaching. It unnerves me and causes me to tremble for the safety of my country . . . the Money Power of the country will endeavor to prolong its reign by working upon the prejudices of the people, until the wealth is aggregated in a few hands and the Republic is destroyed. I feel at this moment more anxiety for the safety of my country than ever before, even in the midst of war."[15]

Five months later, Lincoln would be assassinated. Numerous rumors continue to surround the true reason for his murder.

Salmon P. Chase, the Secretary of the Treasury under Lincoln, later expressed regret at his role in the passage of the National Banking Act when he said, "My agency in promoting the passage of the National Banking Act was the greatest financial mistake in my life. It has built up a monopoly which affects every interest in the country."[16]

Debate over the need for a centralized monetary authority continued to ebb and flow during the decades following the collapse of the Second Bank and the passage of the National Banking Act.

It was not until a series of bank runs known as "the Panic of 1907" that the American public became insatiably eager for banking and monetary reform. The Panic of 1907 would become the catalyst for the birth of the "Third" Bank of the United States.

The "Third" Bank of the United States

One year after the Panic of 1907, President Theodore Roosevelt created the National Monetary Commission by signing it into law. Under the direction of Senator Nelson Aldrich (a friend of J.P. Morgan and the father-in-law of John D. Rockefeller Jr.), the commission turned to the European central banks in an effort to learn how to create one in America. Senator Aldrich personally led his team of experts on a tour of European capitals examining the continent's various central banks. Their findings became the basis for the Federal Reserve Act, which would lead to the creation of the Federal Reserve Banking System — "The Third Bank of the United States."

From its inception, the Federal Reserve Bank has been shrouded in mystery. Many Americans mistakenly believe that the Federal Reserve Bank is simply an agency of the federal government that is regulated at the federal level. However, this is not true. While it is true that the Federal Reserve was created by an act of Congress, the bank is not a government entity. Instead, the "Fed" is a partnership between the federal government and the private banking system. In other words, the Fed is a government-controlled banking cartel and is as federal as Federal Express.

While the Fed was created by an act of Congress on December 23, 1913, the idea for America's new central bank was not debated in the halls of Congress. Instead, it was secretly conceived among a group of bankers on a small island off the coast of the state of Georgia, known as Jekyll Island. On the night of November 22, 1910, Senator Aldrich and seven of his associates boarded a private rail car in Hoboken, New Jersey. They traveled south to Jekyll Island, Georgia. Details of the meeting were kept secret, security was tight, and the media was not invited.

Six years after the Jekyll Island event, B.C. Forbes, of the famed *Forbes* magazine, broke the story of the top-secret meeting. Forbes interviewed one of the meeting attendees, Paul M. Warburg. During the interview, Warburg described the experience: "Picture a party of the nation's greatest bankers stealing out of New York on a private railroad car under cover of darkness, stealthily heading hundreds of miles south, embarking on a mysterious launch, sneaking on to an island deserted by all but a few servants, living there a full week under such rigid secrecy that the names of not one of them was once mentioned lest the servants learn the identity and disclose to the world this strangest, most secret expedition in the history of American finance. I am not romancing. I am giving to the world, for the first time, the real story of how the famous Aldrich currency report, the foundation of our new currency system, was written."[17]

Warburg would later write this in his book, The Federal Reserve System, Its Origin and Growth: "The results of the conference were entirely confidential. Even the fact there had been a meeting was not permitted to become public. . . . Though eighteen years have since gone by, I do not feel free to give a description of this most interesting conference concerning which Senator Aldrich pledged all participants to secrecy."[18]

It is interesting that America's current central bank, the Federal Reserve, was created under such a strict cloak of secrecy. This intentional concealment begs the question: What were the creators of the Federal Reserve hiding? Why did they feel such a strong need for secrecy? What was there to hide?

Perhaps the answer lies in the following statement from another attendee of the secret meeting, Frank Vanderlip. In a February 9, 1935, article in the *Saturday Evening Post*, Vanderlip wrote, "If it were to be exposed publicly that our particular group had gotten together and written a banking bill, that bill would have no chance whatever of passage by Congress."

According to Vanderlip, the Federal Reserve Bank, which controls our nation's money supply and our interest rate targets, was concocted in secret because *Congress would not have passed the bill if they had full knowledge of the bank's true intentions.* Is this a legitimate reason for hiding the deliberations over this piece of legislation from the American public, and its elected leaders? If history tells us anything, control over a nation's money supply is not something that should be doled out to a secretive group cloaked in mystery. It is doubtful that America's founding fathers would have allowed such a bill to ever see the light of day.

A few weeks before his assassination in 1881, U.S. President James Garfield said these words: *"Whoever controls the money of a nation, controls that nation....* Whosoever controls the volume of money in any country is *absolute master of all industry and commerce....* And when you realize that the entire system is very easily controlled, one way or another, by a few powerful men at the top, you will not have to be told how periods of inflation and depression originate."

Despite numerous warnings — and even past failures — on December 22, 1913, the Federal Reserve Act was passed by the U.S. House of Representatives. However, getting the bill passed through the Senate proved to be more challenging. In what appeared to be a crafty ploy to get the controversial bill through the Senate with as little debate as possible, the Senate vote was quietly scheduled for December 23, 1913. Just two days before Christmas, many senators had already gone home for the holiday break. As the bankers had hoped, the bill passed through the Senate with relatively little debate. Later that same day, President Woodrow Wilson signed the Federal Reserve Act into law.

"So the American people, who had suffered through the American Revolution, the War of 1812, the battles between Andrew Jackson and the Second Bank of the United States, the Civil War, the previous panics of 1873 and 1893, and now the Panic of 1907, were finally conditioned to the point of accepting the solution offered by those who had caused all of these events: the international bankers. That solution was a central bank." (Ralph Epperson)[19]

Several U.S. political leaders vocalized their concerns about the true intentions of the Federal Reserve Bank. For example, Minnesota Congressman Charles A. Lindbergh (the father of the famed aviator) said in 1913: "This [Federal Reserve Act] establishes the most gigantic trust on Earth. When the President [Wilson} signs this bill, the invisible government of the monetary power will be legalized. . . . The worst legislative crime of the ages is perpetrated by this banking and currency bill."[20]

Fearing the ultimate control that the private central bankers would now have over the U.S. economy, Lindbergh added: "From now on, depressions will be scientifically created."[21]

True to form and to history, the Federal Reserve doubled the U.S. money supply from in 1914 to 1919. These fresh injections of U.S. dollars into the economy created an era of widespread economic growth. In 1920, when it appeared that the money supply had become too plentiful, the banks began calling in loans, resulting in bankruptcies and foreclosures. Over 5,000 banks failed during the ensuing recession of 1921, leading to a consolidation of the banking industry. Throughout the 20th century, banking failures tended to benefit the larger banks of our nation because they can be purchased for pennies on the dollar. This consolidation of the banking industry in 1921 gave more control to the nation's largest banks, and again served to benefit the Federal Reserve.

Then from 1921 to 1929, the Federal Reserve began inflating the U.S. economy. To accomplish this, the Fed increased the U.S. money supply by over 60 percent.[22] This era, which was marked by an excessive money supply, became known as the "Roaring Twenties." But as our current generation has witnessed, periods of "easy money" always have a downside. When money becomes too easily available in the form of loans and credit, excess is inevitable. Like a bad hangover after one too many drinks, the economy reacts similarly to excessive money supply. And on October 29, 1929, the U.S. stock market crashed. As many Americans feared for the safety of their money, they began withdrawing funds from their local banks. These "bank runs" led to the failure of over 10,000 banks — leading to further consolidation of the banking industry. The Federal Reserve did little to prevent the crash of 1929, and did even less to stabilize the economy once it had weakened. In the face of such desperate economic pressure, this inaction on the part of the Fed confirmed the deep-seated fears that some of America's leaders had regarding the central bank.

One case involved Pennsylvania Congressman Louis T. McFadden, who sought to bring conspiracy charges against the Federal

Reserve Board in 1932. In a speech before the Congress, McFadden declared:

> Mr. Chairman, we have in this country one of the most corrupt institutions the world has ever known. I refer to the Federal Reserve Board and the Federal Reserve Banks, hereinafter called the Fed. The Fed has cheated the government of these United States and the people of the United States out of enough money to pay the nation's debt. The depredations and iniquities of the Fed have cost enough money to pay the national debt several times over.
>
> This evil institution has impoverished and ruined the people of these United States, has bankrupted itself, and has practically bankrupted our government. It has done this through the defects of the law under which it operates, through the maladministration of that law by the Fed and through the corrupt practices of the moneyed vultures who control it.
>
> Some people think that the Federal Reserve Banks are United States government institutions. They are private monopolies which prey upon the people of these United States for the benefit of themselves and their foreign customers; foreign and domestic speculators and swindlers; and rich and predatory money lenders.
>
> There is not a man within the sound of my voice who does not know that this nation is run by the international bankers.[23]

McFadden's concerns were not unusual. Even President Franklin D. Roosevelt was intimately aware of the intense debate over the Federal Reserve. In a letter to Colonel Edward M. House dated November 21, 1933, Roosevelt admitted the extreme tension between the nation and the Federal Reserve Bank: "The real truth of the matter is, as you and I know, that a financial element in the larger centers has owned the Government ever since the days of Andrew Jackson — and I am not wholly excepting the Administration of W.W. [Woodrow Wilson]. The country is going through a repetition of Jackson's fight with the Bank of the United States — only on a far bigger and broader basis."[24]

While the average American was facing financial hardship in the wake of the Great Depression, the central bankers, and their friends, had curiously escaped the downturn. Federal Reserve member Paul Warburg reportedly issued a warning in March 1929 to the central banking community that a U.S. crash was coming. In his book, *The Creature from Jekyll Island*, G. Edward Griffin writes: "Virtually all of the inner club [banking elite] was rescued. There is no record of any member of the interlocking directorate between the Federal Reserve, the major New York banks, and their prime customers having been caught by surprise."[25]

President Woodrow Wilson, who initially signed the Federal Reserve Act into law, would later openly discuss his concern for his nation that he felt was being controlled by a separate "invisible" government. The following three quotes are taken from the writings of President Wilson.

> We have restricted credit, we have restricted opportunity, we have controlled development, and we have come to be one of the worst ruled, one of the most completely controlled and dominated, governments in the civilized world — no longer a government by free opinion, no longer a government by conviction and the vote of the majority, but a government by the opinion and the duress of small groups of dominant men.[26]

DID YOU KNOW?

Fractional-Reserve Faith: Thanks to a banking technique known as fractional reserve banking, banks are not required to keep all of your bank deposits on hand. In fact, they are currently only required to keep 10 percent, **and sometimes less**, of your bank deposit on hand at all times. This means that if every customer of a bank suddenly demanded all their money at the same time, only a fraction of the money would be available. After 10,000 banks went bankrupt due to such "bank runs" during the Great Depression, the federal government created the Federal Deposit Insurance Corporation (FDIC). But as you have seen, our banking system requires the faith of the American people. And if that faith ever fails, so too will the banking system.

Since I entered politics, I have chiefly had men's views confided to me privately. Some of the biggest men in the United States, in the field of commerce and manufacture, are afraid of somebody, are afraid of something. They know that there is a power somewhere so organized, so subtle, so watchful, so interlocked, so complete, so pervasive, that they had better not speak above their breath when they speak in condemnation of it.[27]

The government, which was designed for the people, has got into the hands of the bosses and their employers, the special interests. An invisible empire has been set up above the forms of democracy.[28]

Supreme Court Justice Felix Frankfurter expressed similar concerns when he stated in 1952: "The real rulers in Washington are invisible and exercise power from behind the scenes."[29]

Senator Barry Goldwater identified the international money lenders as the source of this invisible power when he stated: "Most Americans have no real understanding of the operation of the international moneylenders. The bankers want it that way. We recognize in a hazy sort of way that the Rothschilds and the Warburgs of Europe and the houses of J.P. Morgan, Kuhn, Loeb and Company, Schiff, Lehman, and Rockefeller possess and control vast wealth. How they acquire this vast financial power and employ it is a mystery to most of us. International bankers make money by extending credit to governments. The greater the debt of the political state, the larger the interest returned to the lenders. The national banks of Europe are actually owned and controlled by private interests."[30]

Sir Josiah Stamp, the president of the Bank of England in the 1920s and the second richest man in Britain, made this revealing comment: "Banking was conceived in iniquity and was born in sin. The bankers own the earth. Take it away from them, but leave them the power to create deposits, and with the flick of the pen they will create enough deposits to buy it back again. However, take it away from them, and all the great fortunes like mine will disappear and they ought to disappear, for this would be a happier and better world to live in. But, if you wish to remain the slaves of bankers and pay the cost of your own slavery, let them continue to create deposits."[31]

DID YOU KNOW?

In 1933, America was still suffering through the worst of the Great Depression. In an effort to preserve their capital, many Americans were cashing in their gold-backed U.S. dollars in exchange for gold. As demand for gold became crippling, President Roosevelt issued Executive Order 6102, which authorized the confiscation of all privately owned gold held by U.S. citizens. In exchange for their gold, Americans would receive paper money. This despicable act was done under the guise of helping "bring an end to the depression." The penalties for violating this Gold Seizure Law: *a $10,000 fine and/or ten years in prison.*

How America Lost the Revolutionary War

America's early history is one of struggle, courage, and a noble quest for economic, political, and religious freedom. Great Britain's oppressive economic policies eventually led to an American declaration of freedom and independence by way of the Revolutionary War. But it did not take long for America's newfound economic freedom to be threatened by Europe's corrupt central banking system. After several battles with private banking interests throughout its history, America finally lost the war for their economic autonomy with the establishment of the Federal Reserve Banking System on December 23, 1913. Today, the U.S. government is heavily indebted to private banking interests — both domestic and foreign. Similarly, U.S. citizens are no more than indentured servants beholden to the debts that have been created through years of poor fiscal and monetary choices. After all, "we the people" bear the ultimate responsibility for all of the debts incurred by our spendthrift government and their central banking schemes.

Since 1913, the U.S. government has opted to outsource its constitutional obligation to create the currency. Instead of creating its own currency, free of interest, it has chosen a system whereby *it borrows its own currency from the privately held Federal Reserve — at interest!* The U.S. government grants this private banking cartel — the Federal Reserve — the ability to print money out of thin air. And it supports the Federal Reserve Banking System which allows America's banks to do something similar through the magic of something known as "fractional-reserve banking." The greatest fears of our founding fathers have come true. America has become a nation enslaved by private banking interests — and they do not even realize it.

Several questions remain as we prepare to delve into the next chapter. These questions include the following:

- If the Federal Reserve is a private banking cartel that is independent from the government, *who are its owners?*
- Why does the government pay interest to the Federal Reserve for the money that it creates when the government could print the currency itself and not pay a single dime in interest?
- How are banks able to create money out of thin air?
- And finally, what effect has this central banking scheme had upon the average American consumer?

In this chapter you have learned a very brief history of a system that has been at the root of political debates, national struggles, and even wars. In the next chapter, you are going to discover how this system actually works.

Endnotes

1. From a speech by Representative Ron Paul, M.D., "Abolish the Fed," in the House of Representatives, September 10, 2002, http://www.lewrockwell.com/paul/paul53.html.
2. Charles Francis Adams, *The Works of John Adams, Second President of the United States* (New York: Little, Brown & Co., 1853), letter to Thomas Jefferson (August 25, 1787).
3. Ellen Hodgson Brown, *Web of Debt: The Shocking Truth about Our Money System* (Baton Rouge, LA: Third Millennium Press, 2007), p. 36.
4. http://www.planetization.org/prosperity.htm.
5. John McMurty, *The Cancer Stage of Capitalism: And Its Cure* (London; Sterling, VA: Pluto Press, 1999), p. 291.
6. Mike Hewitt, "America's Forgotten War Against the Central Bankers," http://www.financialsense.com/fsu/editorials/dollardaze/2007/1020.html.
7. Richard H. Palmquist, *Einstein, Money, and Contentment* (Bloomington, IN: AuthorHouse, 2005), p. 92.
8. Ellen Hodgson Brown, *Web of Debt* (Baton Rouge, LA: Third Millennium Press, 2008), p. 77.

9. Hewitt, "America's Forgotten War Against the Central Bankers."

10. Olive Cushing Dwinell, *The Story of Our Money* (Boston, MA: Meador Publishing Co., 1946), p. 71.

11. *The Money Masters* (video), produced by Royalty Production Co.

12. "President Jackson's Veto Message Regarding the Bank of the United States," July 10, 1832; http://avalon.law.yale.edu/19th_century/ajveto01.asp

13. Andrew Jackson (Wikipedia); http://en.wikipedia.org/wiki/Andrew_Jackson.

14. Hewitt, "America's Forgotten War Against the Central Bankers," http://www.financialsense.com/fsu/editorials/dollardaze/2007/1020.html.

15. A letter to William F. Elkins, November 21, 1864, Archer H. Shaw, ed., *The Lincoln Encyclopedia: The Spoken and Written Words of A. Lincoln* (New York: Macmillan Co., 1950), p. 40.

16. Mark Hill, *Shadow Kings* (Canada: Trafford Publishing, 2005), p. 107.

17. G. Edward Griffin, *The Creature from Jekyll Island: A Second Look at the Federal Reserve* (Westlake Village, CA: American Media, 1994), p. 9.

18. Paul M. Warburg, *The Federal Reserve System: Its Origin and Growth* (New York: The Macmillan Company, 1930).

19. A. Ralph Epperson, *The Unseen Hand: An Introduction to the Conspiratorial View of History* (Publius, 1985), p. 169.

20. Mike Kirchubel, "Abolish the Federal Reserve System, Treasury Bills, Notes, Bonds, and the National Debt," Independent Media Center, Dec. 10, 2008, http://www.indymedia.org/en/2008/12/917530.shtml.

21. Charles Merlin Umpenhour, *Freedom, a Fading Illusion* (Aurora, WV: BookMakers Ink, 2005), p. 170.

22. Hewitt, "America's Forgotten War Against the Central Bankers," http://www.financialsense.com/fsu/editorials/dollardaze/2007/1020.html.

23. Brown, *Web of Debt,* p. 129.

24. Elliott Roosevelt, editor, *F.D.R.: His Personal Letters, 1928–1945* (New York: Duell, Sloan and Pearce, 1950), p. 373.

25. Griffin, *The Creature from Jekyll Island.*

26. Woodrow Wilson, *The New Freedom: A Call for the Emancipation of the Generous Energies of a People* (Englewood Cliffs, NJ: Prentice-Hall, 1961), p. 201.

27. Ibid., p. 17–18.

28. Ibid., p. 117.

29. Ibid., p. 118.

30. Barry M. Goldwater, *With No Apologies: The Personal and Political Memoirs of United States Senator Barry M. Goldwater* (New York: Morrow, 1979), p. 281.

31. Robert Harris Brevig, L. Fletcher Prouty, *Beyond Our Consent* (Canada: Trafford Publishing, 2004), p. 149.

Chapter 12
Modern Money Mechanics:
What the Banking Industry Does Not Want You to Know

"It is well that the people of the nation do not understand our banking and monetary system, for if they did, I believe there would be a revolution before tomorrow morning."[1]

— Henry Ford, echoing President Andrew Jackson

*OVERVIEW: Ask most Americans if they believe that their nation has too much debt, and the inevitable answer will be yes. But follow up by telling them that the money in their pocket itself is actually debt, and you will receive confused looks. This is because the American government, along with its banking cartel friend, the Federal Reserve, has done a fabulous job of making the public believe that the U.S. dollar is an asset. In this chapter, you will discover the explosive truth that will hopefully change your entire outlook on the U.S. monetary system. This truth summed in a single statement is simply that **money is debt**.*

Money is debt. And debt is money. The concept that all money in our modern society is actually debt may be foreign to you. It seems to offend everything that you have been taught about money. How can it be? Why would someone work 40 hours a week for money, when ultimately this money itself represents nothing but debt? By the end of this chapter, I believe that this concept of our debt-based monetary system will be so simple to understand that not only will you understand it yourself, you will be able to explain it to others. Let's begin.

Modern Money Mechanics

Running a national government is an expensive endeavor. Like most nations, the U.S. government raises the funds that it needs to function in two ways. The first method of funding is generated by the revenue created through the collection of taxes from the American public. The second funding method is by borrowing.

Since most U.S. citizens pay taxes, we are at least somewhat familiar with that process. But how, and from whom, does the government *borrow* money? When you or I need a loan, we simply contact a consumer bank. If we are deemed credit worthy, then we receive the requested loan. But what about the federal government? Who do they turn to when they need to borrow money?

When the U.S. government needs a loan, it turns to the U.S. Treasury. The U.S. Treasury responds by printing treasury bonds, which it then sells to various buyers through public auctions. These buyers include the U.S. public, domestic banks, foreign central banks, and, finally, the Federal Reserve. When the public — both domestic and foreign — buy U.S. Treasury bonds, they are using money that is already in existence to make the purchase. However, when the Federal Reserve buys a treasury bond, it does so by printing the money. In essence, the Federal Reserve creates money "out of thin air" to purchase government debt.

DID YOU KNOW?
Who Owns the Federal Reserve?

The Federal Reserve Bank is privately owned by shareholders, who all happen to be private member banks of the Federal Reserve System. The U.S. government does not own any shares in the Federal Reserve. While the Federal Reserve was created by an act of Congress, *and can therefore be ended by an act of Congress,* it is not a federal entity. It is a government-run private banking cartel that controls the monetary policy of the U.S. federal government.

Consider this quote from a document put out by the Boston Federal Reserve Bank called "Putting It Simply."

> When you or I write a check there must be sufficient funds in our account to cover the check, but when the Federal Reserve writes a check there is no bank deposit on which that check is drawn. When the Federal Reserve writes a check, it is creating money.

As the nation's central bank, the Federal Reserve plays a large role in government lending. As the U.S. government's "lender of last resort," the Fed is required to purchase all excess treasury bonds that are not sold to the public. These leftover treasuries are then exchanged for newly printed currency from the Federal Reserve. Either way, the federal government gets the money that it needs — even if it has to be printed.

To simplify the process even further, consider the following diagram. It illustrates how the U.S. government borrows money from the Federal Reserve, via the U.S. Treasury. In this example, we will assume that the government needs to borrow $100 million.

As you can see, the process by which the U.S. government borrows money is quite simple. But pay close attention to a couple of key points regarding this process.

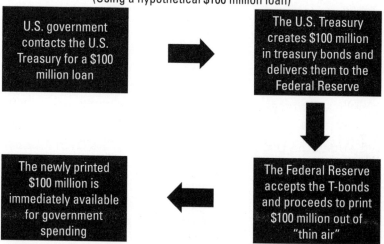

How the U.S. Government Borrows from the Federal Reserve
(Using a hypothetical $100 million loan)

U.S. government contacts the U.S. Treasury for a $100 million loan

The U.S. Treasury creates $100 million in treasury bonds and delivers them to the Federal Reserve

The newly printed $100 million is immediately available for government spending

The Federal Reserve accepts the T-bonds and proceeds to print $100 million out of "thin air"

FACT: U.S. currency is created out of government debt. MONEY=DEBT

First, when the treasury bonds are delivered to the Federal Reserve in exchange for newly printed currency, these bonds are listed as new debts on the federal government's balance sheet. *This means that every dollar that the Federal Reserve prints immediately is a physical representation of an obligation of debt by the U.S. federal government.*

Second, the freshly printed currency created by the Federal Reserve and delivered for the government's use is created out of thin air! Put simply, the Federal Reserve accepts government IOUs in exchange for printing new U.S. currency.

> When the Federal Reserve writes a check for a government bond it does exactly what any bank does, it creates money, it creates money purely and simply by writing a check.[2] (Congressman Wright Patman, chairman of the House Banking and Currency Committee in the 1960s)

So far, this process by which the government borrows money may appear to be legitimate and reasonable to some. But upon closer examination, the more *illegitimate* and *unreasonable* it becomes. This is because when any government relies upon a private bank to print its own money, that government must pay back the borrowed money — *plus interest* — to the private bank. You may be thinking, *What is wrong with paying interest to a bank? That is certainly reasonable. Banks charge interest for borrowing. It is all very normal.*

In response, consider these two very important questions: First, why does the U.S. government pay interest to "borrow" its own currency, when the currency could be created by the government itself, interest-free? And second, where does this interest owed to the Federal Reserve come from? After all, the Federal Reserve only creates the "principal." So where does the money to pay the "interest" come from?

Our answer to these two questions will help unveil the deception behind this unconstitutional government-run banking cartel.

Why Does the U.S. Government "Borrow" Its Own Money?

It is obvious how the Federal Reserve benefits from its commercial relationship with the U.S. government. The private banks that own the Fed profit greatly from the consistent and sizeable income that comes from their willingness to participate in charging interest on money that the Fed creates out of thin air. For centuries, private bankers have known that national governments make the best clients. With their high demand for large loans and their all-but-guaranteed loan payments, what else could a bank ask for? Perhaps only one thing: war. Nothing generates a demand for new government capital like war. Unfortunately, history is replete with stories of sinister involvement of central banking in national conflicts.

So while the Fed's motives are clear, how does the U.S. government benefit from the central banking arrangement?

Perception is everything. There is something wholesome about the U.S. federal government "borrowing" money that it needs to function from a central bank. This veil of normalcy serves to cloak the disturbing reality of the government-run banking cartel. But using economic sleight of hand to deceive a naive public does not make the current arrangement moral, or even legal. According to Article 1, Section 8 of the U.S. Constitution, it is the Congress — not a central bank — that is given sole power "to coin money, regulate the value thereof, and of foreign coin, and fix the Standard of Weights and Measures." Our founding fathers knew the inherent dangers of allowing private banking interests to gain control of the national money supply. Therefore, the Constitution gives express authorization to the Congress alone *"to coin money and regulate the value thereof."* But in 1913, Congress handed over these exclusive powers to the Federal Reserve, and the rest is history. By transferring these powers, Congress maintains the appearance of responsibility while secretly taxing the public through inflation. The Federal Reserve serves as a front to hide the real truth of money creation from the public. It also helps humanize the Congress. Their need to borrow from a bank seems familiar to a naive public.

> I have never yet had anyone who could through the use of logic and reason justify the Federal Government borrowing the use of its own money.... I believe the time will come when people will demand that this be changed. I believe the time will come in this country when they actually blame you and me and everyone connected with Congress for sitting idly by and permitting such an idiotic system to continue.[3] (Wright Patman, Congressman 1928–1976, Chairman, Committee on Banking and Currency 1963–1975)

Where Does the Interest to Pay the Fed Come From?

When the Federal Reserve creates money for the U.S. government, they only create the principal, *not the interest*. As we will see momentarily, it is precisely this issue that imperils the entire American monetary system. Using our previous example, imagine that the Fed lends $100 million to the U.S. government. The government is now indebted by $100 million, plus interest. But since the interest was not created with the principal, the government must raise other funds to repay the loan with interest. In recent years, the interest on the national debt has become an enormous burden. The annual costs are in the hundreds of billions. However, since the total government debts have become too enormous to be paid off, the government simply services the interest on the loan, while leaving the principal unpaid. (This is similar to paying the minimum monthly payments on your credit card each month.)

> The modern banking system manufactures money out of nothing. The process is perhaps the most astounding piece of sleight of hand that was ever invented.[4] (Sir Josiah Stamp, Director, Bank of England 1928–1941)

So far, this explanation of the money creation process between the Fed and the U.S. government has provided us with a perspective of America's banking cartel from a macro-level. But let us now move from Washington to Main Street USA. What about the banks in your town? Do they possess the ability to create money out of thin air, too?

Fractional-Reserve Banking 101

Where does money come from? A large majority of the money in the American monetary system is created by our nation's banks.

For banks to thrive, they need to make loans. If you are like most Americans, you probably believe that banks make their money through a combination of banking fees (monthly maintenance fees, NSF fees, etc.) and the interest spread between loans and investments. For example, imagine that a bank charges 6 percent for a home mortgage loan and offers 3 percent on a CD (Certificate of Deposit). In this scenario, the bank would earn the 3 percent difference between the 6 percent loan and the 3 percent investment in the CD. It is true that the bank makes money on the interest spread and on the fees that they charge. However, if these were the only two ways for banks to earn money, many would go out of business tomorrow. There is a far more powerful method that banks use to earn money. This method is made possible by something known as *fractional-reserve banking*. Since being instituted in 1694 by the world's first central bank, the Bank of England, fractional-reserve banking has come to dominate virtually all banking systems worldwide.

To understand fractional-reserve banking, think of modern banks as money factories. While they do serve other purposes, a bank's primary purpose is to create money. What you may not know is that banks have the ability to create money out of thin air. This is not accomplished by some parlor trick or by illegal counterfeiting. (Of course, that depends on who you ask.) Instead, banks are granted the ability to create

> **DID YOU KNOW?**
>
> Today, some of the Federal Income Tax that you hand over to the government each year actually goes to pay for the accumulated interest on the enormous U.S. national debt. Who receives this interest? Holders of the national debt, which includes the Federal Reserve. Is it a coincidence then that the Federal Income Tax Code was passed in 1913 — the same year as the Federal Reserve?

money out of nothing by the fractional-reserve banking system. What do banks need to work their money creation magic? *Customer bank deposits*. When you and I make deposits into a bank, we are enabling the bank to create new money that did not exist before. The process banks use to create money allows them to take your bank deposit and create nine times more in new money. So, for example, if you make a deposit of $1,000 in your checking account, the banking system is allowed to take that $1,000 and create $9,000 that was never in existence prior to your deposit.

In a nutshell, fractional-reserve banking is a system that allows banks to keep only a "fraction" of customer deposits in reserve. This "fraction" is determined by law and ranges from 3 percent to 10 percent. Assuming that the reserve requirement is 10 percent, banks must keep only 10 percent of all customer deposits. The remaining 90 percent of all customer deposits are considered new assets on the bank's balance sheet. These "assets" are then immediately available to the bank to make new loans. Even more incredible, the new loans that are created with this 90 percent of customer deposits are also considered assets. Why? Banks make loans under the assumption that they will be paid back. Because it is anticipated that bank loans will be repaid, they are considered to be "assets" of the bank. And banks are allowed to make loans from their "assets."

Through the "magic" of fractional-reserve banking, banks are able to create new money out of thin air. Let's see how it is done.

Because banks use such tremendous leverage on customer deposits, this explains why at any point in time, all banks are technically bankrupt. But just because they are all bankrupt on paper does not mean that they will ever become physically bankrupt. Like the early goldsmiths, banks operate under the assumption that not everyone will need to withdraw their money at the same time. This assumption has worked well for them some of the time. And at other times it has not. When fear overcomes faith in a nation's financial system, the fractional-reserve banking system is placed in jeopardy. As bank customers begin withdrawing their funds, the bank's overleverage is finally exposed. When this happens, it is known as a "bank run." Over

FRACTIONAL-RESERVE BANKING 101

Assume that you deposit $100,000 into Bank ABC.
Based upon a 10% reserve requirement,
Bank ABC can lend $90,000 of your deposit.

Deposit	Reserve	Available for Loan
$100,000	$9,000	$90,000
($10,000 reserve)	$8,100	$81,000
	$7,290	$72,900
$9000,000 can be	$6,516	$65,610
created from a single	$5,904	$59,049
$100,000 deposit	$5,314	$53,145

The secret: Banks are allowed to consider new loans as "assets" on their balance sheets, once the loan applicant has signed the loan papers.

Therefore, your single $100,000 deposit can be converted into $900,000 in new bank loans! This $900,000 is created out of thin air. It never existed before your deposit!

10,000 bank runs occurred during the Great Depression in the 1930s. Thousands of Americans lost their life savings during this time due to the overleveraging made possible by fractional-reserve banking.

Remember that our debt-based fiat currency system requires "faith."

Faith in the absurdity of the bankrupt, diseased system is the single most important ingredient for the U.S. monetary system to remain viable. In an effort to restore customer "confidence," the government responded to the 1930s banking crisis by creating the Federal Deposit Insurance Corporation (FDIC) in 1933 under the Glass-Steagall Act. The FDIC, a U.S. government corporation, was created to prevent future bank runs by guaranteeing the safety of most U.S. bank deposits up to a total of $100,000, a figure temporarily raised in 2008 to $250,000.

> I am afraid the ordinary citizen will not like to be told that the banks can, and do, create and destroy money. The amount of finance in existence varies only with the action of the banks in increasing or decreasing deposits and bank purchases. We know how this is effected. Every loan, overdraft, or bank purchase creates a deposit, and every repayment of a loan, overdraft, or bank sale destroys a deposit. They [the banks] control the credit of the nation direct the policies of governments, and keep in the palm of their hands the destinies of the peoples.[5] (The Rt. Hon. Reginald McKenna, former British Chancellor of the Exchequer — Chairman of the Midland Bank)

> The process by which banks create money is so simple that the mind is repelled.[6] (John Kenneth Galbraith)

> The important thing to remember is that when banks lend money they don't necessarily take it from anyone else to lend. Thus they "create" it.[7] (U.S. House of Representatives)

Because the intricacies of fractional-reserve banking can be somewhat difficult to grasp, consider this very simplistic example.

When a customer makes a deposit into a bank, the bank is allowed to classify 90 percent of the deposit as a bank "asset." *Remember, bank assets can be loaned.*

Joe wants to purchase a car for $10,000. After finding a car that meets his criteria, he approaches his local bank, First Bank, for a loan for the full amount. Based upon Joe's good credit, the bank agrees to lend him the full $10,000. Joe signs the loan agreement and walks away with his $10,000 in cash.

Note: *First Bank is eager to loan the $10,000 to Joe for his car purchase. First Bank then inputs the data on the new loan into a computer and instantly the money is created out of thin air. What gives the bank the ability to create this money from nothing? Based upon our current fractional-reserve banking system, banks are allowed to create money based upon the promise of the borrower to pay back the loan. The signed loan agreement creates the money. Another very important thing to note here is that the bank only creates the loan principal — not the interest — that Joe will have to pay back. But if the bank only created the loan principal, where will the loan interest come from? Joe will have to obtain that from the general economy, either through labor — or by borrowing again. The fact that the interest on the new loan is not created along with the newly created loan principal will become an important point toward the end of the chapter.*

Joe leaves First Bank ready to purchase his new car. Joe then meets with the car's owner, Ann. Joe gives Ann $10,000 in exchange for the car. Ann gives Joe the keys and the title and Joe drives off smiling in his new car. Ann immediately deposits the $10,000 cash into her bank, Second Bank.

Note: *When Ann deposits the $10,000 in cash into Second Bank, what happens to the money? According to the reserve requirement rules set forth by the Federal Reserve, the Second Bank is allowed to lend 90 percent of the $10,000 deposit. That means that $9,000 is now available to be lent out to the next borrower in line. The remaining $1,000 is required to remain within the bank to cover transaction costs. Again, the phrase "fractional-reserve banking" means that the bank is only required to keep a fraction of the deposit in bank reserves.*

The banking industry, with help from the government, has effectively programmed Americans to park their money in banking institutions. And when the economy is good, the fractional-reserve banking system appears to be efficient. However, when economic crisis strikes the nation, depositors can become fearful. They may even act on that fear by withdrawing all of their money from the bank. It is in times like these that the flaws in the banking system are exposed. *The truth is that your bank has only 10 percent of your money at any one time.* If all of the bank's customers tried to withdraw their money all

DID YOU KNOW?

According to legal precedents set by the U.S. Supreme Court, the Federal Reserve may be considered an unconstitutional and illegal institution. "Although there has never been a court case that challenged the legality of the Federal Reserve System, there was a challenge to the National Recovery Act or NRA, which was ruled unconstitutional. The U.S. Supreme Court — Schechter Poultry v. U.S., 29 U.S. 495, 55 U.S. 837.842 (1935) — ruled that, 'Congress may not abdicate or transfer to others its legitimate functions.' Article I, Section 8 of the U.S. Constitution states, 'The Congress shall have power . . . to coin money, regulate the value thereof. . . .' By passing the Federal Reserve Act, Congress abdicated and transferred to the Federal Reserve bankers its constitutionally legitimate function of issuing and controlling money. If the Supreme Court ruling on the NRA is applied to the Federal Reserve System, the unconstitutionality and illegality of the Fed becomes obvious."[8]

on the same day, the bank would be shut down. Once again, faith in the system is what is required to keep the illusion going.

Money Is Debt . . . and Debt Is Money

The fractional-reserve banking system has allowed modern economies to have the appearance of "prosperity," but the ugly truth lurks just underneath. By using leverage, our banking system has helped generate a massive illusion of wealth that simply does not exist. The deceitfulness of the system is also compounded when you consider that banks are charging interest on money they did not earn. During his struggles with early attempts at American central banking, Thomas Jefferson said, "No one has a natural right to the trade of money lender, but he who has money to lend."[9] The immorality of charging money on money that is created out of thin air should be apparent.

In his book *The Creature from Jekyll Island*, G. Edward Griffin writes: "When banks place credits into your checking account, they are merely pretending to lend you money. In reality, they have nothing to lend. . . . So what entitles the banks to collect rent (interest) on nothing? . . . We are talking here, not about what is legal, but what is moral."[10]

Griffin goes further by adding, "Every dollar that exists today, either in the form of currency, checkbook money, or even credit card money — in other words, our entire money supply — exists only because it was borrowed by someone. . . . That means all the American dollars in the entire world are earning daily and compounded interest for the banks which created them. . . . And what did the banks do to earn this perpetually flowing river of wealth? Did they lend out their own capital obtained through the investment of their stockholders? Did they lend out the hard-earned savings of their depositors? No . . . they simply waved the magic wand called fiat money."[11]

In summary, every time a bank makes a loan, it creates money. The bank charges interest on this newly created money; and when the debt owed on the loan is paid off, the money disappears from the system. For this reason, debt is encouraged — *and even required* — in our society.

In the August 31, 1959, issue of *U.S. News and World Report*, President Eisenhower's Secretary of the Treasury Robert B. Anderson was asked, "Do you mean that banks, in buying government securities, do not lend out their customers' deposits? That they create the money they use to buy the securities?"

Anderson replied, "That is correct. Banks are different from other lending institutions. When a savings association, an insurance company, or a credit union makes a loan, it lends the very dollar that its customers have previously paid in. But when a bank makes a loan, it simply adds to the borrower's deposit account in the bank by the amount of the loan. The money is not taken from anyone. It is new money, recreated by the bank, for the use of the borrower."

To confirm these absurdities, consider the following exchange. On September 30, 1941, before the House Committee on Banking and Currency, Federal Reserve Board Governor Marriner Eccles was questioned by U.S. Congressman Wright Patman regarding a past Federal Reserve purchase of U.S. government bonds.

Rep. Patman: "How did you get the money to buy those two billion dollars' worth of government securities in 1933?"

Eccles: "We created it."

Rep. Patman: "Out of what?"

Eccles: "Out of the right to issue credit money."

Rep. Patman: "And there is nothing behind it, is there, except our government's credit?"

Eccles: "That is what our money system is. If there were no debts in our money system, there wouldn't be any money."[12]

Stunning, isn't it? If there were no debts in the U.S. economy, there would be no money. This is because our economy is debt-based. It requires debt to survive.

In fact, even if America wanted to pay back all of its debts, it would be impossible. This is because the interest that exists on every outstanding loan is never created to begin with. There is simply not enough money in our monetary system to pay all of the loan principal and interest that we owe.

Where exactly does the money come from to pay the interest on our debts? Because the banks do not create the interest, the only way to obtain money to pay the interest is through human labor. Therefore, human labor produces the banker's profit. With everyone in the system competing for the same limited money supply to pay off their debts, there are bound to be losers. Not everyone can win, because the amount of debt is greater than the amount of money in our system. Think of the old children's game musical

A Completely Flawed System

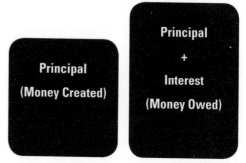

Debts can never be paid off in this type of system because only the principal is created — **not the interest.**

chairs. While the music is playing, there are no losers. But when the music stops, not everyone will find a chair. Sadly, the losers in our society face bankruptcies and foreclosures. But these are simply part of the system. They must occur due to the debt-to-money ratio imbalances that plague our modern monetary system. This exposes one of the most fatal flaws of our modern monetary system.

This is a staggering thought. Someone has to borrow every dollar we have in circulation, cash or credit. We are absolutely without a permanent money system. When one gets a complete grasp of the picture, the tragic absurdity of our hopeless position is almost incredible, but there it is.[13] (Robert H. Hemphill, Credit Manager, Federal Reserve Bank, Atlanta, Georgia)

In our final analysis, it is clear that debt is required to maintain the American monetary system. Our system is built upon the faulty assumption that the economy will expand perpetually. It requires exponential consumption and production. Clearly, this is an unsustainable economic model. This explains why, even in the midst of economic turbulence, the government encourages consumption and borrowing, instead of savings and thrift. The debt-based monetary system has contributed greatly to the demise of the American economic empire. In our next chapter, we will see what happens when our debt-based system goes awry.

Endnotes

1. Ellen Hodgson Brown, *Web of Debt: The Shocking Truth about Our Money System* (Baton Rouge, LA: Third Millennium Press, 2007), p. ix.
2. Ibid., p. 25.
3. Congressional Record, House, Sept. 29, 1941, p. 7583.
4. Moriah Saul, *Plantation Earth: The Cross of Iron and the Chains of Debt* (Canada: Trafford Publishing, 2003).
5. http://www.michaeljournal.org/plenty23.htm.
6. John K. Galbraith, *Money: Whence It Came, Where It Went* (Boston, MA: Houghton Mifflin, 1975), p. 29.
7. Money Facts Subcommittee on Domestic Finance; Committee on Banking and Currency; U.S. House of Representatives, 88th Congress, 2nd Session, September 21, 1964, p. 7, http://www.scribd.com/doc/7547565/Money-Facts-Committee-on-Banking-and-Currency.
8. http://www.buildfreedom.com/tl/rape3.shtml.
9. G. Edward Griffin, *The Creature from Jekyll Island: A Second Look at the Federal Reserve* (Westlake Village, CA: American Media, 1994), p. 190.
10. Ibid., p. 191.
11. Ibid.
12. Ibid., p. 188.
13. Irving Fisher, *100% Money: Designed to Keep Checking Banks 100% Liquid; to Prevent Inflation and Deflation; Largely to Cure or Prevent Depressions; and to Wipe Out Much of the National Debt* (New Haven, CT: The City Printing Co., 1945), p. xxii.

Chapter 13
Bailout Nation

"When you find yourself in a hole, the first thing you should do is stop digging."

— Unknown

In 1999, the stock market was the place to be. With the innovations made possible by the spread of Internet technology, it appeared that the key to a new golden age of economic prosperity had finally been discovered — and it ended in "dot-com."

It was not unusual to hear of long-time employees quitting their jobs to become full-time day traders. Would-be investors salivated as new companies with no earnings history promised huge returns in a short amount of time. To be sure, the dot-com craze did forge quick fortunes for investors who poured money into hundreds of Initial Public Offerings (IPOs) of such companies. For example, in 1999, there were 457 IPOs, most of which were Internet and technology related. Of those 457 IPOs, 117 doubled in price on the first day of trading.[1]

However, as the speculation wore on, so did the concerns about the sustainability of an economy built upon hype with few profits. As America entered the new millennium, the champagne was flowing, but the cash from the profitless dot-com businesses was not. In March 2000, the dot-com craze officially came to an end as former believers in the "New Economy" created a selling frenzy.

The Housing Bubble Bursts

Soon after the illusions of the dot-com bubble had been shattered, our nation faced the horror of September 11, 2001. In the wake of a sinking stock market and a nation panicked by faceless terrorism, the Federal Reserve moved swiftly to alleviate *any and all* economic pain on consumers by providing massive reductions in key interest rates. Throughout 2001, the Federal Reserve cut interest rates a total of *11 times* — 4 of these came in the three months following 9/11. By June 25, 2003, the federal funds rate had been slashed from the 2001 high of 6 percent to a mere 1 percent. Interest rates would not rise to 2 percent until November 10, 2004.

A consumption-crazed public with a love affair with speculation did not have to be instructed on what to do. These historically low rates helped fuel massive overinvestment and speculative buying in the housing market from 2003 to 2007. Although the dot-com bubble had burst in 2000, Americans had found a new — and even riskier — investment bubble to create: the U.S. housing bubble.

On a quantitative level, there has never been a larger investment bubble than the recent U.S. housing bubble. At its height, home values increased by jaw-dropping amounts on an annual basis. Like the heady

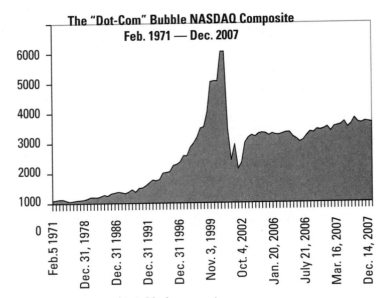

Source: http://en.wikipedia.org/wiki/Nasdaq_composite

days of the dot-com craze, houses could be bought and immediately sold for a profit in many areas of the country. However, under the surface of this housing mania lurked the familiar villain named greed. As interest rates remained low, lending institutions began loosening their lending standards, thus enabling nearly anyone to qualify for a home loan. At the peak of the housing bubble, clever lenders used even riskier loans referred to as "no-doc" loans. These loans, known as "liar loans" in the industry, required no documentation of the borrower's income, net worth, etc. All that was needed was a signature and a very low down payment — and at other times "nothing down." Other loans were knowingly made to households with little or no income and bad credit. These sub-prime loans were packaged into financial products known as "mortgage-backed securities," which were immediately sold off to other private investors as soon as the borrower signed the dotted line. These mortgage-backed securities were categorized according to their risk level, and the buyers of these products included many well-known financial institutions — including Lehman Brothers, Bear Stearns, Merrill Lynch, and Morgan Stanley, among others.

Many new home buyers who had purchased their home with these sub-prime loans soon discovered that their monthly mortgage was not fixed. In 2007, many of the sub-prime loans that were sold in 2005–2006 began to reset. That is, the low teaser interest rates that had lured in the buyers were being reset to compensate for the risk involved to the mortgage investors.

As these adjustable-rate mortgages reset to more realistic rates, many of these sub-prime borrowers found themselves unable to pay the increased monthly mortgages they had signed up for. A large majority of these resets occurred as housing prices were in a rapid decline around the nation. Often owing more than their home was actually worth, many borrowers saw foreclosure as the lesser of two evils. As the foreclosure rate increased to unprecedented levels, holders of these mortgages faced massive financial losses. Mortgage-backed securities purchasers had rolled the dice. And many of them had lost. While the initial total losses appeared to be in the billions, it would later be revealed that these total losses were in the trillions.

In the wake of the bursting housing bubble, it became evident that the effects of this downturn would be sizeable. In 2007 alone, lenders began foreclosure proceedings on 1.3 million properties — up

79 percent from 2006.[2] By August of 2008, 9.2 percent of all U.S. mortgages were either delinquent or had entered foreclosure proceedings.[3] As mortgage delinquencies rose across the nation, the companies who had become overleveraged in these risky loans were facing dire circumstances. Those who had become entangled in the subprime debacle were facing financial ruin as mortgage delinquencies and foreclosures increased dramatically. Some of the major investors in mortgage-backed securities were the large investment banks on Wall Street. By September 2008, the losses had become insurmountable, forcing Lehman Brothers into insolvency. Bear Stearns and Merrill Lynch were sold for pennies on the dollar to J.P. Morgan Chase and Bank of America, respectively.

Additionally, two Government Sponsored Enterprises (GSEs) that were greatly affected by the subprime crisis were Fannie Mae and Freddie Mac. In 2008, these two companies held a combined $5.1 trillion in U.S. mortgages. With the end to the crisis nowhere in sight, the federal government moved to take drastic action to avoid further fallout.

The 2008 U.S. Bailout

The federal government first sought to stop the bleeding by placing Fannie and Freddie into conservatorship. This essentially nationalized the two GSEs — at the taxpayers' expense.

As fears of a deepening mortgage crisis loomed on the horizon, the federal government decided to act. In September 2008, U.S. Treasury

---

DID YOU KNOW?

U.S. Congressman and 2008 presidential hopeful Ron Paul introduced the Free Housing Market Enhancement Act on September 10, 2003, which attempted to put an end to the federal government's support of Fannie Mae and Freddie Mac. In a speech to Congress, Paul predicted that the federal government's support for Fannie and Freddie would eventually lead to a bailout when he stated, "Congress should act to remove taxpayer support from the housing GSEs before the bubble bursts and taxpayers are once again forced to bail out investors who were misled by foolish government interference in the market."[4] His bill was rejected.

Secretary Henry Paulson proposed the Emergency Economic Stabilization Act of 2008, which sought a $700 billion bailout package to purchase bad assets from the balance sheets of private financial institutions who had gambled in subprime loans and had lost. The bailout was presented to the public as a way to restore confidence to the troubled credit markets. Many U.S. congressmen and senators complained of being rushed by Paulson and his team to pass the bill without properly reviewing the bill. Threats of global financial meltdown — and even martial law — were employed to ensure a quick passage of Paulson's bailout bill.

Several senators and congressmen objected, citing similar bills that had been proposed with the same maddening urgency, including the Patriot Act, which had been passed quickly in the days following the tragedy of September 11, 2001.

In a speech before the Congress, Ohio Congresswoman Marcy Kaptur protested against the Paulson bailout package. Her speech sums up well what many of the bill's opponents were feeling:

> Mr. Speaker, here is the latest reality game. Let's play Wall Street Bailout.
>
> Rule one: Rush the decision. Time the game to fall in the week before Congress is set to adjourn and just six weeks before a historic election so your opponents will be preoccupied, pressured, distracted, and in a hurry.
>
> Rule two: Disarm the public through fear. Warn that the entire global financial system will collapse and the world will fall into another Great Depression. Control the media enough to ensure that the public will not notice this bailout will indebt them for generations, taking from them trillions of dollars they earned and deserve to keep.
>
> Rule three: Control the playing field and set the rules. Hide from the public and most of the Congress just who is arranging this deal. Communicate with the public through leaks to media insiders. Limit any open congressional hearings. Communicate with Congress via private teleconferencing calls. Heighten political anxiety by contacting each political party separately. Treat members of Congress condescendingly, telling them that the matter is so complex that they must rely on those few insiders who really do know what's going on.

Rule four: Divert attention and keep people confused. Manage the news cycle so Congress and the public have no time to examine who destroyed the prudent banking system that served America so well for 60 years after the financial meltdown of the 1920s.

Rule five: Always keep in mind the goal is to privatize gains to a few and socialize loss to the many. For 30 years in one financial scandal after another, Wall Street game masters have kept billions of dollars of their gain and shifted their losses to American taxpayers. Once this bailout is in place, the greed game will begin again.

But I have a counter-game. It's called Wall Street Reckoning. Congress shouldn't go home to campaign. It should put America's accounts in order.

To Wall Street insiders, it says no on behalf of the American people. You have perpetrated the greatest financial crimes ever on this American republic. You think you can get by with it because you are extraordinarily wealthy and the

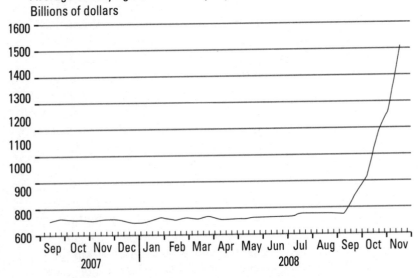

Adjusted Monetary Base
Average of daily figures seasonally adjusted
Billions of dollars

Source: http://research.stlouisfed.org/publications/usfd/

largest contributors to both presidential and congressional campaigns in both major parties, but you are about to be brought under firm control.[5]

On September 29, 2008, the Congress voted down the $700 billion bailout package by a margin of 228 to 205. But in a strange twist of events, on October 1, the Senate voted in favor of the bailout package by a margin of 74 to 25. This forced the bill back into the Congress with added pressure for Congress to respond in kind. Finally, on October 3, the Congress passed the Paulson bailout package by a margin of 263 to 171. Within hours of its passage from the Congress, President George W. Bush signed the bill into law.

The Real Reason behind the U.S. Bailout

As the U.S. Treasury's bailout proposal was debated in the House and the Senate, some very legitimate concerns arose. Many of the bailout's opponents argued that since America's economic crisis had been created by excess credit and debt, a fresh infusion of $700 billion would only further aggravate the problem. The oft-used parable was that of giving more alcohol to someone who was clearly drunk.

The bailout began affecting the U.S. monetary base in the days after its passage from Congress. (Remember, as the monetary base goes up, so does inflation. This is because the definition of inflation is simply "an increase in a nation's money supply.") More importantly, several U.S. congressmen took issue with the Paulson bailout bill, as it gave power to the Treasury to pump bailout money not only to domestic institutions — *but also to foreign institutions and investors.*

One such politician was U.S. Congressman Brad Sherman (D-California). Rep. Sherman discussed the bailout bill during a live television interview on October 2, 2008. The following is a partial transcript where Rep. Sherman expresses his concerns.

Rep. Brad Sherman: "Larry, I am glad you have a few seconds to talk to someone who voted against this bill. I am not changing my mind. I want to thank my colleagues who stood up to the purveyors of panic and voted against a very bad bill and voted with 400 eminent economists, including three Nobel laureates, who wrote to us and said don't panic, don't act hastily, hold hearings, work carefully. The fact is, Larry, if you read this bill, even you would have voted against it.

"It provides hundreds of billions of dollars of bailouts to foreign investors. It provides no real control of Paulson's power. There is a critique board but not really a board that can step in and change what he does. It's a $700 billion program run by a part-time temporary employee, and there is no limit on million-dollar-a-month salaries."

Larry Kudlow: "Let me just ask you one question. I think you are referring to foreign banks headquartered in the United States. I do not see how foreign investors get bailed out."

Rep. Brad Sherman: "Larry, you have to read the bill. It's very clear. The Bank of Shanghai can transfer all of its toxic assets to the Bank of Shanghai of Los Angeles, which can then sell them the next day to the Treasury. I had a provision to say if it wasn't owned by an American entity, even a subsidiary, but at least an entity in the U.S., the Treasury can't buy it. It was rejected.

"The bill is very clear. Assets now held in China and London can be sold to U.S. entities on Monday and then sold to the Treasury on Tuesday. Paulson has made it clear he will recommend a veto of any bill that contained a clear provision that said if Americans did not own the asset on September 20 that it can't be sold to the Treasury.

"*Hundreds of billions of dollars are going to bail out foreign investors. They know it, they demanded it, and the bill has been carefully written to make sure that can happen.*"[6]

But why would the United States want to bail out foreign investors? Should taxpayers really be footing the bill for soured foreign

SEC. 112. COORDINATION WITH FOREIGN AUTHORITIES AND CENTRAL BANKS

The Secretary shall coordinate, as appropriate, with foreign financial authorities and central banks to work toward the establishment of similar programs by such authorities and central banks. To the extent that such foreign financial authorities or banks hold troubled assets as a result of extending financing to financial institutions that have failed or defaulted on such financing, such troubled assets qualify for purchase under section 101.

investment into the United States? The answers to these questions would expose what many had known all along about the real reason behind the Paulson bailout package. *America's dependence on continued foreign investment means that America's foreign investors are a top priority to our continued national economic security.* Because foreign investors own such a large portion of our nation's assets, and because America's lifestyles and consumption habits are made possible by foreign financing, soothing their occasional pain is now a *necessity*.

For example, consider the case of the government-sponsored mortgage lender Fannie Mae. In August 2008, one month before the bailout of Fannie Mae, Bloomberg reported that Asian investors, the largest foreign investor of Fannie Mae bonds, "were asking the Treasury to bolster the government-sponsored company [Fannie Mae] and its smaller competitor, Freddie Mac."

The report continues: "The next afternoon, before financial markets opened Monday in Asia, Paulson announced the rescue plan, saying he would seek authority to buy unlimited equity stakes in the companies and their bonds if needed, while the Federal Reserve would lend directly to Fannie and Freddie."

The report concluded by stating that Asian investors "were among the most important groups to soothe because central banks, financial institutions, and funds in the region own $800 billion of Fannie Mae and Freddie Mac's $5.2 trillion in debt."[7]

Mark Zandi, chief economist for Moody's/Economy.com, wrote: "It was the mounting evidence that central banks, sovereign wealth funds, and other global investors were growing [increasingly] reluctant to invest in the debt that was the catalyst for the Treasury Department's actions."[8]

In an interview with the Washington Times, Council of Foreign Relations Geo-Economic Fellow Brad Sester stated: "I suspect this is the first case where foreign central banks exercised their leverage as creditors to push the U.S. government to make a policy decision that protected their interests."[9]

By nationalizing Fannie Mae and Freddie Mac, the debt obligations of these two enterprises effectively became U.S. Treasury debt. But rest assured, the investors who made financial miscalculations were rewarded with a bailout. With the stroke of a pen, U.S. taxpayers became 100 percent financially responsible for the poor monetary policies of the Federal Reserve. After all, the Fed's decision to lower interest rates to 1 percent in 2003 ultimately led to the speculative housing bubble. This is just one of a growing number of reasons why the Federal Reserve Act should be repealed.

U.S. Senator Jim Demint (R-South Carolina) has also gone on record stating that the U.S. bailout was primarily about appeasing America's foreign creditors, namely China. In a September 2008 interview, Sen. Demint was questioned about the root cause of the bailout. He replied: "What happened over the years is Fannie Mae and Freddie Mac together processed over 5 trillion dollars' worth of loans and sold them as securities all over the world. This easy credit inflated the cost of homes and created over-building and an over-supply of homes until we finally hit a wall. The values of people's homes started to go down, which means the mortgages were over-priced. Now these banks want to unload these securities in order to have money to loan. . . . But they can't sell them for what they got them for."

Demint added, "The biggest creditor is China and that's a big part of this equation that's not being talked about. If America was not in such deep debt, we could deal with this problem much more effectively — but China has essentially told the U.S. that we make good on all the debt that they're holding, which is nearly a trillion dollars, or they're going to stop lending us money. To show that they're serious, they've already stopped lending us money and if we can't borrow money every day, literally hundreds of billions of dollars, we default on the loans that are coming due."[10]

Senator Elizabeth Dole (R-North Carolina) voted against the U.S. bailout bill, stating, "It bails out foreign investors before American homeowners struggling to pay their mortgages."[11]

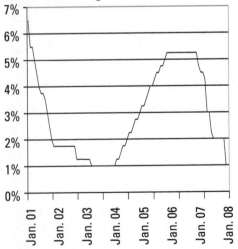

Federal Funds Target Rate

Source: www.moneycafe.com/library/fedfundsrate.htm

Concerned about the foreign bank bailout provision, Senator Pat Roberts (R-Kansas) stated, "The plan permits taxpayer dollars to be used to buy assets of foreign financial institutions that have a presence in the United States. If U.S. taxpayer dollars are going to be put at risk, those dollars should be used to shore up U.S. based companies."[12]

The Emergency Economic Stabilization Act of 2008, promoted by the U.S. Treasury, the Federal Reserve, and the Bush administration, was a scam perpetuated on the American people. What began as a $700 billion rescue plan has morphed into an $8.5 trillion handout of U.S. taxpayer money. While it was touted as a way to save U.S. homeowners, it has only served to pay off foreign investors who have incurred major losses due to the poor U.S. monetary and fiscal policies that have led to America's immoral financial excesses. This is because the U.S. government knows that America's economic future is held hostage by foreign investment. If foreign investors begin to perceive that they will lose money in financing American overconsumption, they will look to invest elsewhere. And the U.S. government cannot allow that because this would cause America's financial house of cards to collapse even sooner.

The Federal Reserve — Above the Law?

The Federal Reserve had a major role to play in the Paulson bailout. Primarily, the Fed's role was to provide massive amounts of liquidity to the markets. The Federal Reserve first responded to the financial crisis by reducing interest rates. And once again, these rate cuts were drastic. In August 2007, on the eve of the mortgage crisis, the Federal Funds Rate was 5.25 percent. One year later, it had reached 2 percent. And by December 2008, rates were hovering near zero — *for the first time in U.S. history.*

Of even more concern was the fact that low rates had caused the housing bubble in the first place. Americans had become inebriated on the easy credit of the early 2000s. Like a drug addict who is desperate for his next high, the Federal Reserve appeared to be acting as the "pusher" of this easy credit. Why would the Fed treat a credit crisis with more credit?

In addition to cutting rates to fuel further consumption and debt, the Fed sought to increase the available money supply in the United States. To achieve this goal, the Federal Reserve made over $2 trillion of "emergency" loans to banks in the weeks following the passage of the bailout plan. While the amounts of these Fed loans were made public, the names of the recipients were mysteriously withheld by the Federal Reserve. It soon became apparent to the American media that the Fed would remain tight-lipped regarding the identity of the loan recipients. On November 7, Bloomberg News filed a federal lawsuit against the Federal Reserve demanding the requested information under the Freedom of Information Act.[13] Under the lawsuit, Bloomberg petitioned the Federal Reserve for the identities of the loan recipients. And second, Bloomberg inquired what type of collateral was being accepted by the Federal Reserve for these large "emergency" loans. If the recipients, or the collateral used to secure the loans, were foreign, the Fed's cover would be blown. Or even worse, perhaps these "emergency" loans were not backed up by any collateral at all.

On December 8, 2008, in classic Fed style, the central bank denied Bloomberg's requests, claiming that they are allowed to withhold such information. Further, the Federal Reserve sought to protect the privacy of the loan recipients in order to maintain "consumer confidence."

The Fed had assured a skeptical Congress that it would maintain transparency in its actions. But when transparency was requested by the public, they immediately used the legal system to enshroud their actions. But the lack of transparency by the Federal Reserve should come as no surprise. This unconstitutional central bank has been cloaked in secrecy since the days of its inception. Its failure to maintain a sound currency — the U.S. dollar — for the people of the United States has proven its ineptness. The Fed refuses to abide by sound economic principles. Instead, it uses socialistic tactics while draping itself in a robe of democracy. The mysterious $2 trillion that they had doled out without accountability or oversight is a sham. It is not their money. It is taxpayer money. It belongs to the people, and the transparency of its use should be demanded.

The Federal Reserve System is a disgrace to America. It has proven, once again, that it is unaccountable for its reckless actions. And when their unaccountability is coupled with their clear incompetence in managing the U.S. money supply, it becomes increasingly obvious that the Federal Reserve System should be abolished.

American Socialism

While America claims to ascribe to free-market principles, our government's actions have exposed the true economic system operating in America. America uses free-market principles when they are convenient. However, when the losses of the free market mount, America opts for socialism. Those whom we have elected to the highest political offices in America now sit behind the wheel of the world's current global empire. Unfortunately, they have steered our nation into complete bankruptcy. Our nation has been bankrupted by poor fiscal policies that discourage savings and encourage debt. And it has been hoodwinked by poor monetary policies, which have made our money "cheap" and therefore worthless.

The examples that could be given regarding the vacuum of economic leadership in our nation's capital are numerous. Here's just one example: One month before President George W. Bush left the White House, in the wake of the great credit crisis of 2008, he admitted in a CNN interview that he had "abandoned free-market principles to save the free-market system." He continued, "I feel a sense of obligation to my successor [President-elect Barack Obama] to make sure there is not a, you know, a huge economic crisis. Look, we're in a crisis now. I mean, this is — we're in a huge recession, but I don't want to make it even worse."[14]

This admission of the failure of the free-market was a reversal of Bush's own stance from one month earlier when he stated, "History has shown that the greater threat to economic prosperity is not too little government involvement in the market, it is too much government involvement in the market. . . . It would be a terrible mistake to allow a few months of crisis to undermine 60 years of success."[15]

As Bush should know, it is *not* possible to save free-market capitalism with socialism and then expect the nation to remain capitalistic in nature. Once the markets know that the federal government is willing and available to bail them out of their financial missteps, the proverbial cat is out of the bag. In economics, this principle is called *moral hazard*.

Are we to believe that our nation's romance with socialism is a one-night stand? Of course not. In fact, far from a one-night stand, it could be effectively argued that America has been "engaged" to socialism for the last several decades. We live in a nation that is free-market in name, but socialistic in policy.

Sorting It All Out

Consider the charts on the following page compiled by Casey Research. In the first chart, the current total impact of the 2008 bailout is measured.

Total 2008 Bailouts = $8.5 Trillion
($3.1 trillion of which is committed pledges)

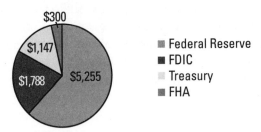

- ■ Federal Reserve
- ■ FDIC
- ■ Treasury
- ■ FHA

Total Large U.S. Projects/Wars = $8.4 Trillion
(Inflation Adjusted)

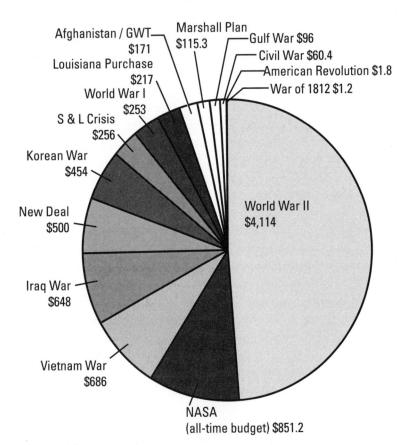

Afghanistan / GWT $171
Louisiana Purchase $217
World War I $253
S & L Crisis $256
Korean War $454
New Deal $500
Iraq War $648
Vietnam War $686
NASA (all-time budget) $851.2
Marshall Plan $115.3
Gulf War $96
Civil War $60.4
American Revolution $1.8
War of 1812 $1.2
World War II $4,114

Source: CRS Report for Congress, "Cost of Major Wars" by Stephen Daggett and western-standard.blogs.com/shotgun/2008/11/us-bailouts-now.htm.

In the second chart, the total cost of the 2008 bailout, $8.5 trillion, is compared to the costs of past U.S. wars and government programs.

Now consider for a moment that this $8.5 trillion bailout was largely motivated to protect foreign investors and private banking interests. This makes this bailout one of the worst financial crimes ever perpetrated upon the American people.

Republicans, who are inevitably in this reading audience, are probably now elated that someone is finally pointing the finger at their "socialistic" nemesis, the Democratic Party. However, accept my sincere apologies for my unwillingness to comply with this political coup d'état. If only it were that simple. Instead, the majorities in both of America's political parties — Democratic *and* Republican — have been all too willing to sacrifice free-market principles at the altar of socialism.

It is a disgrace that our nation is, once again, bailing out the reckless rich in order to "save the working poor and the middle class." This approach to the economic crisis has produced socialism for those who are in power and feudalism for the rest. President Bush and his cronies asked for a "blank check" to solve America's economic problems. In addition, the Bush administration sought "unreviewable" authority for Treasury Secretary Henry Paulson, as he is allowed to write checks to corporations as he sees fit. And the Federal Reserve secretly provides trillions of dollars of "emergency loans" with U.S. taxpayer money with *no oversight and no accountability*.

Indeed, not all of the rich have been, or will be, bailed out of their misery. *Only those who made financial miscalculations*, often with other people's money, were considered for the bailout. Instead of letting these backward financial institutions fall under the weight of their own greed, the working poor and the middle class — if they can really be separated — will get to pay the price for this economic maliciousness through huge future tax burdens.

Many Americans now stand and applaud the efforts of our incompetent government as they dig an even bigger hole of debt for future generations. *"If we can only delay the pain for a few more decades,"* they pray. Instead of demanding real sacrifice from the living, our nation's economically defunct leaders have sought to maintain the status quo. Let the unborn sort out the details.

The burden of future tax increases is not the only surprise in store for the working poor and middle class of this nation. In an effort to keep the free-market system alive through socialistic means, *our na-tion's leaders have made the ultimate mistake of believing that our current crisis can be solved by printing more money.* This logic goes through the heart of every sound economic principle known to man. Our nation's crisis cannot be solved by printing more dollars. By printing more money, our government is sending the signal to the average American that our crisis is due to a lack of money in the system. Again, if that were only true. America's problem is one of *too much* credit, not an absence of it. In truth, what our nation's leaders fear is the drying up of the "easy credit" that has been available to the working poor and middle class for the last several years. It was this easy credit, coupled with lax lending standards of financial institutions, that made the housing bubble possible.

Who ensured that this easy credit was available to any and all who desired it? The Federal Reserve System and America's banking industry. How did they accomplish this heroic feat? By driving down interest rates targets. The lending institutions took advantage of this historic moment to lend this easy money to anyone who could fog up a mirror. The explanations can go deeper. But for the purposes of this book, do they really need to? Understanding the difference between a Collateralized Debt Obligation and a Mortgage-backed Security are not necessary to understand the gravity of America's economic plight. Other books will explain the various nuances of these derivatives. As usual, a recommended reading list is provided at the end of this book for those who wish to delve further into the details.

What Americans need to understand now is that their beloved nation is bankrupt. And it has been bankrupted at the hands of those who have been placed with the charge of protecting the public.

Wealth cannot be created through a printing press, despite what the "Washingtonites" proclaim. And the dollar crisis cannot be solved by printing more dollars.

"We the people" have become a nation ensnared by our own greed. And we have been blinded to all the exit doors from this trap by our lust for more.

And lest we erroneously think that the public has been an in-nocent bystander in this scheme, let us now turn our attention to the American public's role in the bankruptcy of America: *consumer debt.*

Endnotes

1. "Crashes: The Dotcom Crash" http://www.investopedia.com/features/crashes/crashes8.asp.
2. "U.S. Foreclosure Activity Increases 75 Percent in 2007," http://www.realtytrac.com/ContentManagement/pressrelease.aspx?ChannelID=9&ItemID=3988&accnt=64847.
3. "Delinquencies and Foreclosures Increase in Latest MBA National Delinquency Survey," http://www.mbaa.org/NewsandMedia/PressCenter/64769.htm.
4. "Hon. Ron Paul of Texas in the House Financial Services Committee," September 10, 2003; "Fannie Mae and Freddie Mac Subsidies Distort the Housing Market," http://www.house.gov/paul/congrec/congrec2003/cr091003.htm.
5. "The Latest Reality Game — Wall Street Bailout," House of Representatives, September 22, 2008, http://www.kaptur.house.gov/index.php?option=com_content&task=view&id=289&Itemid=1.
6. "Rep. Brad Sherman On Bailing Out Foreign Investors," http://globaleconomicanalysis.blogspot.com/2008/10/rep-brad-sherman-on-bailing-out-foreign.html.
7. "Fannie's Mudd Soothed Asian Investors as Yields Rose," http://www.bloomberg.com/apps/news?pid=20601109&sid=azswcZQvmUX0&refer=home.
8. "The Fannie-Freddie Takeover: A Latter-Day RTC by Mark Zandi." http://www.economy.com/dismal/article_free.asp?cid=108515&src=hp_economy.
9. "Overseas Debt Drives Bailout of Fannie, Freddie." http://www.washingtontimes.com/news/2008/sep/09/overseas-debt-drives-bailout-of-fannie-freddie/.
10. "An Interview with Jim DeMint on the Bailout Crisis," http://community.adn.com/adn/node/131928.
11. "Banking Bill Bails Out China," http://www.aim.org/aim-column/banking-bill-bails-out-china/.
12. Ibid.
13. "Fed Defies Transparency Aim in Refusal to Disclose," http://www.bloomberg.com/apps/news?pid=20601087&sid=aatlky_cH.tY&refer=home.
14. "Bush Says Sacrificed Free-market Principles to Save Economy," http://www.breitbart.com/article.php?id=081216215816.8g97981o&show_article=1.
15. "Bush Defends Free Market, Calls for 'Smarter Government,'" http://www.cnsnews.com/public/Content/article.aspx?RsrcID=39322.

Part V
The End of the Consumption Gospel

14
Maxed Out:
The New American Slavery

"The only reason a great many American families don't own an elephant is that they have never been offered an elephant for a dollar down and easy weekly payments."

— Unknown

"The rich rules over the poor, and the borrower is servant to the lender."

— Proverbs 22:7

"None are more hopelessly enslaved than those who falsely believe they are free."[1]

— Johann Wolfgang von Goethe

Americans pride themselves on being a free people. But in reality, we are enslaved. However, the notion that Americans could be "slaves" probably is offensive to our sensibilities. The word "slave" conjures up the image of a poor soul being treated as a number and then sold on an auction block to the highest bidder. This is an example of physical slavery. Today, approximately 27 million people live in this type of slavery around the world.[2] But slavery can exist in more than just one form. And it is not always visible. Quite simply, a person is a slave if he has lost control over his life and is dependent upon someone else for his sustenance. For example:

> We are cultural slaves . . . when we are afraid to question the status quo.
>
> We are religious slaves . . . when we are fearful of questioning our own beliefs.
>
> We are entertainment slaves . . . when we mindlessly spend billions on good times.
>
> We are political slaves . . . when our own political persuasions are not truly our own, but those of the media or other persuasive individuals or groups.
>
> We are wage slaves . . . when we feel trapped in a job that pays just enough to survive, but not enough to ever break free.
>
> We are consumer slaves . . . when our disposable spending is determined by corporations and the media.
>
> And most importantly, we become debt slaves . . . when we are unable to dictate our own destinies due to our ever-mounting debts.

Debt slavery has become more pronounced in America over the last several decades as the purchasing power of the dollar has decreased and as consumers have been encouraged to go further into debt to enrich corporations and the credit industry. Many falsely believe that they can escape this debt slavery by paying off all of *their own* debt. But becoming "debt-free" in America is a complete illusion. In truth, you and your children are ultimately responsible for the debts incurred by this generation's immoral financial excesses. The debts that America owes are *yours*. *You are America.* The Congress and the Senate are not spending "Monopoly" money to drop bombs and bail out the rich. They are using *your* tax dollars. And their frivolous spending is done with the checkbook of the U.S. citizenry.

The illusion is further perpetrated upon Americans when we falsely believe that the U.S. economy will always rebound.

That the stock market will always go up perpetually.

That your job will always be available.

That your labor skills will always be in demand.

That foreigners will always be our lenders.

That inflation will never get out of control.

That grocery stores will always be stocked full of food.

That gasoline will always be cheap.

It is all an illusion.

Think about it: *How can you be free and at the same time be a full-fledged citizen of the greatest debtor nation in world history?*

And likewise, how can a man be free who *owes* on everything he *owns?*

> There are two ways to conquer and enslave a nation. One is by the sword. The other is by debt.[3] (President John Adams)

The enslavement of the American population has been further perpetuated by the emphasis upon over-consumption that pervades our society. This consumption-driven culture has literally programmed Americans to believe in the virtue of "more."

More money.

More sex.

More food.

More alcohol.

More work.

More houses.

More cars.

More wealth.

Good, patriotic Americans who love their country are led to believe that their support of their nation is best demonstrated through random acts of consumption.

Even worse, "more" consumption has become closely associated with "godliness." Those who have consumed "more" goods are thought to be more greatly blessed, while those who have relatively little are thought to be cursed.

What deception!

The financial excesses attached to this Gospel of Consumption have dwarfed the true joys of life: spending time with your spouse and your children or volunteering your time for the benefit of others.

DID YOU KNOW?

Shopping centers have become the new houses of worship in America. Seventy percent of Americans visit a mall each week — more than attend church.

While writing this book, I had the pleasure of traveling to Greece, Turkey, and Israel for ten days. While I was invited there to speak about the global financial meltdown, I made sure to take in lots of sightseeing opportunities. As I roamed through the ancient ruins of Athens, Ephesus, Jerusalem, and Galilee, I began to wonder: if America was ever reduced to ruins, what would future travelers find from our civilization? The ancient ruins of Greece and Ephesus magnified the gods and goddesses that the Greeks worshiped. Jerusalem and Galilee gave strong hints of a former Roman occupation. By examining ancient archaeological sites, we are able to determine what was important to the people of that culture. So back to my original question: using this same logic, what if America's buildings and cities were all covered by a super volcano, only to be discovered 2,000 years from now? What would archaeologists discover about America? What could be determined about our values based upon what exists today? The Greeks worshiped a number of gods, including Zeus and Athena. The Jews worshiped the Hebrew God. But who, or what, would America be accused of worshiping by future discoverers of our artifacts and ruins?

The answer should be evident. Americans serve the god of money and consumption. We worship this god in our modern-day houses of worship, known as shopping centers. Banks, which fuel these acts of consumptive worship, are peppered throughout every community. High-rise bank buildings fill the skylines of every major American metropolis. While we may want to think of ourselves differently, the truth is obvious. We worship money and all that it can do for us.

America's Addiction to Consumption and Credit

Let's face it, Americans love to shop. We love our 50-inch plasma televisions, our iPhones, laptops, Playstations, fancy automobiles, McMansions, name-brand clothes, designer jewelry. And what's

con-sume [kuhn-soom]
  1. to destroy, as by decomposition or burning: (as in the fire
     "consumed" the forest; or the cancer "consumed" the
     organ).
  2. to spend (money, time, etc.) wastefully.

better than being able to buy all of these great things now and to pay
for them later? Simply tell us the monthly price and we will sign the
dotted line.

Welcome to America: the "buy now, pay later, no credit check" society.

But somewhere between the "go-go" 1980s and the "me-me"
2000s, America's love affair with easy credit turned from an inno-
cent "crush" into a bad marriage in desperate need of professional
counseling.

Sadly, Americans have been indoctrinated to consume — *or totally
destroy* — their finances for the benefit of corporations and the credit
industry. We have been successfully trained by the media, advertisers,
corporations, the credit industry — and even our own government —
to hand over our hard-earned money with no questions asked. The
problem stems from the fact that we are programmed to be *consumers*
in this country from the time we are very young. And the program-
ming comes from all sides. It is estimated that the average American
is bombarded with over 500 advertising messages every day.

- When Americans watch television, they are urged to spend
  money.
- When driving in their vehicles, billboards urge them to
  spend.
- When picking up their telephones, a telemarketer urges them
  to spend.
- When reading through their favorite magazine, they are told
  to spend.
- When listening to the radio, they are urged to spend.
- And in the middle of an economic crisis, their own government urges them to keep borrowing and spending.

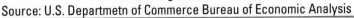

Personal Savings Rate (PSAVERT)

Source: U.S. Departmetn of Commerce Bureau of Economic Analysis

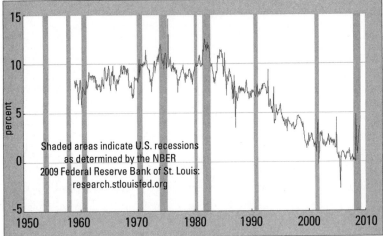

Source: http://research.stlouisfed.org/fred2/series/PSAVERT

It has become so socially acceptable for Americans to consume more than we need that it feels almost like second nature. Sadly, our nation has become so obsessed with consumption that we have forgotten the wisdom and discipline of saving even a small portion of our money. The chart above illustrates America's savings rate since around 1960 — *or lack thereof*. It shows the savings rate has been declining sharply since the 1980s. Remarkably, America's savings rate actually went negative in 2005 — for the first time since the Great Depression.

America is, by all standards, the greatest debtor nation the world has ever known. And while much of this is seen in our national debt of nearly $11 trillion, it is also seen in our record consumer debt levels. As of September 30, 2008, the Federal Reserve reported that total U.S. consumer debt stood at a whopping $2.6 trillion.[4] This breaks down to $8,500 per U.S. citizen. What qualifies as consumer debt? Credit cards, bank loans, student loans, auto loans, loans from finance companies, etc. This amount does not include U.S. mortgage debt. As of 2008, mortgage debt in America totaled $12 trillion.[5]

The chart on the following page demonstrates the increase in U.S. consumer debt and mortgage debt from 1990 through 2007.

Additionally, U.S. household debt has increased dramatically since 1965. The next chart shows U.S. household debt as a percentage of Gross Domestic Product.

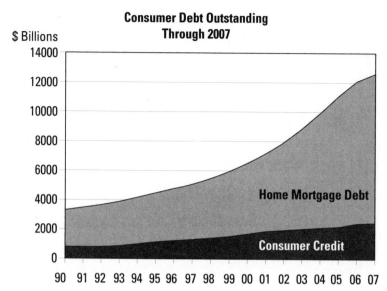

Consumer Debt Outstanding Through 2007

Source: CRS Report for Congress — "Consumer Bankruptcy and Household Debt," by Mark Jickling

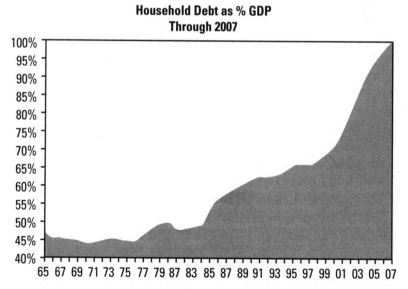

Household Debt as % GDP Through 2007

Source: www.prudentbear.com; source: Federal Reserve Z-1, Bureau of Economic Analysis.

According to the U.S. Bureau of Economic Analysis: "Starting in 2005, American households have spent more than 99.5% of their disposable personal income on consumption or interest payments."[6]

While driving down the road, I saw a bumper sticker that said: "Winning is dying with your credit cards maxed out." Maybe so, but try telling that to the 850,912 U.S. consumers and businesses that filed for bankruptcy in 2007.[7] And thanks to the bursting of the U.S. housing bubble and the ensuing sub-prime crisis, America should expect record numbers of bankruptcies in 2008–2009.

According to Samuel Gerdano, executive director of the nonpartisan American Bankruptcy Institute, "It looks pretty clear that we will have more than 1 million bankruptcy filings by consumers in 2008. . . . Consumers are laboring under a heavy burden of both credit card debt and home mortgage debt. People are concerned about their economic future and shaken by the inability to rely on their homes as a backstop."[8]

Without a doubt, times are tough and will get tougher. But Americans seem to respond to stress with more spending. To soothe their stress, the average American consumer will no longer settle for plain comfort — they want luxury. Of course, funding a luxurious lifestyle requires money, and lots of it. In order to afford these lifestyles of mass consumption, Americans have had to work more hours, further increasing their stress levels. Whether we realize it or not, this consumption-crazed generation has reversed it priorities. Today, many Americans value their money more than the time spent with their loved ones. This is demonstrated by the increasing number of hours that Americans spend working for a living.

In addition to working more hours, Americans are also borrowing more money than ever before. They have also had to borrow more money to afford the luxuries they see everyone else enjoying. Trying to keep up with the Joneses is expensive. The truth that no one seems to understand is that the Joneses are going broke. This is because no one, not even the Joneses, can continue to spend more than they earn forever. According to an October 2008 *Newsweek* article, "During 2008, the typical USA household owned 13 credit cards, with 40% of households carrying a balance, up from 6% in 1970."

How the U.S. Government Discourages Personal Savings

Surprisingly, despite all of this hard work and consistent borrowing, most Americans are just one paycheck away from bankruptcy or foreclosure. And age does not seem to help the problem. In fact, according to the U.S. Department of Health and Human Services, 95 percent of today's 65-year-old Americans retire dependent on family, friends, or the federal government — or they are still working. Only 5 percent are able to sustain themselves financially during retirement.

How can this be possible when we live in the wealthiest nation on earth? How can so many people work so hard all their lives and still reach retirement with so little to show for it?

The truth is we are living in a different era. Gone are the days of job stability and pension plans. Today, most people are left to fend for themselves. Their financial planning consists of a question via e-mail to their Human Resources Department at work. When they turn on the television, the "stock jockeys" send these poor souls to the glorious casino of Wall Street. With few retirement dollars in hand, and thousands of different choices before them, it is no wonder so many feel discouraged. The odds are stacked against an uninformed public. According to the U.S. Commerce Department, 40 percent of American households now believe they could accumulate $500,000 more easily through the lottery than by savings.

But America's aversion to saving is not solely to blame on their drive to consume. The U.S. federal government itself discourages personal savings based upon its policies. How? Consider the U.S. Tax Code. It has an inherent bias toward consumption by penalizing savings and investment. If you take your paycheck and decide to do the responsible thing and save it, you will pay a penalty in the form of a tax on interest. If you choose to invest it, you will also be taxed. However, if you take your paycheck and buy a big-screen television with it, the government never gets involved. By taxing consumption and not productivity, the U.S. government would be more responsible stewards of our national economy.

And what about Social Security? By giving Americans the false hope that their retirement expenses will be covered, they provide a strong disincentive for Americans to save money for their future. Not that a social safety net in retirement is wrong by any means. But when this is coupled together with all of the government's other policies, it only makes sense that Americans consume big, and save little. Their own government rewards this behavior.

The Real Problem: Debt-Based Wealth

Over two-thirds of the American economy is built upon consumption. This means that the future economic growth of America is dependent upon growing amounts of consumption. But is it possible to increase our consumption forever? Is this a sustainable model for future economic growth?

The answer is clear. Without our continued consumption, our economy would collapse. We are held hostage by our own way of life. We are a nation dependent upon borrowing and consumption. We are slaves to debt. One Christian financial radio show that I have heard has its listeners call in and scream: "I'm debt free!" when they pay off all of their debts. And while their plight is better than most, they are still on the hook for the massive debts our nation has created through obsessive spending and reckless borrowing.

As we discussed in chapter 12, our modern banking system creates money out of debt. This debt-based money is then lent out to the American public in the form of loans and lines of credit. However, when a consumer borrows money from a bank or other financial institution, they are only borrowing principal. The interest that will need to be paid back on that loan is not created by the lender. Lenders only create the principal of the loan — *not the interest. So all borrowers in our nation are trying to pay back a **large** pool of principal plus interest from a **smaller** pool of only principal.* For this reason, bankruptcies, repossessions, and foreclosures are guaranteed. According to the current banking system of debt-based money, losers are required. Not everyone can win. Only those who can go out into the marketplace and find the interest to pay back on their loans have a chance at coming out even. Like musical chairs, there are never enough chairs for everyone who is playing the game. Likewise, there is never enough money in the system for everyone to pay back both *principal and interest* — because only the principal exists.

The Tax Man Cometh

So far we have established that many Americans are drowning in consumer debt and all are facing a debt-based monetary system that is stacked against them. If that were not enough for a "free" people, they are also subject to a whole host of taxes from their federal, state, and local governments.

Here is a list of some of the taxes that most Americans are subject to:

Accounts receivable tax
Automobile registration tax
Building permit tax
Capital gains tax
CDL tax
Cigarette tax
Corporate income tax
Court fines (indirect taxes)
Dog license tax
Estate tax
Federal unemployment tax (FUTA)
Fishing license tax
Food license tax
Fuel permit tax
Gasoline tax
Hunting license tax
Inheritance tax interest expense (tax on the money)
Inventory tax
IRS interest charges (tax on top of tax)
IRS penalties (tax on top of tax)
Liquor tax
Local income tax
Luxury taxes
Marriage license tax
Medicare tax
Parking meters
Property tax
Real estate tax
Septic permit tax
Service charge taxes
Social security tax
Road usage taxes (truckers)
Sales taxes
Recreational vehicle tax
Road toll booth taxes
School tax

State income tax
State unemployment tax (SUTA)
Telephone federal excise tax
Telephone federal universal service fee tax
Telephone federal, state, and local surcharge taxes
Telephone minimum usage surcharge tax
Telephone recurring and non-recurring charges tax
Telephone state and local tax
Telephone usage charge tax
Toll bridge taxes
Toll tunnel taxes
Traffic fines
Trailer registration tax
Utility taxes
Vehicle license registration tax
Vehicle sales tax
Watercraft registration tax
Well permit tax
Workers compensation tax

Whew! And that is just to name a few. And there is one more important tax that Americans are required to pay: *the federal income tax*. Every April 15, Americans have a rendezvous with reality. This is the day when all Americans are required to give an accounting to their government of how they performed financially throughout the year. No hiding allowed. If you think you are not a slave, try evading your taxes for a few years. If you are caught, the penalties will be severe.

Inflation — The Hidden Tax

There are many eroding factors that are attacking your money from every angle. One of these eroding factors is inflation. In his book *Lifetime Economic Acceleration Process*, Robert Castiglone states: "Math is not money, and money is not math."[9] This is true, as money is not static, but instead it is tangible. A U.S. dollar is more like a commodity than a mere number. For example, if I placed an apple and a U.S. dollar on a table and then came back ten years later, what would I find? The apple would have disintegrated. What would have happened to the U.S. dollar? Would it still buy a dollar's worth of goods? No, it would have lost value due to inflation.

Inflation is a stealth tax. And the fact that it is hidden makes it even more dangerous to your wealth potential. Every time the Federal Reserve Bank increases the money supply higher than the nation's overall productivity, they create inflation. Inflation eats away at your savings — and it does so invisibly. The great American economist Milton Friedman put it best when he said, "Inflation is one form of taxation that can be imposed without legislation."[10]

Over the course of their working lifetimes, most American citizens will spend a very large majority of their income on three things:

1. Interest
2. Taxes
3. Inflation

Interestingly, each of these three are created and collected by the federal government and their controlled banking cartel, the Federal Reserve.

> **DID YOU KNOW?**
>
> The U.S. Tax Code was developed in 1913, the same year as the Federal Reserve. When it was originally written, it was a mere 400 pages. Today, it consists of over 60,000 pages, making it well over 50 times longer than the King James Bible!

- Banks collect interest on money that they do have and collect interest they did not create.

- Governments extract taxes from the pockets of their citizens on a consistent basis.

- As the government and the Federal Reserve increases the money supply, they create inflation.

In the long run, the American economy is in trouble and the lifestyle of the American consumer is endangered. Only through proper planning can you even attempt to avoid the fallout that will strike this nation as it has every other in history.

Endnotes

1. Johann Wolfgang von Goethe, Otto von Wenckstern, trans., *Goethe's Opinions on the World, Mankind, Literature, Science, and Art* (London: J.W. Parker and Son, 1853), p. 6.

2. http://www.freetheslaves.net.
3. Ellen Hodgson Brown, *Web of Debt: The Shocking Truth about Our Money System* (Baton Rouge, LA: Third Millennium Press, 2007), p. 47.
4. "There Is a Silver Lining," http://www.newsweek.com/id/163449.
5. Federal Reserve Statistical Release: G.19 Release — Consumer Credit — December 5, 2008, http://www.federalreserve.gov/releases/g19/Current/.
6. "Mortgage Debt Least of Bad Bets as Investing Sinks," http://www.bloomberg.com/apps/news?pid=20601087&refer=home&sid=aIFGZELZtWpQ.
7. Bureau of Economic Analysis, NIPA, Table 2.9, 100 - line 46, http://www.bea.gov/national/nipaweb/TableView.asp?SelectedTable=294&ViewSeries=NO&Java=no&Request3Place=N&3Place=N&FromView=YES&Freq=Year&FirstYear=2000&LastYear=2007&3Place=N&Update=Update&JavaBox=no#Mid.
8. "U.S. Bankruptcies Soared 38 Percent in 2007," http://www.reuters.com/article/telecomm/idUSN155757020080416.
9. Robert Castiglone, *Lifetime Economic Acceleration Process* (Canada: Castle Lion Publishers, 2005).
10. Jay M. Shafritz, *The HarperCollins Dictionary of American Government and Politics* (New York: HarperPerennial, 1992), p. 296.

Chapter 15
Shattering the Myths of the American Mindset

"There never was a democracy yet that did not commit suicide."[1]

— Henry David Thoreau

"God does not show favoritism."

— Romans 2:11; NIV

OVERVIEW: The illusion of prosperity created by the U.S. consumption bubble has been built upon a deceptive premise: perpetually low interest rates and a globally accepted paper currency with no intrinsic value. When the U.S. dollar fully collapses, interest rates will be driven to sky-high levels in order to attract demand for worthless U.S. paper. Americans, who have become accustomed to easy money, no down payments, and cheap foreign imported goods, will be shocked back into economic reality and will be forced into a sacrificial lifestyle of consuming less and saving more.

The Twilight of American Hegemony

Since 1945, America has been the supreme global economic power. However, as this book has sought to demonstrate, the days of American hegemony are entering their twilight years.

219

For far too long, Americans have operated under the assumption that the economic good times would never end. These assumptions have been manufactured inside an illusion that now holds our nation spellbound. The noise created from America's long economic boom has fully awakened a host of emerging nations. As technological advances have leveled the global economic playing field, many of these emerging nations are now eager — and, more importantly, able — to walk the path of mass consumption, Western-style. *Ironically, it is not America's over-consumption that will bring it to its knees. It is the world's attempts to emulate the consumption patterns of the West that will destroy America.* Instead of being the land of more than enough, as it has for the last several decades, America will be forced to watch from afar as more nimble nations rise in economic dominance. These nations will rise unfettered by the crushing weight of unpayable debts, unsustainable monetary policies, and an entitlement-minded population.

Those who continue to believe in the perpetual resilience of the American empire must face facts. And facts are stubborn things.

- America is confronted by an insurmountable energy crisis and has no strategy.
- America is fighting an expensive global war on "terrorism" with no end in sight.
- America has a weakening currency with no clear strategy on how to revive it.
- America's debt-based monetary system requires exponential growth, debt, and production in order to expand. This is clearly unsustainable.
- America's trillions of dollars in consumer debt have placed massive constraints on future consumption.
- America is faced with trillions of dollars in government debts — multiplying with interest by the second — that can never be repaid without completely debauching its currency, wiping out vital social safety nets, or taxing the American population into oblivion.

Like a race car heading straight toward a brick wall with the driver asleep at the wheel, the gradual collapse of American hegemony will not be a pretty sight.

What Goes Up, Must Come Down

As stated in chapter 1, Scottish historian Alexander Tyler documented the typical life cycle of a democracy:

> *A democracy cannot exist as a permanent form of government. It can only exist until the voters discover that they can vote themselves **money from the public treasure**. From that moment on, the majority always votes for the candidates promising the most money from the public treasury, with the result that a democracy always collapses over **loose fiscal policy followed by a dictatorship**.*[2]

All of the world's former empires have risen only to fall later. Many have fallen by military conquests. Others by the weight of their own miscalculations.

The Egyptian Empire rose . . . then gave way to the Assyrian Empire.

The Assyrian Empire rose . . . then gave way to the Babylonian Empire.

The Babylonian Empire rose . . . then gave way to the Medes-Persian Empire.

The Medes-Persian Empire rose . . . then gave way to the Greek Empire.

The Greek Empire rose . . . then gave way to the Roman Empire.

The Roman Empire rose . . . then fell at the hands of others.

Then we fast-forward through history.

In 1709, Holland was a great place to be as the Dutch dominated European trade.

In 1809, Britain was a great place to be as the British Empire rose like the sun across the globe.

In 1909, the United States was a great place to be as America prepared to dominate the 20th century.

In 2009, where will the next great empire be? China? Europe? The Middle East?

Time will tell. But believing that America will extend its hegemonic role far into the 21st century is sheer fantasy. We are clearly an empire in decline. The sooner "we the people" awake to this fact, the more time the nation will have to slow the inevitable.

Global War and Disney World

On the morning of December 7, 1941, Japanese naval forces launched a surprise attack against the United States Naval Base at Pearl Harbor, Hawaii. The attack came in the form of two aerial waves that included over 350 Japanese planes launched from Japanese aircraft carriers. The surprise attack left more than 2,400 dead and more than 1,200 wounded. This act of terror by Japan lured a reluctant United States into World War II. To fund the war, the U.S. government, under President Franklin D. Roosevelt, immediately began a rationing program that sought to restrict American consumption of essential products. In addition, Roosevelt ended production of new automobiles, new homes, and new appliances. Why? To free up American manufacturing plants, materials, and labor for the war. During this same time, gasoline was rationed and war bonds were issued to provide the necessary military funding.

During World War II, Americans were expected to sacrifice for the war effort, even to the point of limiting their travel. A great war demanded much from a great people, and they complied willingly.

A 1943 Office of Defense Transportation poster urging U.S. citizens to limit travel to help the war effort

In contrast, consider the American response to a more recent surprise terrorist attack. Few Americans will ever forget the tragic events that unfolded on the day of September 11, 2001. That day, 19 radical Islamists hijacked four commercial passenger jet planes. Two planes were flown into the World Trade Center buildings in New York City. One plane was crashed into the Pentagon in Washington, DC. The fourth hijacked plane was brought down in a field in Shanksville, Pennsylvania, while en route to Washington, DC. Americans viewed the horrific scenes of terror on their television sets as they unfolded. Nearly 3,000 Americans died in the worst terrorist attack on American soil in history.

But in the wake of a national tragedy, the American people rallied around New York City and the families of the victims who lost their lives that September day. In the days after the attack, blood donations across the United States rose dramatically and many houses of worship were filled to the brim. The American people saw a need and were ready to unite behind their nation and its leader.

Within weeks, the U.S. military had embarked on a new global war on terror. However, with this war came no call for sacrifice. No war bonds were issued, and no gasoline was rationed. Instead, in the midst of a global war on terror, President George W. Bush stood before a large televised audience and told American citizens to go shopping and to take vacations: "Fly and enjoy America's great destination spots. Get down to Disney World in Florida. Take your families and enjoy life, the way we want it to be enjoyed."[3]

While the case could be made that Bush was attempting to remobilize a fearful nation, still the question remains: where is the economic sacrifice in this new massive worldwide war on terrorism?

Ask yourself: which of our nation's leaders are asking you to curb your consumption in an effort to fund our current global war?

This is really not a trick question. Instead, it is just straight and simple mathematics. If you are not being asked to pay for this modern war, then who is funding it? The same people who have been funding America's extravagant lifestyles for the last several decades: *foreigners.*

Today, foreign countries like China, Japan, and others fund America through massive capital inflows that serve to prop up U.S. consumption and conquest. The capital inflows from China alone are over $3 billion per day. *In other words, foreign countries, like China and Japan, are financing American consumption and American conquest.*

In addition to foreign capital inflows that fund our over-consumption, America is doing something even more regrettable. Today, American politicians promise the unborn grandchildren's money to pay for the luxuries of the grandparents through the use of massive entitlement spending programs. Of course, it is much easier to borrow from our future than to demand sacrifice from the living. Our politicians are aware of this and exploit this tendency toward human selfishness to secure their own re-election. Because America's economy is imperiled, economic sacrifice is the answer. Unfortunately, corrupt government policies and poor fiscal stewardship have created an entitlement-demanding generation that is highly resistant to the idea of sacrifice.

> **Think About It:**
>
> Imagine a man walking into the finest restaurant and ordering the most expensive entrée and bottle of wine on the menu. Then upon receiving the bill from his waiter, he proceeds to yell and scream about how unfair life is. He then says: "Put this expensive meal on my unborn grandchild's bill."

Today, American citizens want low taxes while they fight numerous wars.

They want low taxes but expect no cuts to be made to their entitlement benefits.

They want low taxes but they want national healthcare.

They drive SUVs but they want cheap gasoline.

They expect interest rates to remain low but they want the government to print more money.

Sadly, our politicians have been all too willing to comply with these requests in exchange for our votes.

Eventually, the American people will have to come to terms with the fact that our current economic policies are unsustainable. And the longer the economic insanity continues, the more severe the economic pain will be in the end.

In essence, the resistance to economic sacrifice in America has become so strong that our nation now borrows from foreign nations, and unborn American citizens, to fund their current lifestyles.

Shattering the Myths of the American Mindset

As this book has demonstrated, America is living in massive monetary deception, and hallucinations are a common side effect of the deception that pervades the inside of a declining economic empire. In conclusion, let us examine several of these illusions that still persist in American society.

Illusion: Most Americans view foreign nations and their governments as inherently inferior to America.

Truth: God is not partial, and He is no respecter of persons (Acts 10:34; Rom. 2:11). Instead of playing favorites, the Bible is clear that *all* nations will be judged (Zech. 12:3; Rev. 16:14). Therefore, the God of heaven views all national governments as an offense to His wisdom and holds them in derision (Ps. 2:4).

Illusion: America is "one nation under God."

Truth: America is not one nation under God. We have never been a Christian nation, and we are certainly not a Christian nation today.

Illusion: Bombing countries to spread "democracy" is justified.

Truth: Try to find anywhere in the New Testament where Christianity is called to support war and revenge. Instead, we should let the nations do as they may. A Christian's concern should be for God's Kingdom. Beating the war drums "in Jesus' name" is an offense to the true gospel. Christian ministers who advocate war "in Jesus' name" have misplaced their hope in this world's kingdoms. Instead of a solution of war, they should proclaim the coming Kingdom of Christ as the answer.

Illusion: America is a peaceful nation. We are not militant.

Truth: The U.S. military is a war machine with military bases in over 130 nations. It protects both the national and global interests of the American empire. While the continent of North America has experienced long periods of peacetime, those whom America dislikes have not.

Illusion: God is on America's side.

Truth: President Abraham Lincoln once said: "My concern is not whether God is on our side; my great concern is to be on God's side."[4] When Christ returns in His glory, He will smite all of the nations and kingdoms of this world in His wrath. To believe that His wrath will be selective in that day is the height of arrogance and presumption. The Bible is clear: no nation will be spared, including America (Zech. 12:3; Rev. 16:14, 19:15).

Illusion: Cheap oil will never run out.

Truth: Oil is a finite resource. When it becomes more expensive to pull it out of the ground than it can be sold for, cheap oil will be gone forever. And according to credible sources, this could happen within the next couple of decades, if not sooner.

Illusion: Gasoline prices should always remain cheap.

Truth: It takes four barrels of oil to produce two and a half barrels of gasoline. As demand for oil goes up and supplies continue to dwindle, gasoline prices must go up. Because America uses 50 percent of the world's gasoline supplies each year, these price increases will affect America dramatically.

Illusion: America's huge national debt is completely normal for a nation of our size.

Truth: The Bible says that a borrower is a servant of the lender (Prov. 22:7). The American federal government will not, and cannot, pay off its mounting debts because debt is a vital part of maintaining our crumbling economy. But having over $60 trillion in debt certainly does not indicate a normal and healthy economy.

Illusion: China needs America.

Truth: China is no stranger to being a global empire. In centuries past, the Chinese empire has risen and fallen. Today, it is rising on the backs of American consumption; however, this is clearly an unsustainable long-term growth strategy. China is smart enough to know how to navigate the global economic waters. If it must use force, it will. But China will rise, regardless of America's demise.

Illusion: The Middle East needs America.

Truth: America needs the Middle East. The Middle East sits atop the majority of the world's oil supplies. America satisfies its enormous oil demand by large amounts of imports from the Middle East. The U.S. military installations in the Middle East exist primarily to protect the oil that America desperately needs. The Middle East has other customers who buy oil. And as the demand from these other nations continues to grow, America will become increasingly less important to the Middle East.

Illusion: America's central bank, the Federal Reserve, is a federal institution.

Truth: The Federal Reserve is as federal as Federal Express. It is a privately owned banking enterprise that has colluded with the federal government to print the nation's currency while charging U.S. taxpayers interest.

Illusion: The U.S. dollar will always be accepted by all nations.

Truth: The dollar's days are numbered. The U.S. dollar is a fiat currency backed up by nothing. It is worthless paper that the world is currently willing to accept. When the world finally awakens to America's bankrupt status, it will gravitate toward other, more stable currencies.

Illusion: Banks make money honestly.

Truth: False. Thanks to the fractional-reserve banking system, today's banks create money out of thin air. (See chapter 12 for more details.)

Illusion: The U.S. dollar is honest money.

Truth: The U.S. dollar is a fiat currency backed by nothing. As a fiat currency that is printed at will, it is therefore defined as a "false balance" and an "unjust weight," according to the Bible (Prov. 20:10).

Illusion: Hyperinflation will never occur in America.

Truth: Hyperinflation is impartial. It visits all nations who greedily overprint their currency. When a nation's money supply wildly outpaces its productivity, hyperinflation is just around the corner.

Illusion: Government entitlements are good and should be expected.

Truth: Many Americans are infected with an entitlement mentality, falsely believing that society owes them something. Throughout history, governments have been destroyed by the crushing weight of the financial promises they have made to support the public. We need fewer entitlements, not more.

Illusion: If Republicans/Democrats could just gain majority control, everything would be fixed.

Truth: Both Democrats and Republicans have failed America. The reason has less to do with good policy and more to do with the fact that men cannot rule men. In all of history, never has a nation been able to govern itself with stability and righteousness for a sustained period of time. The "conservative-liberal" argument is a fool's game that distracts the citizenry from the real issues facing America. Those who are prone to this argument should learn its lessons from the American church. The "conservative-liberal" game has effectively divided the American church. And in so doing, it has completely marginalized and masked the real message of Christ and Him crucified.

Illusion: War will never occur on our own soil.

Truth: On September 11, 2001, this illusion should have been shattered. However, many still believe that America could never be the theater of a future full-scale war. Think again.

Illusion: Shopping is patriotic.

Truth: Seventy percent of America's annual productivity (GDP) is based upon its consumption. To maintain future GDP growth requires that Americans continue to borrow money and shop uncontrollably. This is a recipe for disaster for any nation. Patriotism is found in saving a portion of your income and living within your means, which are both discouraged by current government policies.

Illusion: If we pay off our personal debt, we are "debt-free."

Truth: FALSE. How can you be a full-fledged citizen of the greatest debtor nation in world history and consider yourself "debt-free," simply because you paid off an automobile loan? America's poor fiscal policies have created a huge liability for every American citizen. And as the nation continues to further enslave itself and its citizens in more debt, the situation will grow even more bleak.

Over the next several years, as the illusion of American prosperity begins to crumble, millions will be rudely awakened. America is an empire in decline. History never seems like history when you are living through it. Yet, together, we are witnessing the end of an age — we are living at the end of an empire.

Endnotes

1. Robert Wuthnow, *American Mythos: Why Our Best Efforts to be a Better Nation Fall Short* (Princeton, NJ: Princeton University Press, 2006), p. 19.
2. Durham W. Ellis, *Big Government — Poor Grandchildren: How Democrats and Republicans Are Impoverishing You and Yours* (Birmingham, AL: Wealthy World Publishers, 2005), p. 232.
3. "At O'Hare, President Says 'Get On Board,' Remarks by the President to Airline Employees, O'Hare International Airport, Chicago, Illinois," http://www.whitehouse.gov/news/releases/2001/09/20010927-1.html.
4. http://www.famousquotes.com/show.php?_id=1033002.

Chapter 16
Why the Message Of "Sacrifice" Is Coming to the American Church

"There is no means of avoiding the final collapse of a boom brought about by credit (debt) expansion. The alternative is only whether the crisis should come sooner as the result of a voluntary abandonment of further credit (debt) expansion, or later as a final and total catastrophe of the currency system involved."[1]

— Ludwig von Mises

"The people who walked in darkness have seen a great light."

— Isaiah 9:2

OVERVIEW: As the American economic empire enters its final stages of decline, the message that arises will be one of sacrifice. This coming era of "sacrifice" will do more than simply reveal the absurdity of America's immoral financial excesses. It will expose the American Church's reliance upon man-made kingdoms. Instead of focusing their adherents upon the necessity of the coming Kingdom of God, the American Church has often misplaced its hope in worldly kingdoms. When the government is finally forced to demand sacrifice from the living, the American Church, inebriated by a false prosperity, may finally awaken to the need for the coming Kingdom of God. Then, various versions of the message of sacrifice will ring loudly across the United States of America. Some will be genuine, but many will not be.

Awakening from the American Dream

What is strangely missing from the majority of today's churches is solid teaching regarding the most pressing issues of our day. This list would include: the global food crisis, movement toward global political integration, and the threat of worldwide economic collapse. These, and other important issues, are bearing down on our nation. Ignoring these matters does little to reduce their size and their scope. In the midst of the chaos and confusion confronting our world, the Church of the Lord Jesus Christ is mysteriously quiet. I am convinced that this silence exists for a number of unfortunate reasons. I will not go into all of those reasons here, with the exception of one, which I feel is the most important and relevant to our discussion: the idea of *American exceptionalism.*

According to the idea of "American exceptionalism," America is such a unique and special nation that it will not face the same fates as nations and empires that preceded it. Of course, every empire that has existed before America has fallen. However, according to the idea of American exceptionalism, America will not have to face those same challenges. Instead, America is an exception to the rule of history.

On what basis does the Church subscribe to these beliefs? Some in the Church have attributed America's exceptionalism to God's divine protection due to America's stance on Israel. They quote God's words to Abraham in Genesis 12:3 — *"I will bless those who bless you and I will curse him who curses you"* — to defend America's insulation from the trends of history. I will certainly not debate the merit of this logic from Genesis 12 because I do believe firmly that God has future plans for the nation and people of Israel. *Therefore, I believe it is in our nation's best interests to pray for the peace of Israel.* However, to claim that America's economy is failing due to our stance on Israel is absurd and plainly uninformed. America's economy is in peril due to the same poor monetary policies that have taken down every fiat empire before it. The logic behind this becomes even more suspect when we question it further.

Does America's support for Israel negate God's displeasure of America's obsession with sacrificing 5,000 unborn children every day through abortion in the name of convenience?

Does America's support of Israel mean that God will suspend His disgust with the abomination of our fiat currency system?

Does supporting Israel get our nation off the hook for its unfathomable obsession with, and its exportation of, the most obscene forms of pornography?

Will God turn His head while the American Church ignores the poor and the needy simply because of our "support" for Israel?

This thinking is obviously very dangerous. I have heard many Christian leaders and mega-church pastors succumb to this teaching by telling their followers that God *will never allow America's economy to fail* as long as our nation supports Israel! Not only are these types of teachings at the pinnacle of arrogance, they are also extremely illogical.

"God Is Not an American"

I still remember my first lecture in which I explained that God was not an American, and that God's throne was not draped in an American flag. Many in the audience that day later informed me that they had never thought about it in that way before. This concept is important to grasp. America, like all empires before it, views everything through its own special "Americanized" lenses. Simply put, Americans are America-centric. Unfortunately for Americans, the Bible is not. It is Israel-centric. It is Middle Eastern-centric.

To many, the logic goes something like this:

> Is America facing calamity? It must be a fulfillment of biblical prophecy!

> Did America have a major natural disaster? It must be that God is sending us a special message.

Never mind that many nations around the world are facing severe tribulation today. In Sudan, millions of Christian men, women, and children are facing great tribulation and are suffering in silence. However, this means virtually nothing to the America-centric. Now let's reverse the roles. Imagine that white American Christians were being physically persecuted for their faith. The Church would declare the "end of the world" to be at hand.

In North Korea, Christians face death camps and horrific persecution for their faith in Christ. But unfortunately, this does not pass the America-centric test.

Christians attending China's underground churches number in the millions. Each week, these Chinese brothers and sisters meet in secret due to the threat of intense persecution from China's intolerant Communistic regime. However, this is not enough to get the attention of the American-centric mindset.

To the American Church, "real" persecution is defined in the following ways:

> Walking into a non-Christian retail store during the Christmas season and being greeted with the words "Happy Holidays" instead of "Merry Christmas."
>
> Threats and/or the removal of a Ten Commandments display from a local courthouse.
>
> Outspoken protests regarding nativity displays during the Christmas holiday season.
>
> Threats of removing "In God We Trust" from the U.S. currency.

Amazingly, the American Church wants those whose minds have not been enlightened to the gospel of Jesus Christ to still "act" like Christians. Should Christians expect those who do not believe in Christ to promote Him? By forcing non-Christians to act like Christians, the American Church exposes its own Achilles' heel. Is not this acting what they expect from their own as well?

Missing the Point?

As the American economic empire completely collapses, many may point to its demise as proof that God is "judging" America for its immorality and other sins. Or perhaps for its lack of support of Israel. The truth, however, is that the American economic empire will fall due to its faulty foundations. Because of these flawed foundations, the prosperity that America has enjoyed has in fact been an illusion of paper wealth. Other paper currency empires have enjoyed similar (albeit) smaller periods of prosperity prior to their collapse.

This means that the prosperity that America has enjoyed up to this point has been an illusion of wealth. Does the Christian God "bless" nations with illusions of prosperity? And will the Christian God threaten to remove this "blessing" of fake prosperity dependent upon our treatment of Israel?

The fact that the American Church has misjudged this brings us right to the heart of the matter. I will submit to you that the American Church has bought the "illusion of prosperity" that has been packaged and sold to America as fact. *Do we really believe that God's "blessing" involves extending our nation's economic delusion and our debt-based paper money system which has enslaved us — and which He calls an "abomination" in His Word?* (See chapter 4.)

> Hear this, you who swallow up the needy, and make the poor of the land fall. . . . Making the ephah small and the shekel large, falsifying the scales by deceit (Amos 8:4–5).

How the "Prosperity Gospel" Feeds the "Consumption Gospel"

Finally, it should be noted that the American Church's fascination with "prosperity" has helped create the financial excesses of America itself. In their haste to get rich, "in Jesus' name," many deluded ministers inadvertently taught their flocks to value over-consumption. Many of these ministers teach that Christians should not settle for less, and instead, they should expect the best. Bigger houses, bigger cars, more money, etc. In other words, personal spirituality is enhanced through a pursuit of visible blessings. This focus upon mass consumption by many churches has exacerbated the financial problems of millions of their loyal adherents. The prosperity message emitting from the American Church is like an open sewer to the nostrils of a righteous and holy God. He clearly warns in His Word: "You cannot serve both God and Money" (Matt. 6:24; NIV).

Of course, the clever ones from this bunch (and there are several) will quickly jump to defend the promotion of financial excess as the "blessing" from God. "We are not promoting riches for riches sake," they say, as they boast of the financial blessings they have received as a result of their strict religious adherence to their false gospel. Indeed, their exploitative shenanigans will be fully exposed, and their day of reckoning is at hand.

Then Jesus went into the temple of God and drove out all those who bought and sold in the temple, and overturned the tables of the money changers and the seats of those who sold doves. And He said to them, "It is written, 'My house shall be called a house of prayer,' but you have made it a 'den of thieves'" (Matt. 21:12–13).

But as the U.S. economy begins its all-but-certain chaotic economic descent, how will those who promote the prosperity gospel respond? How will they explain to their congregations that they have promoted a fiat currency as God's blessing? How can they say that the unjust weights and balances that fueled American "prosperity" are "God's best" when He clearly calls it an "abomination" in His Word? Will they pray for more of the abomination with which to fill their bank accounts? How will they explain their lack of wisdom in such evil and perverse days?

While confronting such questions would be the responsible thing to do, it is also the most unlikely. Instead of examining their theology, it is more likely that they will search for new ways to pick the pockets of those who believe their rhetoric. The transformation will occur before our very eyes. Those who once promoted the failed prosperity message will turn to their new message of choice: *the message of "sacrifice."*

Why the Message of "Sacrifice" Is Coming to the American Church

Today, much of the American Church has embraced the economic delusion that will ultimately lead to our nation's downfall. Unfortunately, this blind trust that has been placed in the American illusion of prosperity has rendered the Church impotent in offering solid biblical solutions to a clueless public regarding the economic crisis. Undoubtedly, the crisis that is unfolding offers the American Church a strong evangelistic opportunity to expose the modern version of the Tower of Babel that America has built upon its economic prowess and political exploits. But while the "Tower of America" stood strong and deceived many, much of the Church instructed its members with shallow teachings on finances that rarely pointed to the futility of man-made kingdoms.

When America needed to hear a strong message of "sacrifice" from the American church, what they got instead was feel-good messages designed to stroke the ego and stoke the fire of over-consumption. Besides, in our modern era of "positive thinking," messages on sacrifice could be taken as "intrusive," "demeaning," or just plain "mean." Obviously, this is no way to grow a church. Teaching on sacrifice would be an obstruction to church growth. Apparently, messages on sacrifice do little to add numbers to declining churches. So the American Church continues its fixation on "growing" its numbers, building more buildings, and spreading the worldly kingdom of republicanism to the nation.

As the economy moves into a downward spiral over the coming years, it will catch most off guard. Not because they were not warned, but because the severity of the collapse will complicate their lives by ruining the effectiveness of their philosophies. Many of the philosophies that will be most under attack will be financial and theological philosophies. Those who have believed in American exceptionalism and perpetually inclining financial markets will be rudely awakened.

One of the benefits of the coming economic hardships that America will face will be found in our rediscovery of community. Neighbors will once again know each other's names. Communities will have the chance to rally together in an effort to bring aid to the financially destitute. In the coming era of "sacrifice," life will consist of more than simply working, consuming, and sleeping. Instead, Americans will have the opportunity to band together in community-organized social networks to solve local challenges. In a day where Hollywood, the media, and corporations urge Americans to please themselves through mass consumption, the message of sacrifice is coming.

But what about the American Church? Surely while the masses shopped till they dropped and lived above their means, the Church in America was calling for fiscal restraint, right? Haven't they been urging sacrifice from Americans for decades? Well, perhaps a few. However, we live in an hour where much of the American Church has urged its adherents to "live their best life now," to "love their life," and to consume "big," as only "the King's kids" should. It should be noted that the American Church's promotion of unsacrificial living is at the height of irony. This is especially true when one considers that the entire Christian religion is rooted and grounded in the idea of self-sacrifice.

But the real indictment against the American Church is their sheer lack of insight into the failed kingdoms of this world. As the false prosperity bubble got bigger, the American Church believed it to be real. *In fact, most evangelical Christians unknowingly consider the fiat-fueled, debt-based economy to be a divine "blessing" from God.* Only because America was "special" were they able to possess such a large bubble economy. Even worse, many thought that God might prematurely terminate this false prosperity if gay people were allowed to marry, or if "In God We Trust" were ever removed from the worthless fiat U.S. dollar.

It is important to note that much of the American Church's numerical growth in the 20th century came from the explosion of interest in the health and wealth gospel. When the growth of this prosperity movement is measured against the growth in American consumption, one finds a curious thing indeed. America's explosion in credit, debt, and money supply is *directly* tied to growth of the prosperity movement. This means that when the economy goes up, times are good in the prosperity movement. However, when economic conditions become difficult, the prosperity gospel will suffer. The economy's effect upon the prosperity movement will render it impotent in the face of the coming economic chaos that will strike America. As the economic pain becomes evident to all, those who have promoted the prosperity message will use a new message of "sacrifice" to sustain their ministries. Amazingly, those ministers who had promoted over-consumption to their adherents for decades will discover the ancient principle of sacrifice. But when these former prosperity preachers begin to wax eloquent on their newfound message of sacrifice, it will be far from sincere. Instead, it will be designed to continue the cash flow.

In our current environment, leaders who refuse to speak truth, and instead continue to strive for top placement in popularity contests, will fail the people that they have been commissioned to lead. Once the American Church is purged of the career charlatans that control it, it can finally arise with real answers. Until then, the American evangelical church will remain a declining subcultural phenomenon, a voting bloc easily manipulated by certain keywords uttered by informed politicians that are designed to elicit the right response. Until the American Church desires the coming Kingdom of God as desperately as it wants the American kingdom to reflect its own glory, it will remain irrelevant. But despite their irrelevance, the message of sacrifice is *still* coming.

The ancient principle of "sacrifice"— proclaimed by Christ Himself — will ring throughout this land as America's sins of excess and immorality become evident through the "false weights and balances" created by its economy. Sacrifice will not be the natural response from a people accustomed to over-consumption. However, it will be the only possible response.

Facing the Facts

> How long, ye simple ones, will ye love simplicity? And scoffers delight them in scoffing, and fools hate knowledge? (Prov. 1:22; ASV).

What is at the root of the problem in the American Church? I submit to you that the root of our problem is the American Church's ignorance to God's coming Kingdom and ignorance of the greatest issues facing mankind. For decades, the American Church has been pillaged due to its lack of knowledge. As it says in the Book of Hosea: "*My people are destroyed for lack of knowledge*" (Hos. 4:6).

> Through wisdom a house is built, and by understanding it is established; by knowledge the rooms are filled with all precious and pleasant riches. A wise man is strong, yes, a man of knowledge increases strength; for by wise counsel you will wage your own war, and in a multitude of counselors there is safety (Prov. 24:3–6).

A loss of strong theological teaching in the American Church has bred a new generation of "believers" who seek self-satisfaction instead of sound doctrine. Instead of treating the kingdoms of this world with godly suspicion, many have believed the satanic lie that men can rule men. Instead of pointing people to the hope of the coming Kingdom of Christ, many churches have been all too willing to promote the counterfeit kingdoms of this world. The result has been disastrous.

> Her princes within her are like wolves tearing the prey, by shedding blood and destroying lives in order to get dishonest gain. Her prophets have smeared whitewash for them, seeing false visions and divining lies for them. . . . The

people of the land have practiced oppression and committed robbery, and they have wronged the poor and needy (Ezek. 22:27–29;NASB).

In truth, the fiat currency and debt-based economic growth that have fueled America to the stratospheres of this world system were *never* blessed because they were flawed from the beginning. They were doomed to failure from the start. Therefore, when the house of cards collapses, it will not be because we stopped supporting Israel, or because same-sex marriage became legal. *Instead, the system will collapse because it is a man-made system.* And as this book has sought to demonstrate, man cannot rule man. The entire American economic system is laughable in the eyes of God because of its ineffectiveness and unsustainability.

Our failed man-made systems are clear testaments to mankind's need for God's Kingdom. Those who seek to blame particular political philosophies, corporate scandals, immorality, etc., are completely missing the point. Their media-inspired focus upon the "effects" have blinded them to the real culprit: the "cause." The reason that our systems are failing is because *man cannot rule man.* Sin is taking hold of our society and is choking it before our eyes. This is the gospel, not according to the culture at large, but according to the Bible.

Those who are *aware* are able to view the problems as they truly are. And they realize that these problems are rooted in man's inherent deficiencies in ruling himself. Let's make an important distinction: awareness is not the equivalent of activism. *However, those who favor activism will always have the loudest voices.* They are quickly recognized as the ones who insist on re-arranging the furniture on the sinking *Titanic.* In contrast, the aware recognize the root problem and see God's Kingdom as the *only* real solution.

Are You an "Activist" or Are You One of the "Aware"?

The **activists** are biblically aware but politically motivated.

In contrast, the **aware** are politically aware but biblically motivated.

The **activists** insist that by getting the right political party into office we can "take back America for God."

In contrast, the **aware** realize that no matter which political party gets elected, nothing can slow man's sin problem. They avoid political games, knowing their futility.

The **activists** think that getting prayer back into America's schools will change the nation.

The **aware** pray with their children at home and do not expect government-controlled institutions to teach their children spiritual values.

The **activists** *extol* the virtues of man's kingdoms (political platforms) and follow them with a religious fervor.

The **aware** *endure* man's kingdoms, all the while praying and longing for God's Kingdom.

The **activists** demand "Merry Christmas" be spoken — even in secular settings. The phrase "Happy Holidays" is viewed as religious persecution.

The **aware** do not expect non-Christians to promote Christ.

The **activists** want "In God We Trust" to remain plastered on the U.S. fiat currency.

The **aware** realize that fiat currency systems, such as the U.S. dollar, are "unjust weights and balances" and therefore are an "abomination" to God.

The **activists** take their cues from, and measure themselves by, their culture.

The **aware** know that God will never judge anyone based upon their culture, only based upon God's Word, the Bible.

Endnotes

1. Richard Duncan, *The Dollar Crisis: Causes, Consequences,* Cures (Singapore; Hoboken, NJ; Chichester, England: J. Wiley & Sons (Asia), 2003), p. 5.

Chapter 17
Forecasting the Future

"The art of prophecy is very difficult, especially with respect to the future."[1]

— Mark Twain

"The people who were honored in the Bible were the false prophets. It was the ones we call the prophets who were jailed and driven into the desert."[2]

— Noam Chomsky

OVERVIEW: In this chapter, current global events are used to predict future economic, political, and spiritual trends.

Throughout this book, we have covered a lot of ground together. My purpose in writing this book is rooted in a deep desire to issue a general warning to the public regarding the danger of the times that we are living in. Undoubtedly, some may characterize the nature of the material that I have presented as unnecessarily alarmist. If the trends and facts that have been presented were untrue, I would agree wholeheartedly. Unfortunately, the facts that have been presented reveal the new economic and political realities that are facing America. It is in our best interest to come to terms with these new realities so that we may effectively protect ourselves — *and even prosper* — in the coming years.

In this brief chapter, I would like to offer my own observations on what the future may hold for America. Admittedly, I was hesitant to include this chapter because I am acutely aware of the futility of what I call the "predictive arts." Rarely is one correct in being able to determine where the current winds of destiny are leading. No one has a crystal ball, and no one can know what tomorrow holds. However, I do believe that one can make some very strong educated guesses based upon the analysis of current trends.

For each of the following trends, I will include a brief sentence or two to explain my reasoning. Be aware that my biblical knowledge and my personal love for and relationship with Jesus Christ inform my insights. Where appropriate, I will include the biblical foundations for my reasoning. I will avoid using specific dates and/or years in these forecasts. Instead, I will use specified time frames, such as a four-year time window.

Finally, it should be understood at the outset that I reserve the right to adjust these forecasts as new developments arise. All of the forecasts included in this chapter are based on current realities. As the world further evolves toward its ultimate destiny, which it does on a daily basis, these forecasts will obviously need to be re-adjusted to correspond to the new realities.

The following forecasts are based upon my own analysis of economic and political data coupled with biblical knowledge. These trends should not be viewed as investment advice. *You should always consult your trusted financial advisor prior to making any financial decisions.*

2009–2013 Forecasts

"Free market capitalism" will continue to be bailed out by the shadow socialistic nanny state.

Everybody believes in free markets, *until they lose money.* Unfortunately, America's skin is too thin to make it as a free-market economy, as economic pain is avoided at all costs. But America will never admit to being socialist either. So let's just make this a nice and quiet prediction, as I don't want to rock the boat. America will continue the use of socialism to bail out financial mistakes made in the free market in the coming years. Ironically, China has become more capitalistic than America in recent years. I expect this trend to continue.

The U.S. economy will experience a sucker rally, then utterly collapse.

The massive capital infusions that the U.S. government is relying on to solve America's financial crisis is the equivalent of giving crack cocaine to a drug addict. Certainly the cash infusions will provide a temporary fix to challenges facing our nation. However, in the long run, government bailouts will only serve to further enslave the American public financially. The American economic empire is a financial house of cards that is teetering on the brink of disaster.

Expect further fallout in the U.S. real estate market as Alt-A loans and Option ARMs create a new "subprime" crisis.

The years 2009 to 2011 will bring more pain to many U.S. homeowners and the U.S. mortgage industry. For example, Option ARM's (Option Adjustable Rate Mortgages) were sold to prospective homeowners with the use of low teaser interest rates. These lower teaser rates allowed homeowners to buy a more expensive home than they could actually afford. Many of these low introductory interest rates will begin resetting to higher rates in 2009, and these resets will continue through 2011. These higher rates will mean higher monthly mortgage payments for millions of Americans in the middle of a severe economic crisis. Additionally, the implosion of many Alt-A loans (Alternative A) are going to present a serious challenge to the housing market in the near future. Expect many more mortgage defaults and foreclosures in the coming years.

Fears of short-term deflation will instead give way to hyperinflation.

America's economic crisis until 2013 will ultimately be marked by inflation, not deflation. While future bouts of deflation are likely during this period, they will be short-lived. The real concern will occur when the dollar loses its status as the global reserve currency. Foreign dollar holdings will come flooding back into the national economy. This dramatic increase in the national money supply will spell hyperinflation.

The global food crisis will deepen.

Increasing global poverty, political corruption, and corporate monopolization of the world's food systems will mean the global food crisis will get worse in the coming years. As the crisis worsens, billions will go hungry.

The deepening economic crisis will provoke a newfound American awareness of sound money principles.

I expect that the problems that have been discussed in this book will eventually be defined in such a way that the average American can easily understand the issues. Hopefully, this book has contributed to this cause. This awareness will create an entire subculture (much larger than currently exists) that will seek localized economic solutions. The last time that America had a true sound money revolution was in the 1890s. A similar awareness will sweep the nation as many Americans are awakened to the systematic destruction of the purchasing power of their savings. As the economy worsens, many will even develop community currencies that will supplant the need for local dollar exchanges.

The $180+ trillion U.S. derivatives market will threaten to unwind.

When U.S. banks want to gamble with their (your) money, they don't head to Vegas. Instead, they use high-powered financial instruments, including foreign exchange contracts, interest rate contracts, equity-linked contracts, and commodity contracts. These insurance contracts are known as derivatives. Warren Buffett has another name for them: "weapons of mass destruction." Credit default swaps are the most widely traded form of derivatives — with over $62 trillion of these in existence. In total, there are at least $180 trillion in derivatives owned by U.S. banks alone. Over $500 trillion of derivatives exist globally. When you consider that the entire world's annual GDP is only $60 trillion, the problem becomes clear. *U.S. banks hold three times the amount of the entire world's GDP in the form of derivatives.* As the severe structural problems in the global economy continue to be ignored, or patched with Band-Aid answers, the trillion-dollar derivative market will begin to break down. When this happens, it will make the mortgage crisis look like the glory days.

Calls for "sacrifice" will emerge.

After years of consuming like mad and surviving on debt, the U.S. consumption party will come to an end. When America's credit-induced hangover finally arrives, economic sacrifice will be the only available option. This constraint on needless and mindless consumption will be more than a huge inconvenience for most. But this will be especially true for a new American generation who has never been asked to sacrifice anything for anyone. How America responds to the coming required economic sacrifice will directly determine our nation's viability to exist peacefully in the 21st century.

2009–2020 Forecasts

The dollar will lose its global reserve status.

During the last half of the 20th century, the dollar reigned supreme as the world's currency of choice — technically known as the global reserve currency. Throughout history, few nations have experienced the financial exhilaration of having such an artificial demand for their currency — *and no nation has ever survived the ride.* The dollar's reign as the global reserve currency has allowed America's consumption levels to reach unprecedented levels. This rampant over-consumption has led to trillions and trillions of dollars in debt. As foreign nations awake to America's inability to service these unsustainable debt levels, their money will gravitate to safer currencies. And when this happens, the dollar will become a second-rate currency. A law in economics states that "money always flows to the rate of highest return." When the dollar collapses, the United States will be forced to raise interest rates to encourage foreign capital inflows.

The U.S. government will lose its AAA credit rating.

As a shocked world community comes to terms with 21st century economic realities, foreign investors will begin withdrawing their long-term financing of American over-consumption. *Even U.S. government bonds will be suspect to investors.* Speculators will remain, but few will be willing to trade 30 years of currency risk with a U.S. government bond offering a sheer 4 percent. In order to prevent massive foreign capital outflows, the United States will be forced to drastically increase interest rates.

U.S. interest rates will skyrocket to double digits.

While a dollar collapse and a downgrade of the U.S. credit rating would both force an increase in U.S. interest rates, so will the impending threat of inflation. And thanks to the recent federal government bailout, which has chosen to fight a credit crisis with more credit, *massive inflationary pressures are just around the corner.* By raising interest rates, the United States will hope to save the dollar. But higher interest rates will crush the housing market and business spending. Likewise, the average debt loads carried by most Americans will be aggravated by interest rate increases.

The petrodollar system will break down as oil-producing nations turn to gold, the euro, or a basket of currencies.

In the face of a weak and worthless dollar, *oil-producing nations will finally detach themselves from the petrodollar system.* (See chapter 9.)

The system, which requires oil-producing nations to accept only U.S. dollars for their oil and to then place their profits in failing U.S. debt instruments, could be replaced by a variety of different systems. *It is possible that oil could be priced in euros, gold, or even a basket of currencies that could include the dollar.* But the petrodollar system will collapse, ending the global artificial demand for U.S. dollars that has caused neurotic U.S. over-consumption.

Oil prices will skyrocket as global peak oil becomes a full-blown reality.

The threats posed by global peak oil (see chapter 8) have not currently gone mainstream — as seen in the lack of an effective U.S. energy policy. In the next several years, however, continued declining oil supplies and growing global demand will force the American public to face the long-term economic realities of oil. As peak oil gets into full swing, oil prices will reach levels well above $200 per barrel by 2013.

The spotlight will move from the West to the East.

As the American economic empire begins to lose its grip on the globe, the global spotlight will slowly shift from the bloated American empire to an ascendant European Union, an oil-rich Middle East, and a labor-rich Far East.

The Middle East will develop an economically integrated monetary and political union.

Sitting atop 62 percent of the world's oil supplies, the Middle East is poised to capture the largest amount of wealth in history as the reality of peak oil is realized. Middle Eastern integration and articulation is greatly feared by Western nations due to the overwhelming economic and political power a solidified Middle East could possess. Despite constant Western (oil-motivated) interference designed to bring continued division, it appears that the Middle East is finally seeking serious political and economic integration. Interestingly, I expect this Mideast integration to be initiated and led by Iraq. A unified Middle East, flush with oil cash, will be a force to be reckoned with. It is coming in our lifetime.

China will continue to drive global demand.

Despite some hiccups, *China's growth will continue to drive global demand for commodities.* Many believe that China cannot survive without a prosperous America. But was America prevented from rising despite a declining British empire one hundred years ago? Once again, this American exceptionalism has blinded many. China's economy will continue to grow exponentially despite America's self-inflicted demise.

Global resource wars lie ahead.

Our future of unlimited wants and limited resources will only mean one thing in the future: resource wars. As global demand for all commodities continues to grow in the future, nations will revert to armed conflict to satisfy their own demand requirements. Expect "wars, and rumors of wars" in the future (see Matt. 24:6).

Iraq's massive oil discoveries will greatly enrich the country.

It is believed by some that Iraq sits upon the largest conventional oil reserves in the world. With the stabilization of Iraq will come the exploitation of Iraq's oil reserves. I firmly believe that the coming oil discoveries in Iraq will make this nation one of the wealthiest nations on earth in the coming years. Expect Iraq to be the major economic power in the Middle East within the next decade.

Endnotes

1. Patrick J. Buchanan, *The Death of the West: How Dying Populations and Immigrant Invasions Imperil Our Country and Civilization* (New York: Macmillan, 2002), p. 97.
2. Norm Chomsky (b. 1928), U.S. linguist and politcal analyst, interview in *Guardian,* London (Nov. 23, 1992).

Chapter 18
Twelve Key Strategies for Weathering the Impending Economic Storm

"The wise have wealth and luxury,
but fools spend whatever they get."
— Proverbs 21:20; NLT

"The time to repair the roof is when the sun is shining."[1]
— John F. Kennedy

In this final chapter, I want to provide you with some key strategies that you can use to safeguard yourself and your family in uncertain financial times.

In the Book of Proverbs, wise King Solomon writes:

> A prudent person foresees danger and takes precautions. The simpleton goes blindly on and suffers the consequences (Prov. 22:3; NLT).

As I have documented in this book, the economic turmoil facing our nation will almost certainly intensify in the coming months and years. Through a combination of applied biblical wisdom and common sense, you *can* prepare yourself and your loved ones for the coming economic storm.

The most common question that I receive after lecturing on the topic of America's economic crisis is: *"What should I do with my money?"* Since I do not believe in a one-size-fits-all approach when it comes to your personal finances, I am very hesitant to give specific advice. However, I believe that after a thorough reading of this book, you will find that there are some common-sense life strategies that nearly everyone should take into consideration. *Of course, you should always consult with a professional financial advisor prior to making a financial decision.*

With that said, let's now consider 12 key strategies that I believe will help protect you and your family from the inevitable economic storm looming on the horizon.

1. Admit that man cannot rule man . . . and then actually believe it.

Our deceptive generation has convinced us that man can rule himself. Sadly, millions of Christians today blindly believe this lie. But the Bible makes it abundantly clear that mankind was created and designed to be led by God Himself. However, in response to man's fall in the Garden of Eden, man opted for self-rule. This act of defiance has led to nearly 6,000 years of failed human government, beginning with the Tower of Babel. Since then, mankind's attempts at self-rule have only intensified. And the consequences have been tragic. One thing that our supporters always hear me say is that "man cannot rule man." I say this because man was never designed to rule himself. Instead, he was designed to be led by our Heavenly Father.

Today, we live in the chaotic and confusing environment of man's rule gone bad. Politicians promise peace and deliver war; they promise certainty and deliver chaos. And yet what is so amazing is that Christians today still believe the lie that men are quite capable of ruling themselves. It should come as no surprise that God disagrees with this line of reasoning because at His return He will come and smite the nations with His wrath. Then He will set up His own Kingdom on the earth in which He will reign for 1,000 years. I often wonder when the Body of Christ will awaken to the fact that this world and this life offer no real lasting hope. As Christians, our *only* hope is found in Christ and in His soon coming Kingdom. Like the patriarch Abraham, we too are looking and longing for that city "whose builder and maker is God" (Heb. 11:10). This world is not our home and could never even come close. In fact, in the Book of 2 Peter, the Bible tells us that Christ's final act of judgment upon this failed world system will be full annihilation. It says that "the elements will melt with fervent heat; both the earth and the works that are in it will be burned up" (2 Pet. 3:10). With this in mind, ask yourself this question: According to the Bible, which one of this world's governments will be shielded from the wrath of God's anger on that great "Day of the Lord"? The answer is none. This world is doomed because people have dared to defy the supreme rulership of the living God of heaven. Man's failed quest for self-rule will end in absolute annihilation. That is why the man-made earthly hopes and values promoted by this world are vain and empty. *The world's leaders, its politics, bureaucracies, organizations, religions, pleasures, and philosophies are all going to be destroyed by fire at the coming of the Lord Jesus Christ!*

The Apostle Peter continues by asking: "Since all these things [earth and all of its works] will be dissolved, what manner of persons ought you to be in holy conduct and godliness?" (2 Pet. 3:11). I believe that this question is highly relevant to our current generation. Peter's question is one that every church in America should be asking from its pulpits. Sadly, many churches in America encourage friendship with the world. But the Bible says that those who are friends of this world are the enemies of God.

So how should we, as the friends and followers of Christ, respond? Our response should be twofold: (1) awareness and (2) extraction.

The first step in any direction begins with awareness. Becoming and remaining aware of man's need for God's leadership will help you properly evaluate man's aspirations and hopes of self-rule. If anyone in this world should know that man cannot rule himself, it should be the followers of Christ. The Bible is so clear on this point. The only way that we can lose awareness on this issue is to ignore the Bible's clear teachings.

The second step is to extract yourself from the deceitful illusion that is found in this world. We can do this by becoming conformed to the likeness of Christ (see Rom. 12:1–2). There is great reward found in immersing yourself in the Father's business. As Christians, we are to be in this world, but not of it (see John 17:14–15). This means that we must operate here but simply as pilgrims and sojourners. We are not deceived by man's great swelling words and false promises of utopia. We

Man Cannot Rule Man

Now Samuel said to all Israel: "Indeed I have heeded your voice in all that you said to me, and have made a king over you. And now here is the king, walking before you." . . . you said to me, "No, but a king shall reign over us," when the LORD your God was your king. Now therefore, here is the king whom you have chosen and whom you have desired. . . . your wickedness is great, which you have done in the sight of the LORD, in asking a king for yourselves" (1 Sam. 12:1–17).

— The words of the prophet Samuel to the nation of Israel when they demanded a human king instead of keeping God as their King.

know that his end is destruction without Christ. We know that Christ's kingdom will be far better than anything here. So why settle for a poor substitute? Why not live in great expectation of Christ's kingdom?

By admitting that man is incapable of truly ruling himself, your eyes will be opened to the deceptive nature of our day. You will no longer be shocked at man's failures at self-government. Instead, you will expect them and make preparations for them. In these wicked times, deception permeates our world so greatly that it is impossible to quantify. Obviously, these days call for great discernment. Without discernment, you will be susceptible to this world's deception, and you too will follow the world's herd mentality. And without discernment, your judgment on economic and political topics will be impaired, thus placing your future financial health in danger.

2. We the people need to get informed and stay informed.

For far too long, Americans have been economically illiterate. This is not acceptable if we desire to be wise financial stewards of the finances and resources that have been placed in our hands by God. As Americans, each of us live at a higher standard than much of the world outside our nation's borders. However, this blessing comes with responsibility. The Bible says that "to whom much is given, from him much will be required" (Luke 12:48). The journey toward becoming good stewards of our God-given resources begins with information. There is much you can do to help inform yourself and others.

Dedicate yourself to economic awareness. By reading this book, you have demonstrated that you are committed to your economic health and to good financial stewardship. But don't stop here. Commit yourself to remaining aware and to doing what you can to safeguard your financial future. Remember, there are very few people really looking out for you in this world. And no one cares about your financial future as much as you do.

Keep current with financial news both here and abroad. Life in the information age is interesting. On one hand, it means that we have information literally at our fingertips. But it also means that we must be careful in what we believe and who we choose to listen to. The more you read about finances, the more you will discover that much of the financial news is not worth the paper it is printed on. Much of the financial press contains contradictory advice on investing and can confuse you more than it helps you. However, I do recommend a few news sources. The *Wall Street Journal* is still one of the best financial news sources for getting solid reporting on global economic issues. Another U.S. publication I recommend is *Investor's Business Daily*. As far as international news sources, I highly recommend the *Financial Times*. It is based in London and provides a European perspective to the global economy.

Take an economics or money management course. Check with your local community college for a beginner's course on economics or money management. This is such an important step because most of us have never learned how money really works. I believe that every high school student should have to pass an economic and money management test before obtaining his or her diploma. It is simply amazing how little real world training goes on in most of our public schools. Many high school students get out of school and don't know how to make a basic budget, or even how to write a check!

Study personal finance books. An abundance of books have been written designed to help individuals become better money managers. And many of them offer great insights and are worth reading. But the best recommendation I can make is to study what the Bible has to say about money management. Before you say that studying about money in the Bible is unspiritual, know that the Bible has over 2,350 verses directly dealing with money and possessions. That's around twice the amount of verses that the Bible spends on faith, prayer, and love combined! If this topic is that important to God, then shouldn't it be important to us? Find out what God's Word has to say about the topic of money. It will revolutionize your views on money and will anchor you in times of volatility with financial wisdom.

Share what you have learned with others. I hope that through the reading of this book, your eyes have been opened to the harsh realities facing America's economy. If you have benefited from reading this book, then perhaps others may, too. Who do you know that could benefit from being exposed to this information? Pass this book on to them. And share what you learn through your future studies with those you love and care about.

See the recommended reading list at the end of this book.

3. Create a network of friends and family that you can trust in a time of crisis.

Americans have gained a reputation around the world of being highly individualistic creatures. Our culture places great value upon self-sufficiency and self-reliance. While these are admirable traits when properly applied, they are attitudes that are foreign to the Christian faith. Christianity is a faith that emphasizes community. It is a faith that is dependent on the parts to make the whole. It is a faith that finds its great strength in unity of its parts. It is not a "lone ranger" faith. Christianity also emphasizes love for one's neighbor. But it is certainly difficult to love your neighbor if you don't even know his name!

Historically, times of great crisis have galvanized the Christian community. The Body of Christ in America should begin preparing for very difficult financial times ahead. Having a network of godly friends and loved ones will become one of the most valuable assets that you, as a Christian, could ever hope to possess in a time of crisis. Update your rolodex and reconnect with long-lost friends. Invite your neighbors over for dinner. Join a small group in your church with the purpose of seeking intimate friendships.

In 2008, our ministry unveiled a home fellowship network called the *Acts 20:20 Network*. Through this network of home fellowships, we are seeking to reach out and provide physical aid and spiritual growth to people in neighborhoods all over the city of Tulsa. Our vision is to have "a church in every neighborhood." As these home church fellowships grow and mature, we expect to see those attending to form new friendships and have deep spiritual intimacy with one another.

I believe that this network, and others like it across the country, will greatly serve those in the Christian community in times of need and crisis. As the economy gets worse, churches, small communities, and neighborhoods will be required to work together. *Why not get started now?* If you would like to learn more about the Acts 20:20 Network, contact Jerry Robinson Ministries International in Tulsa, Oklahoma.

4. Worship the Lord with your giving.

One of my favorite scriptures on generosity is found in 2 Corinthians 9:6–7. There, the Apostle Paul states:

> But this I say: He who sows sparingly will also reap sparingly, and he who sows bountifully will also reap bountifully. So let each one give as he purposes in his heart, not grudgingly or of necessity; for God loves a cheerful giver.

One of the greatest hallmarks of true Christianity is generosity. The Bible tells us true happiness is found when we give. And when we give, we are simply imitating God who is the biggest giver of them all. As the Scripture says, "For God so the loved the world that He gave His only begotten Son . . ." (John 3:16).

It can be tempting to slow your giving to the work of the Gospel when you are dealing with a time of lack. But this is a dangerous practice to get into because the Bible tells us that God watches how we use the money that He places into our lives as a way to examine our hearts. The money that has entered your life is a test, pure and simple. We know that God owns everything. Everything is His, including the money sitting in your bank account. He is not a tyrant that demands all of your money. Instead, He is a loving Father who knows what's best for His children. And He knows that the greatest joy in the world is found in giving of ourselves and our resources for His divine purposes.

The first thing we must do is change our thinking on giving. Our beliefs on Christian giving have been beaten into us many times by well-meaning preachers who need funds to pay a utility bill and who view you, not God, as their source. As such, they ask you to reach deep down into your pocket to receive God's "extra special" blessings. This is absurd and must end. God is not concerned with *how much* you give. Instead, what He cares about is what your gift *costs* you. Again, God is not impressed with the size of your gift. Instead, what He cares about is what your gift costs you. The reason God cares about what your gift costs you, and not about the size of the gift, is because *giving is worship*. And for giving to become worship, *it must cost you something*. But obviously, if worship must be commanded, then it is not truly worship. You can give but not worship. (Consider the Pharisees of Jesus' day.) But it is impossible to worship and not give. Think about it this way:

- When you give because you *have* to . . . it is law.
- When you give because you feel like you need to . . . it is an obligation.
- But when you give simply because you want to out of the depths of your heart . . . it is love.

If you are currently giving to a church or to a ministry, examine why you are giving to that particular ministry. Are you giving simply because you feel like you *have to*? Or because you *need to*? Or are you giving because you simply *want to* bless the Lord with your gift?

If you are not currently giving any money to further the cause of Christ, you should search your heart to find out why you are not giving. Eliminate every obstacle to giving.

It has been said that Christians show who they *are* by what they *do* with what they *have*. That is true because "where your treasure is, there your heart will be also" (Matt. 6:21).

5. Save at least 15 percent of your income now!

Overheard in a Starbucks coffee shop: "Yesterday's a cashed check, tomorrow's a promissory note. Today's the only cash you've got."

Let's face it: Americans are not good savers. Apparently we think that we don't need to worry about having a "rainy day" fund because the sun will always shine. Nothing could be further from the truth. According to a February 2008 report from the U.S. Department of Commerce Bureau of Economic Analysis, the average American saved a dismal 0.3 percent of their income that month. That's a mere 30 cents for every $100 earned. It's even worse if you go back to January 2008. In that month, the savings rate was negative, which means that Americans were actually spending more than they were earning. This lack of saving has been a chronic problem in America since the 1990s. In fact, the U.S. savings rate today is at its lowest level since the Great Depression more than 70 years ago.

The Book of Proverbs says: "Go to the ant, you sluggard! Consider her ways and be wise, which, having no captain, overseer or ruler, provides her supplies in the summer, and gathers her food in the harvest" (Prov. 6:6–8). Saving money is a biblical principle that helps insulate us from times of economic uncertainty.

How much money should you save? I believe that the *minimum* anyone should save is 15 percent of their monthly income. *Why 15 percent and not 10 percent as most financial advisors recommend?* I recommend 15 percent because of the various eroding factors that affect our money. For example, the combined impact of inflation and taxes alone is a good enough reason to save more than 10 percent. These two eroding factors have a tremendous wealth-destroying effect and must be fought against aggressively. Those who recommend a 10 percent savings rate may mean well, but 10 percent will barely keep your financial head above water over the long run if inflation creeps over 10 percent and when, *not if*, taxes increase.

When we talk about saving money, we are really talking about *planning*. And in order to plan, you have to get serious about your money. You have to take control, and you have to want to save. But planning to save your money is just the first step. Someone once said, "You can be on the right track, but if you just sit there, you may get run over." Being on the right track by planning to save money is good. But if it just remains a plan that never gets put into action, it will never bear fruit. However, once we do begin to work our plan by saving money, we will often find distractions all along the way. The road to success is marked with many tempting parking spaces. Something will always come up that will compete with your plan to save. *This is why I recommend that you automate your savings plan.* This is easily accomplished now with direct deposit and automatic debiting of specified percentages of your paycheck into your savings account.

Finally, I understand that it may be difficult to begin saving 15 percent of your paycheck, especially if you are not used to saving anything at all. However, let me urge you to start your savings plan *immediately*, regardless of the amount you are able to save. *And don't become discouraged if you can only begin with putting 3 percent or 5 percent of your paycheck into savings.* You can always increase your savings to the 15 percent goal slowly over a period of time. The most important thing is just to begin saving *now*!

6. Build a six-month diversified liquid cash reserve and hold it in safe places.

Once you commit to a 15 percent savings plan, it won't be long before you begin to accumulate a nice sum of money. Your initial goal will be to save 50 percent of your annual gross income (or six months of income) through your monthly contributions. Building a six-month reserve of liquid cash will help shield you from the uncertain times that lie ahead. This means that if you earn $30,000 per year, you should build and maintain a minimum of $15,000 in liquid savings, *at all times.* As your savings continue to grow, you will want to begin diversifying the funds in safe places. These funds will need to remain in highly liquid accounts in case you need to access it quickly. The diversification model that I personally like is:

- 1/3 — U.S. dollar denominated assets (interest-bearing accounts, CDs, properly structured cash value life insurance, etc.)

- 1/3 — hard assets (precious metals, real commodities)

- 1/3 — select stable foreign currencies (CDs, etc.)

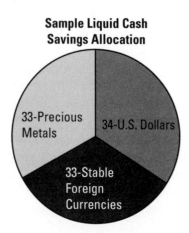

Sample Liquid Cash Savings Allocation

33-Precious Metals
34-U.S. Dollars
33-Stable Foreign Currencies

By spreading your liquid savings across a variety of savings vehicles, you will help to ensure that your money is not too highly exposed to risk in any one area. And by keeping only 1/3 of your money in U.S. dollar denominated assets, you will protect yourself from further declines to the dollar's purchasing power.

Just as diversifying your money is important, so is keeping it in a safe place. Just ask anyone who lived during the Great Depression when over 10,000 banks closed their doors. Many of these banks did not allow people to take out their funds. Why was that? Well, it's a little known fact that the *banks do not actually have all of your money*. This is due to a legal practice known as *fractional-reserve banking, which was covered in chapter 14.*

I recommend that you periodically investigate the bank or financial institution that is holding your money. You want to make sure that the financial institution is FDIC-insured. The FDIC is a government corporation that insures the majority of the nation's banks. If your money is on deposit in a FDIC-insured bank, then your money is insured up to a amount that is regulated by the federal government. Currently, this maximum is set at $250,000; however, this maximum is set to decrease to $100,000 on January 1, 2010.

Recently, there have been many concerns about the FDIC's ability to handle a major banking crisis. According to a September 2008 official FDIC press release, the FDIC currently *has only $45 billion to cover $4.5 trillion* of FDIC qualified deposits. For this reason, you should consider not keeping more than the government-set maximum amount in any one bank. *Also, take note that items placed in a safe-deposit box at the bank are not considered a deposit account and are therefore not FDIC insured.*

In addition, it would be a very good idea to investigate the banks you are doing, or considering doing, business with. This is especially important as I believe we are going to witness a large number of bank failures in the not-too-distant future.

7. Get out of DEBT.

> The rich rules over the poor, and the borrower is servent to the lender (Prov. 22:7).

The Bible views debt as bondage, but Americans have come to view it as a way of life. Many Americans have no idea what it is like to have enough money in the bank to cover unexpected expenses. Instead of having an emergency fund, most Americans simply use credit cards to get them through rough financial times. This is a recipe for disaster. In fact, the American consumer's dependence upon debt has made the debt servicing industry one of the largest and most profitable in the nation. We are truly a nation enslaved by *debt*. Today, credit card companies encourage more consumer debt slavery by flooding the mailboxes of American families with *four billion credit card offers a year.* Banks alone have made available *$3 trillion of credit* on their credit cards.

While occasional borrowing is normal, and even necessary in our nation's economy, I am warning against chronic debt.

Do you find that there is not enough money at the end of every month? Do you feel like you are constantly behind on your bills and debt payments? Do you receive phone calls from your creditors at home and at work inquiring about your late payments?

If so, you should do all you can to pay off your high-interest debts as soon as possible. Out-of-control debt is going to become a very big problem for our modern consumption-driven economy that relies upon easy financing. Many banks are up against the wall due to the lingering credit crisis. I would expect them to become more and more intolerant of late payments as the economy gradually worsens.

8. Become a wise bargain shopper.

Americans are master consumers. Shopping is a competitor sport in this nation, as many feel the need to have the latest and greatest gadgets, whether or not they can afford them. Due to this obsession with overspending, more Americans will declare bankruptcy than will divorce, graduate from college, or get cancer this year alone. It should not be surprising that an estimated *43 percent of American households spend more than they earn every month.*

When the economy turns south, it will catch many American consumers off guard. If you find yourself often buying things that you don't necessarily need, begin searching for new cheaper hobbies. It is certainly okay to treat yourself occasionally, but does everything you buy have to be brand new?

Are you a voracious reader? Take a trip to your local library and you'll find all of the latest books and movies available free of charge. I am always amazed at the great selection of books, audio books, DVDs and CDs at my local county library.

DID YOU KNOW?

If you have internet access you can visit http://www.veribanc. com or http://www.bankrate.com to verify the safety of your bank. Check your bank's health today.

Garage sales, thrift stores, and flea markets still provide the "shopper's high" without the hefty price tag. Also, online shopping through ebay.com and craigslist.org offers online shoppers a great alternative to higher priced items.

My wife and I enjoy getting bargains and we shop at garage sales and on craigslist.org often. We get a thrill from spending less for high-priced items. Notice I did not say that we "saved" money — I said we "spent less." *"Saving" never occurs when you are shopping.* Saving 50 percent on that new pair of jeans is not really "saving." *It is spending, pure and simple.* Real saving only happens when you place money back into your *own* hand, *not* into the cashier's.

Facts about Debt

› U.S. consumer debt totals $2.3 trillion as of 2007.

› 43% of American households spend more than they earn every month.

› This year, more Americans will declare bankruptcy than will divorce, graduate from college, or get cancer.

9. Stock up on food, water, and medicine.

The convenient lifestyle that America affords means that many of us eat out at restaurants quite often, maybe even several days a week. In fact, studies show that most Americans only keep a few days' worth of food at home. I think having an absolute *minimum* of one month's food supply is vital in the event of some unforeseen disaster, food shortage, or pandemic. You should also keep a month of fresh water supply.

Some time ago, I would have been laughed at for recommending that people stock up on food supplies. But today, everyone knows that this is no laughing matter. Many are slowly awakening to the fact that storm clouds are appearing in the once sun-filled sky. Without a doubt, there is an economic storm heading for the shores of America, and it will be devastating to those of us who have not prepared. It will strike

Top 10 Money Drains

1. **Coffee** — According to the National Coffee Association, the average price for brewed coffee is $1.38. There are roughly 260 weekdays per year, so buying one coffee every weekday morning costs almost $360 per year.

2. **Cigarettes** — The Campaign for Tobacco Free Kids reports that the average price for a pack of cigarettes in the United States is $4.54. Pack-a-day smokers fork out $1,660 a year. Weekend smoker? Buying a pack once a week adds up, too: $236.

3. **Alcohol** — Drink prices vary based on the location. But assuming an average of $5 per beer including tip, buying two beers per day adds up to $3,650 per year. Figure twice that for two mixed drinks a day at the local bar. That's not chump change.

4. **Bottled water from convenience stores** — A 20-ounce bottle of Aquafina bottled water costs about $1. One bottle of water per day costs $365 per year. It costs the environment plenty, too.

5. **Manicures** — The Day Spa Magazine Price Survey of 2004 found that the average cost of a manicure is $20.53. A weekly manicure sets you back about $1,068 per year.

6. **Car washes** — The average cost for a basic auto detailing package is $58, according to costhelper.com. The tab for getting your car detailed every two months: $348 per year.

7. **Weekday lunches out** — $9 will generally cover a decent lunch most work days. If you buy rather than pack a lunch five days a week for one year, you shell out about $2,350 a year.

8. **Vending machine snacks** — The average vending machine snack costs $1. Buy a pack of cookies every afternoon at work and pay $260 per year.

9. **Interest charges on credit card bills** — According to a survey released at the end of May 2007, the median amount of credit card debt carried by Americans is $6,600. Rate tables on bankrate.com indicate that fixed interest rates on a standard card average 13.44 percent. Making the minimum payment each month, it will take 250 months (almost 21 years) to pay off the debt and cost $4,868 in interest. Ouch!

10. **Unused memberships** — Costhelper.com reports that the monthly service fee at gyms averages between $35 and $40. At $40 per month, an unused gym membership runs $480 per year.

Source: bankrate.com

FREE STOCKPILE LIST!

Pre-planning is key to an effective emergency supplies list. Need help in preparing your list? Get a free comprehensive stockpile list today by visiting www.jrmi.org.

especially hard those who have become dependent upon 24-hour grocery stores that are always stocked full to the brim (which may include nearly all of us). Apparently the federal government agrees, along with many public health agencies, that we should begin stockpiling food. They have recently begun urging Americans to stock up on nonperishable food, like canned goods and dried fruit, to ensure they have food during any future unexpected shortage. Even the *Wall Street Journal* chimed in back in April 2008, stating that everyone should begin stockpiling food. The glaring fact here is that most Americans are simply not prepared because they have never faced a crisis like the one I am describing.

I often think how, as Christians, we should be ahead of the game on things of this nature. Wouldn't it be a great testimony if you were so well prepared in advance of a major food shortage, or pandemic, that you could help your neighbors and friends in a time of great need?

Also consider keeping an extra supply of common over-the-counter medications that may be in short supply in the event of some crisis or disaster. Remember the Boy Scout motto: *Be Prepared.*

10. Diversify your income

Millions of Americans are one paycheck away from foreclosure on their homes. If you lost your job today, would you still have an income a month from now? If not, you should definitely consider diversifying your income by adding another income stream. Just as you should diversify your savings, I also believe you should diversify your income. Like the old saying goes: "Don't put all of your eggs in one basket." It is my personal belief that everyone should have a minimum of two streams of regular income during their working years, and a minimum of five streams at retirement. Abraham exhibited this quality in that the Bible tells us that he was rich in cattle, in gold, and in silver (Gen. 13:2, 24:35).

The nice thing is, you don't have to have a lot of money to create multiple streams of income. But what you do need is some creativity and to not be afraid of hard work. By diversifying your income through the creation of multiple streams of income, you will be creating a safety net under you and your family in the event of unforeseen circumstances. People who have diversified income also enjoy not feeling trapped in their job and constantly being at the mercy of their employer. When you have multiple streams of income, you can breathe a lot easier knowing that if one stream dries up you still have other steady sources coming in.

So how do you create multiple streams of income? Let me give you some examples of income streams that you can add to your life:

MORE IDEAS FOR EARNING EXTRA MONEY

- Do you have a knack for landscaping? Consider starting a seasonal landscaping business during the summer and putting most of the proceeds back into your savings plan.
- Are you computer-savvy? Consider moonlighting as a computer consultant or website designer. With technology getting more complicated by the day, many people are overwhelmed and desperately need help. This could be a lucrative career with a steady supply of work if you are good.
- Do you have an eye for design? Consider the growing field of graphic design as a side business.
- Are you good with animals? Pet-sitting is becoming an in-demand service for many busy people today.
- Are you good with a camera? Consider starting a small photography business. In addition to weddings, parties, and family portraits, you can also sell your photos through special online services to people around the globe, 24 hours a day. For example, check out http://www.istockphoto.com.
- Are you a book lover? Sell books online through amazon.com, half.com, ebay.com, or craigslist.org. It is a fairly straightforward process and can be a lot of fun if you love to read.
- Do you like to garden? Find your niche by specializing in some fruits or vegetables and selling them at your local farmer's market each weekend.
- Do you like to garage sale? Consider setting up a booth at your local flea market and selling your great finds each week.

- Income from a rental property
- Part-time job
- Royalties and patents
- Selling information online
- Selling used items on ebay.com or craigslist.org

The list is really endless. Examine your hobbies and passions and determine if there is a way in which you can turn them into a steady stream of income. The whole point of diversifying your income is to generate a number of different paychecks. When the economy weakens, you will be glad you did.

11. Be cautious of government-controlled, tax-deferred savings plans — IRAs, 401(k)s

In the past, American companies took responsibility for their employees' retirement by paying for, managing, and placing a guarantee on the retirement benefits for their employees. Not so in today's fast-paced and cutthroat business world. Gone are the days of company-paid pension plans and other defined benefit plans. Today, the responsibility for retirement savings has been placed squarely upon the American worker. Instead of the company-funded pension plans of yesteryear, many employees are turning to a variety of other retirement savings vehicles to save for their golden years. Two of the most popular financial products used for retirement that usually come to mind are IRAs (Individual Retirement Accounts) and employer-matching 401(k) plans.

What you should know about these two retirement savings vehicles is that they are both government created and, therefore, government-controlled plans. *Under these government-controlled plans, the federal government makes all of the rules, both on the money going in and on the money coming out.*

To understand why I am cautious about aggressively funding these plans, you must first understand what it means that these two products are "tax-deferred." When a financial product offers tax-deferred savings, this means that all of the taxes that will be owed on the growth of the savings are allowed to be "deferred" or "delayed" until the person begins receiving distributions at retirement. So good, so far?

Today, most financial advisors are advising their clients to "max out" their contributions to their company 401(k) plan and to traditional IRA plans. Their motive in advising their clients to contribute to these tax-deferred plans is likely rooted in the desire to help them accumulate enough money to retire comfortably. This is a good goal, but I believe that this method may have more risks than meet the eye.

Many financial advisors consider the tax-deferral provided by the 401(k) and the IRA to be a huge benefit to their clients. The logic goes something like this: since the client will be spending his entire working lifetime in a higher tax bracket and will retire in a lower tax bracket, doesn't it make sense to delay the payment of taxes until he retires and is in a lower tax bracket? Since the tax bracket will be lower in retirement than it was during the working years, many consider the tax-deferral provided by the 401(k) and the traditional IRA to be the greatest retirement savings vehicles ever invented.

Sounds good, right? Then let me ask you a question: *Based upon what you know so far about the economic crisis facing America, do you think taxes are going to be higher or lower in the future?* (If you said lower, then proceed to page 1 of this book and begin reading this book again, a little more slowly this time.) But if you said that you think taxes will be higher in the future, then you now realize one of my main concerns about these popular retirement savings plans.

In addition, why start with the premise that you are going to be in a lower tax bracket upon retirement? Shouldn't your trusted financial advisor be creating a pool of money for you so that you will be in an even higher tax bracket when you reach the retirement finish line? The whole logic behind these plans seems a bit counterintuitive.

These plans also lack cash flow and provide you with little liquidity. If you have to access this cash, or to begin a cash flow stream, at any point prior to the government-mandated distribution age (currently 59-1/2), you will be hit with a penalty, with few exceptions. These tax-deferred plans are also huge targets of estate taxes, which means that if you pass any of this qualified money on to your heirs at death, the government will take a nice chunk for themselves, again with few exceptions. If you desire to have more control over your own finances, these plans are poor choices.

And don't forget, since they are government-controlled plans, guess who makes all of the rules? What if the federal government decided in 2020 to help solve the Social Security crisis by placing a 40 percent surcharge on all withdrawals from 401(k)s and IRAs? Could they do it? Sure, they could. And while no one can predict future tax law, I am certain that something will need to be done. Always remember, he who makes the rules, wins. And your government controls every aspect of the 401(k) and IRA savings vehicles. I personally do not want to gamble with the government. I would rather pay the hungry beast now and walk away. I certainly do not want to feed them taxes decades from now when they are completely desperate due to their bad spending choices.

Therefore, it is my recommendation that you at least consider all of your options before simply placing all of your retirement money into a government-controlled tax-deferred plan. Those who wish to pay taxes up front on a portion of their retirement savings can consider funding a Roth IRA. A Roth IRA is simply an IRA in which you pay the taxes up front and take the money at the end, tax-free. Of course, the government knows that this is a sweet deal so they have strict income guidelines on who can participate in these types of plans.

But even the Roth IRA has its risks. There are other creative strategies for creating tax-free money at retirement. For more information on these strategies, consult your trusted financial advisor. Or you can also contact me with your questions through our website at www.jrmi.org.

Finally, understand that your retirement savings plans are not part of your six-month savings reserve that I have recommended you

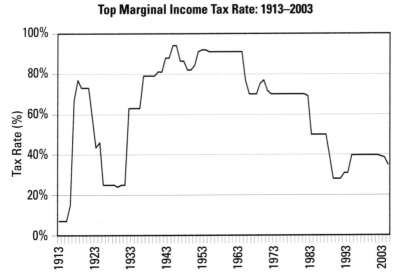

Top Marginal Income Tax Rate: 1913–2003

Source: www.truthandpolitics.org/top-rates.php

maintain at all times. Retirement is a long-term need and should not be 100 percent liquid, as a rule. Your six-month savings reserve is for short-term needs and should remain liquid at all times. Because our nation has such poor savings habits, many people only save for retirement but have no liquid savings plan for emergencies. Confusion over this matter has been the reason that many Americans have had to begin borrowing from their 401(k) or their IRA (long-term savings) just to cover short-term needs. You can avoid falling into this trap by choosing to save for both short-term needs and long-term needs.

12. Begin positioning your investments within industries that will benefit from U.S. inflation.

Once you have built up your six-month savings reserve, then, *and only then*, it is time to think about "investing." As you approach investing, you will be looking for investments that will provide you with protection from the coming inflation on the not-too-distant horizon.

One of the best hedges against inflation is hard assets. Hard assets include precious metals, commodities, fine art, real estate, and more. Basically, hard assets are tangible assets that you can physically touch and handle. One of the more exciting areas of hard assets right now is precious metals. Precious metals are items like gold, silver, platinum, etc.

What I find interesting about precious metals is their current lack of ownership. For example, consider the following chart detailing the breakdown of global liquid wealth.

Across the globe, investors now own the largest amount of liquid "paper" wealth in recorded history. Out of all of the liquid assets owned globally, gold makes only a fractional 1.4 percent. According to Anthony Allison from the PFS Group, "If just 1 or 2 percent of the world's liquid wealth moved into gold in future years, the price rise would be explosive."[2]

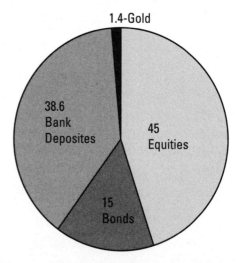

Breakdown of Global Liquid Wealth

1.4-Gold

38.6 Bank Deposites

45 Equities

15 Bonds

Precious metals are typically scorned by governments that churn out fiat currencies. That is because precious metals have been used throughout most of recorded history as a way to constrain the overproduction of fiat currencies. In today's economy, U.S. dollars are printed at will and devalued as needed. *Regardless of the government's opinion, precious metals, such as gold and silver, outperform in the midst of economic uncertainty*. And if anything is certain, it is that the outlook for the global economy in the coming years is uncertain. *Precious metals always have been, and always will be, the beneficiary of poor monetary policies*. So as America's economy continues to worsen over the coming months and years, I expect more investment dollars to pour into the safe haven of precious metals, thus driving their prices up to very high levels.

Where gold is heading in 2009:

- Investors are fleeing the dollar, which will cause gold to rise.

- Demand is greater than gold production. Production was down 3 percent in 2006 and remained flat in 2007. Demand, however, is not abating.

- Gold producers are buying gold.

- The gold/oil ratio is lower than normal. Lately it has been 10:1, but historically it has been as high as 50:1.

- The safest countries to buy gold in are those countries in which the legal system makes government takeovers of mines very difficult. This list includes the United States, Canada, Mexico, and Australia.

While I am on the topic of investing, allow me to issue a cautionary note about stock investing in general. Many good men and women who want to get ahead financially come to the stock market with dollar signs in their eyes. They simply want to provide a better future for themselves and their families. But before they know it, they are accosted by numerous "Wall Street" stock gurus who claim to have the ability to predict the markets with precision . . . *for a small fee of course*. Be warned up front: no one knows what the stock market will do, not even the professionals who manage money for a living. No one owns a crystal ball when it comes to stock prices. Wall Street is a well-oiled machine in which a novice investor can lose his shirt overnight. Like many people, I have made money in the stock market; and I also lost money. Investing should be approached only after due diligence. *Before investing in anything, you should consult a trusted financial advisor.*

Like never before, it has become vital to read between the lines of the news coming at you daily from the American media machine, especially in the business world. The majority of the American media is economically illiterate. And they push "doctored" government numbers for a living. I cannot even begin to tell you how many contradictions I see in the business media on a monthly basis.

If you desire to invest in the markets, do so carefully and after much research. You owe it to yourself and your family to distinguish between fact and fiction in the stock market. Not only will a keen awareness of the economy allow you to protect your current assets, but your future wealth depends on it.

Special Bonus: Strategy #13 — Commit to Learning "the Rules of the Game"

As you have gathered from this book, the economic system of the United States of America is flawed in a number of ways. The reason that the system is so completely flawed is due to the nation's faulty financial foundation. Once you truly grasp the fatal flaws within the system, you may be tempted to become angry. This is especially true if you have a great patriotic love for your country. Some may seek to react to this newfound awareness by engaging in activism in the political and economic arenas. While I would certainly not want to discourage anyone from becoming involved with informing the public regarding the impending collapse of our nation's economy, I would urge you to protect your own interests first: yourself and your family. The fragility of our nation's economy should also cause those who seek to become involved in activism to question whether their efforts are worth the time invested. After all, only a fool would rearrange the furniture on a sinking *Titanic*. Instead of activism, I believe that consistent awareness is the most important and effective response to the information regarding America's economic crisis. Followers of Christ should seek awareness on these matters. Awareness does not necessitate activism. While activism may appear to be a valid response to our nation's crisis, we must remember that we are not members of the faulty kingdoms of this world. We belong to the Kingdom of God. True reform for this world will only come when men stop trying to rule it and allow God to be King. Of course, mankind's pride and sinfulness would never allow him to collectively submit fully to the kingship of God. Therefore, it is necessary that God execute judgment upon this world for humanity's sin and arrogance. This judgment of the world will come in the form of the greatest battle in mankind's history. The Bible refers to this as the battle of Armageddon. Mankind's attempts at self-rule will finally come to a climactic close. The curtain will be drawn on man's stubborn pride and rejection of God. This reason alone makes activism seem fruitless as a constructive long-term strategy. Awareness, however, is a powerful strategy that will aid anyone in understanding how to react to the days of economic uncertainty that lie ahead.

The most effective form of practical awareness is to begin learning what I will refer to as "the rules of the game." This is similar to a child's board game. Since my first daughter was very young, she has enjoyed playing board games. But until she fully learned the rules of her favorite board games, guess who won nearly every time? Her daddy! Why? Because I was mature enough to understand the rules of the game and to use them in my favor. Similarly, the American economic system operates according to a very specific and complex set of rules. Anyone who expects to succeed at this game must understand the rules. While you need not master them, you must certainly understand a few basic concepts before playing the game.

The rules to our financial system are found in the nation's tax code. While no one but tax professionals has the time (or the desire) to keep up with the constantly changing tax code, you and I can certainly determine some basic economic rules by which to "play." For example, what does the government favor when it comes to the tax code? There are a number of things, but two very important ones are business ownership and real estate.

Conclusion

Thank you for reading this brief book on the growing American economic crisis. As a minister of the gospel, and as an economic advisor, I am genuinely concerned about the economic, cultural, and social path that America is currently heading down. If you feel the same, please contact us at our ministry and let us know that we are not alone in our concerns for this great country. We need your help to warn the nation about the crisis that is facing all of us.

You can contact us with any questions, comments, or speaking requests by visiting our website at www.jrmi.org.

Endnotes

1. John C. Maxwell, *Talent Is Never Enough: Discover the Choices That Will Take You Beyond Your Talent* (Nashville, TN: Thomas Nelson Inc., 2007), p. 96.
2. Tony Allison, "The Year of Living Dangerously: Printing Our Economy Back to Prosperity?" published March 17, 2008, http://financialsense.com/Market/allison/2008/0317.html.

Recommended Reading

Newspapers
Wall Street Journal
Investor's Business Daily
Financial Times

Books
Basic Economics by Thomas Sowell (New York: Basic Books, 2004).
Empire of Debt by Bill Bonner (Hoboken, NJ: Wiley, 2006).
I.O.U.S.A.: One Nation. Under Stress. In Debt by Addison Wiggin (Hoboken, NJ: Wiley, 2009).
The Creature from Jekyll Island by G. Edward Griffin (Westlake Village, CA: American Media, 1994).